WITHDRAWN
HARVARD LIBRARY
WITHDRAWN

THEOLOGICAL REFLECTIONS
OF A CHRISTIAN PHILOSOPHER

THEOLOGICAL REFLECTIONS
OF A CHRISTIAN PHILOSOPHER

by

JOSEPH J. SIKORA, S.J.

MARTINUS NIJHOFF / THE HAGUE / 1970

© 1970 by Martinus Nijhoff, The Hague, Netherlands
All rights reserved, including the right to translate or to
reproduce this book or parts thereof in any form

PRINTED IN THE NETHERLANDS

PREFACE

The essays which follow, as theological reflections of a Christian philosopher, are essays of inquiry concerning the ontological reality of and underlying truths revealed by God. Divine revelation of course cannot be encompassed within a few dogmatic formulae in any adequate manner; it is the mysterious plenitude of the historical human encounter with the self-revealing God Who has revealed His salvific designs for men. This revelation can be approached from many viewpoints of scientific study, such as those of religious psychology, historical theology, Scriptural study, the history of dogmas, but also that of the philosophical thinker seeking to understand what he has already believed – so far as this be possible in regard to the mysteries of God's inner life and of the new creation that He works in us by His grace. In our rather non-metaphysical age such an inquiry into the underlying ontological reality opened to us by the revelation of God is somewhat unfashionable; but the issues remain, and in fact one can only choose between a rather unconsciously and uncritically accepted attitude about the ontological significance of such dogmatic truths as the existence of the Trinity and the hypostatic union and created grace, and a consciously and critically developed analysis in the light of, and with the help of such understanding of being as the philosophers can offer. Metaphysical theology of this kind is here to stay, regardless of some "prophets" who would cut away the ground on which they stand. We have only to choose between rational elaboration of such a theology and a rather non-rational acceptance of attitudes produced by the play of chance factors.

We do not confuse this effort of understanding with the acceptance by divine faith of revelation itself. It is this last that is the root and foundation of Christian life, and the former is to a large extent unnecessary for the individual Christian (though what Christian is there, alive to his faith, who is never to the slightest degree concerned to understand a little better what it is that he believes?). But in the life of the Church this effort of rational understanding is necessary for the well-being of the Church and its treasure of revealed truth. How else could the Church move out of a particular cultural reference frame to understand its own message in such a way that it could truly make the adaptations needed to preach the Gospel to all nations of all times even while preserving intact the truth that has been confided to it for this proclamation? How else could this revelation be and remain more than a code of ritual and practice, of which each might make what he could? But in a book of this kind it is unnecessary to dwell at length on such points, since they are well-known to its likely readers.

As the theological reflections of a Christian philosopher these essays belong to what I conceive as the necessary dynamism of the Christian philosopher, who could hardly stop at a purely philosophical elaboration of his reflections but would be compelled by his *elan* to pass over into, if indeed he had not already begun his thought with, properly theological reflection on the revelation that holds absolute primacy in his intellectual as well as moral life. As theological reflection of this kind, the presuppositions of these essays are to be found in my earlier philosophical work, especially in *Inquiry Into Being*.* There a fundamentally Thomist development arising out of confrontation with various other philosophical traditions led to a new formulation of the metaphysics of existence and the existential subject. The analysis of the dimension of subjectivity (and that of activity) led to the key distinction – already made by Jacques Maritain – between the mere possession and the actual exercise of the act of existence. This metaphysical distinction in fact also offers much valuable light for the partial theological understanding of the mysteries of the three Persons subsisting in the one divine nature, the two natures of the Second Person, and the general nature and modes of created grace. This can best be appreciated by consideration of the essays themselves.

Metaphysical analysis of subjectivity in the *Inquiry* led on to the consideration of the spiritual subject as such. The reflexivity and autopresence of spiritual being, as well as the necessary intentionality of all finite spirit, which appeared in the course of that analysis, also offer much light for the treatment of the theological problems that follow in the present work. So also, the relation between intellect and will which was seen in the light of this analysis of the spiritual subject, and

* Loyola University Press, Chicago, 1965.

the consequent role of the will and of affective connaturality as principles of special new modes of knowing things, are most important tools for the understanding of the act of faith, mystical experience, and other psychological aspects of the supernatural life. The importance of understanding this philosophical base (without however requiring a pre-reading of *Inquiry Into Being*, since these themes are reconsidered in the present work) cannot be sufficiently emphasized. To receive what is said in the context of a more essentialist and purely objectivist metaphysics would almost surely lead to such objections as that the will is here treated as a faculty of knowing, as "another intellect." Such an objectivist metaphysics, which ignores the obscure recesses of the preconceptually attained dimensions of being in favor of the already and more directly objectified, perhaps precisely because the latter is more readily accessible, is still very much with us even among large numbers of Thomists. Indeed, if this work were to contribute toward some greater appreciation of the theological (and philosophical) possibilities for Thomism in the analysis of the preconceptual domain of knowing and the transobjective dimensions of being, this would already be a great gain even apart from acceptance of the positions to be elaborated in the course of these essays.

This work is not an attempt to present an overall systematic view in terms of which to approach the whole range of theological problems. Such a theological system might hopefully be the fruit of reflection upon a much larger series of essays upon a much wider range of theological problems. I do hope to continue these special theological reflections in another volume or series of volumes. In all of them the fundamental aim will be simply to push forward such reflections in particular domains in accordance with such opportunity as presents itself. I am at this time rather fearful of the grand generalizations that would be necessary for the ordering of a theological "system." This kind of empiricism may seem too plodding for some, but it seems to result from a proper respect and reverence for the height and breadth and depth of the mystery that has been revealed to us in Christ Jesus.

JOSEPH SIKORA, S.J.
Bellarmine School of Theology
North Aurora, Illinois

TABLE OF CONTENTS

PREFACE		v
1.	AM I A PHILOSOPHER OR A THEOLOGIAN?	1
2.	SOME REMARKS ON THEOLOGICAL METHOD	13
3.	FAITH AND INTERSUBJECTIVITY	27
	I. INTRODUCTION	27
	II. THE SO-CALLED "TRADITIONAL" DOCTRINE AND ITS DIFFICULTIES	36
	III. SOME POST-VATICAN I TENDENCIES	46
	IV. AFFECTIVE CONNATURALITY AND INTERSUBJECTIVITY	51
	V. INTERSUBJECTIVITY AND HUMAN BELIEF	58
	VI. INTERSUBJECTIVITY AND DIVINE REVELATION	63
	The Analysis of the Act of Faith	67
	Supernatural Consciousness in the Act of Faith	73
	Personal Belief in God and Belief in Propositions	74
	VII. THE FAITH OF PURE INTERSUBJECTIVITY	77
	APPENDIX. *The New Testament and Interpersonal Faith*	91
4.	THE TRINITY	95
	I. THREE PERSONS — ONE NATURE	95
	II. ARE THE PERSONS RELATIONS OR ABSOLUTES?	109
	III. THE SELF-CONSCIOUSNESS OF THE THREE PERSONS	120
5.	THE HYPOSTATIC UNION AND THE CONSCIOUSNESS OF CHRIST	136
6.	THE FINITE SUPERNATURAL AND ITS MODES	156
7.	THE WAYS OF GRACE OUTSIDE THE CHURCH	184
8.	THE BASIC MORAL OPTION AND THE AMBIENCE OF GRACE	195
9.	LITURGY AND THE SPIRIT OF MAN	208
10.	SACRAMENTS AND ENCOUNTER	213
	Analysis of the Sacrament as Cause of Grace	215
	Encounter	219
	Encounter, Communion, and Dialogue with God	227
	Sacramental Encounter	228

11.	SOME ONTOLOGICAL PRINCIPLES OF MYSTICAL EXPERIENCE	234
	I. PHENOMENOLOGICAL INVENTORY: THE DIMENSIONS OF BEING	238
	II. SELF-CONSCIOUSNESS	243
	III. UNION WITH THE FINITE OTHER	245
	IV. NATURAL MYSTICAL EXPERIENCE OF GOD	251
	V. CONTEMPLATIVE SUPERNATURAL MYSTICAL EXPERIENCE	254
	1. *Faith and Mysticism*	256
	2. *Charity and Mysticism*	260
	3. *The Mystical Light*	261
	4. *Ordinary Charity and the Presence of God*	262
	5. *The Nature of the Mystical Light*	264
	6. *The Gifts of the Holy Spirit and Mystical Experience*	268
	VI. SOME REMARKS ABOUT MYSTICAL EXPERIENCE IN ACTIVE LIFE	271

INDEX   274

I

AM I A PHILOSOPHER OR A THEOLOGIAN?

I propose to set down some theological reflections of a Christian philosopher. This may well prompt one to ask whether I here present myself as a theologian or as a philosopher, and leads me to write this little introductory essay in a somewhat more personal style than those which follow. The question must be answered in this more personal and concrete manner, for it is a personal question. Most of us at least will admit readily enough the sharp distinction between philosophical reason and theology as the search for and achievement of some understanding of the divine revelation accepted in faith. But here there is question of the basic orientation and drive of a concrete human intellect, not of this well-known distinction between philosophy and theology.

Obviously, one man might pursue both philosophical and theological truth; he could be both a philosopher and a theologian. But unless he is an intellectual schizophrenic, his intellectual life should take on a fundamental form, a deep unity first of all in the line of finality but encompassing other lines of causality and influence as well. It is wisdom that gives this fundamental form and unity. There are diverse wisdoms marking out diverse universes of knowledge and love, and the existential choice that such-and-such a view of life and hierarchy of values be wisdom *for me* determines (so long as I am loyal to this basic option) the form and unity not only of my practical life but of my intellectual life as well. I have elsewhere treated of four generic types of such wisdom governing diverse universes of knowledge and love.[1]

This existential choice is not necessarily, or even in most cases, an explicitly conscious one made in the light of clear, formulated conceptual and propositional knowledge. Rather, it is preconditioned, even predetermined – may we even say, precontained – in the degree of openness to being, truth, and goodness in the attitude assumed even in the very

[1] *The Christian Intellect and the Mystery of Being* (The Hague, 1966), p. 152–169, 178f.

first moment of truly moral choice (an attitude subsequently confirmed, changed, strengthened, weakened, at every moment in which we are called upon to consent to the being and order of reality). This openness or lack of openness in the heart of man is a freely chosen attitude, free despite the obscurity in which it is assumed and in which it continues to exist at the base of all other free choices we make. But this free attitude is already the prefiguration, the anticipation, and the outline of a wisdom. For the truth we attain, the view of life with which we settle down, the goods for which we strive and are willing to exert ourselves and depart from established and quasi-mechanical routines, all these are already indicated by the degree to which we remain open to and consent to the total being and order of things.

But of course this openness is not simply an openness of nature to being; it is for us always an openness of a free person to and under the grace of God. Openness to the plenitude of being, truth, and goodness is openness to the Infinite God, receptiveness to His activations, and submissiveness to His designs. But such a total consent to being is possible for us only under the solicitations and help of divine, supernatural grace. God has revealed to us that the conditions of its possibility are faith, hope, and charity, and first of all faith. If one does, in the first or in any subsequent instant of genuine moral decision, actually desire the true and good in an unqualified way without any reservation, however obscure and "implicit" this desire be, this can only be so because divine faith, hope, and charity are already operative in some manner or other. The boy reaching the use of reason and never having heard of God, never having been baptized, perhaps even indoctrinated already so as to hate the very name of God, this boy in his very first moral decision opts at least obscurely and implicitly for or against God in opting for or against the unqualified moral good; and in doing so he accepts or rejects supernatural graces of faith, hope, and charity offered to him in the dark and without his full realization (indeed with almost no realization at all at the level of formulated knowledge) of what is going on. But his decision is truly free and makes him truly worthy of the love or hatred of God. The obscure consciousness with which it is made does not destroy this freedom; although this consciousness of this basic existential option may be entirely pre-conceptual, pre-propositional, unformulated in any manner at all, even while it is concomitant with a formulated moral decision in some lesser matter, still this consciousness is sufficient for a free act. May it not be said that the very obscurity of this consciousness results from its profundity?

It exists at a level at which the deepest reality of human freedom is found to be engaged with the ultimate and absolute, far below the levels at which the play of conceptual and propositional reason can be manipulated so as to obscure issues and induce ignorance. St. Paul recognized the obscurity of this basic existential option when he said that he did not know whether he was worthy of love or hatred; the Church recognizes it at Trent when she says that we cannot know with the certitude of faith that we are in fact justified.

But however obscure, this existential option, the basic moral choice of one's end, is a fact; and the degree of openness to being that this choice ratifies does in fact already commit one, if he consistently follows out the dynamism of this choice, to a certain view of life and to a certain hierarchy of values. Unless there is total openness to and under grace, and as a result total openness to being, there is some partial closing-in of the intellectual horizon and narrowing of the range of values. Of course, hardly any of us succeed in escaping this predicament entirely; our self-centeredness usually takes some toll, distorting our vision and rendering us cold to so much of the true and the good, leading to a hierarchy of values that is to some degree false and the principle of moral disorder in our lives.

The extreme case of such non-openness is that of the man who seeks, and who sees, nothing more than the world of subjective impressions, the world of phenomena. Questions of being, of truth, of moral principle, are relatively meaningless to him; life is to be lived for what satisfactions it can bring in the line of these subjective impressions. Outside of this, and beyond this, there is only the dark; but one must not ask too many questions. In his non-openness to being, absolute truth and ontological goodness, such a man has in fact decided for a certain kind of wisdom – a pseudo-wisdom it is true – but still a view of things and a hierarchy of values. I have elsewhere called this wisdom the wisdom of the flesh,[2] for it refuses to pay any heed to that transcendence of phenomena and subjective impressions which is the prerogative of spirit.

It is not necessary for us to here consider some intermediary kinds of wisdom, natural wisdoms of the spirit which presupopse diverse degrees of openness to being. Non-Christian literature and history are full of examples of even very sublime triumphs of the spirit in rising to high degrees of openness to being and therefore to profound

---

[2] *Ibid.*, 164f., 178f.

understanding of the truth of things and noble appreciation of genuine moral good.

What is of concern to us is to consider the implications of Christian wisdom, the wisdom of faith and charity, with its total openness and consent to being and to the plenitude of being which is the Triune God. We would like to see something of the meaning of the Christian commitment in its impact on the intellectual order, on the life of the Christian intellectual. But I propose to speak of what should be and not simply of what is, of the intrinsic dynamism of Christian wisdom and not of the impediments to this dynamism which we can and do throw up against it.

The primary truth of Christian revelation is a sublime and totally unexpected expansion of a natural truth, that God calls us to Himself, not simply to know Him through creatures "from outside," but even to enter into the inner life of the Trinity in a mysterious, though still finite and personal way. It is vision of and joy in God that is *the* good for us. The being of the world remains true and good, but we cannot rest in it; for all of it is finite *participation* in the riches of God, the chief value of which (without denying its value in itself) is to point to and lead us to God. It is helpful here to speak of the sacramentality of creatures. Employed by God in the service of divine grace, these creatures are sensible signs (at least those in our material world) of the spiritual reality of God, of the Trinity, of the Word through Whom all things were made. In contemplating the being, truth, and goodness of creatures we should rise to a higher understanding of the being, truth, and goodness of the Triune God. Divine grace also renders these sacramental creatures to be *efficacious* signs of spiritual reality, insofar as, under the action of grace, these very creatures can be so many lures toward God, so many calls to love and praise Him, so many means to use in our progress toward Him. At this point, one can say that God's grace is actually *conferred* through all these creatures, not in the special manner in which grace is channeled through the seven sacraments of the Church but in the sense that "all is grace," that "all things work together unto good for them that love God." From this perspective, the intrinsic goodness of creatures is not in any way diminished; indeed it is this very intrinsic goodness of creatures that at the same time make them to be apt means, suitable as sacraments which manifest and render present to us even now the divine mystery of the Trinity and their designs. There can be no question of slighting the intrinsic goodness of creatures in order to focus upon a certain "extrinsic" goodness, for these are only two aspects of one total goodness of creatures which is both intrinsic and wholly pointed toward the Infinite Goodness of God of which this finite goodness is entirely a participation, reflection, and beckoning call.

If this be the genuine Christian view of the world and of created truth and goodness, then the intellectual life of a Christian should bear a unique stamp, making it altogether other than the intellectual life of an unbeliever. If there are Christian scholars for whom this is not so, for whom research and scholarship are purely "secular" activities in another sphere quite removed from supernatural life, this can be only because such scholars do not understand the all-embracing character of Christian wisdom. Faith exercises primacy not only over the moral order but also, and indeed first of all, over the intellectual order. Faith communicates to us that vision described in the preceding paragraph, a vision of the world in which all other knowledge falls into its place and is allowed its proper role in speaking to us of the glory of God. It is this sapiential ordering and directing activity of faith that makes sacred theology as the profound understanding of the content of faith truly the "queen of the sciences." Often enough, when Theology is given this name, all that is meant is that it is concerned with God, the highest object of knowledge. But a queen must reign, order, and direct. Too little attention has been given by many theologians to this, which perhaps partially explains why Christian education so often fails to communicate to students a vision of the world in faith in which all the sciences, far from conflicting with revelation, find in the Christian universe their natural (and supernatural) places on the ladder which ascends to God. This is why the humanism inculcated in Christian schools is not infrequently a merely natural achievement on which faith is somehow superimposed, which grace inspires from without. A fully Christian humanism will not neglect such natural values, but it will see them from the start in their supernatural context, as themselves already supernaturalized and rendered sacramental by the Spirit Who fills all things.

Christian wisdom acknowledges the distinction between nature and supernature, between "natural" knowledge and supernatural knowledge. But at the same time it reveals that everything in the natural order, including such natural knowledge, should be seen and treated in relation to the self-revelation of God to faith. This is in fact, as regards the intellectual order and the entire range of human knowledge, to recognize a higher synthetic view of things in which all knowing becomes theological knowing. He in whom the wisdom of faith holds absolute primacy in the intellectual order is always theologizing, be he a theologian, a philosopher, a physicist, a mathematician, a sociologist, a student or scholar of whatever kind. It is not that he is distracted by some alien preoccupation when he finds God in new ways in all these activities, for this is only to apprehend the deepest meaning of every creature. Nor does this mean that he pays less attention to the so-called "secular" aspect of such study or research. For God is also there – this is the whole point, that there is absolutely nothing in the creature in any of its aspects which does not also speak of God. Indeed, to ignore the so-called secular significance of creatures is to ignore many of the words they utter to us about God. If a church is a special dwelling-place of God, in which one even "feels" more easily the presence of God, then we must say that for the Christian the entire world and the entire universe and all the sciences and all other human achievements exist in a church, in the cosmic temple of God, and that every such creature should evoke, and be approached with, a sense of reverence at the nearness of the Lord. Such should be the fruit of total openness to and under grace, to all being and to the plenitude of being, under the light of Christian wisdom.

In the customary manner of speaking, there are two levels of knowing, one terminating in the light of reason alone – purely natural knowing, and the other terminating in the light of faith (although the light of reason may here be employed in a subordinate role too) – this is the knowledge of faith and theology. Let us say that from the viewpoint of the abstract distinction of formal objects, such a distinction is adequate enough. But at the same time the distinction, in the sense in which it is frequently enough understood, is also grossly inadequate. Granting that such purely natural objects of knowledge exist (and therefore recognizing a certain validity in the distinction drawn), still in the light of all that has been said above one cannot help but feel a sense of unreality about the concept of a purely natural knowledge in a man in whom Christian wisdom is allowed its full scope. For him the purely natural formal object of knowledge is – how shall we say it? – elevated and transfigured by being subalternated to a higher light in Christian wisdom. From the subjective, psychological point of view, I have elsewhere [3] suggested that natural habits of knowing continue to exist in their natural being but that they are now caught up in a synergic operation of both supernatural and natural habits at once, so that natural knowing is at the same time supernatural knowing; and

[3] *Ibid.*, 176f.

reflection upon physical laws, for example, is a filling-out of the vision given by faith and more deeply plumbed by theology. So it is that physics remains physics and yet at the same time becomes theology.

There are then two manners of theologizing. The first, which is what has most commonly been called theology, seeks to examine carefully and understand more deeply the very truth which was historically revealed and communicated to us through Scripture and Tradition. One could here conceive the contents of this revelation as embodied in a determinate set of propositions communicated to certain men, and then distinguish between the implicitly and explicitly, and the actually and virtually revealed, in the manner of the older theological schools. Or one could better conceive this revelation as first of all the revelation of certain realities, so that together with determinate propositions uttered at determinate points of space and time there is also a certain *"mitgesagt,"* communicated in diverse ways – by the total life-context, by silence as well as by words, by gestures, by whatever means were available. On this latter supposition, the scope of the revealed can be broadened considerably, and it is impossible for us to assign precise limits to it; we can only affirm what we know and observe the development of dogma, holding firm to the conviction that this development takes place under the close guidance of the Holy Spirit leading us to a fuller understanding of what was already communicated in some manner even to the early Christians. But with either understanding of revelation, the following remarks concerning theology remain generically true.

Theology seeks to attain the meaning and adequate intelligibility of revelation, so far as this be possible for us. Christians have always felt, and it was reaffirmed by Vatican I, that some understanding – partial and analogical – of the revealed mysteries is possible. This understanding can exist at three levels. There is an intelligibility immanent in the very formulae of revelation themselves, in the truth which is formally and actually revealed. To clarify this initial intelligibility is the work of positive theology, and to accomplish this work better theology makes use of a wealth of natural knowledges as instruments, such as history, anthropology, linguistics, philology, etc. Secondly, there is an intelligibility in the ontological principles of the revealed truths and in the consequences flowing from them, an intelligibility which is somewhat attainable by us with the aid of natural reason and the philosophical light which it can provide. For example, the meaning of nature and person must be plumbed in order the better to understand the mysteries of the Trinity and the Incarnation, and the relation between God's transcendent causality and human freedom must be investigated in order to shed some light on the revealed mysteries of grace and predestination. Going in the other direction, the revelation of an existent moral order, naturally accessible to man, calls for ever greater illumination from the progressive growth in human moral consciousness. There is yet a third order of theological intelligibility, perhaps assimilable to the second, yet perhaps also useful to distinguish and describe by itself. Here there is question of the wider ontological context which grounds the possibility of revelation itself and of the various revealed truths. The general question here might be phrased as follows: What are the intermediary and ultimate conditions for the possibility of such a revelation? The pursuit of such an inquiry, if successful, would lead to the formulation of a "theological metaphysics" which would perhaps exclude certain philosophical positions as radically incompatible with Christian revelation. Indeed, we have already seen the gradual closing off of certain lines of thought by the magisterium of the Church – certain philosophical positions ruled out (although there are seldom lacking those who would try again to see how far they can get in these paths and still hold to the pronouncements of the magisterium, interpreted in at least a minimal sense). Such theological metaphysics may overlap the field of philosophy in a great deal of its area; the Christian philosopher consequently will have to pay close attention to theological truths, not just to avoid certain possibilities of error and conflict with theology, but even more to take advantage of the positive guidance which theology can offer to the inquiry of reason in the domain of philosophy.

The second manner of theologizing, frequently enough ignored by some professional theologians, has already been described above. Here the Christian scholar seeks to locate whatever natural truth he has gained in the all-embracing context provided by Christian wisdom, to view it under the light of faith, charity, and theology in the narrower sense. Here, faith and theology in the narrower sense are seen as providing us with a certain outline-structure of the total truth of reality, an outline-structure to be filled in with the aid of the entire universe of natural truth and goodness of being. Such a structure now filled in with such content constitutes theology in a broader sense, at a moment of greater perfection in which its sapiential, ordering, and directive function as "queen of the sciences" is more fully realized. Theology in this state, as I say, seldom exists among professional theologians – they are preoccupied for the most part with the work of theology in the narrower sense. Yet it does exist, mainly among many Christian scholars in other sciences who are concerned that nothing in their life, not even in their intellectual life, elude the light of faith and the dominion of charity. Such scholars understand the UNUM NECESSARIUM, and with this understanding they seek to achieve a fundamental form and unity of their intellectual life in Christian wisdom. If there are other Christian scholars whose openness to some particular domain of truth does not carry with it such a complete openness to faith and all the light which faith, charity, and theology bring to the special domain of created truth they love, this is a serious error. St. Bonaventure tells us that the knowledge of the creature which does not terminate in knowledge of the creator is death. Yet one may hope that this non-openness at the level of formulated knowledge is much more the fruit of the wound of ignorance dealt us by original sin than the result of any deliberate exclusion. Behind such non-openness at this level may lie a more radical adherence to the Uncreated Truth, an unreserved commitment in the basic existential option, one deeper in some such cases than that of some strong proponents of the idea of Christian intellectualism here described. The judgment is only for God to make; and His judgment respects not the play of conceptual, propositional, and discursive reason so much as the deep commitment of the heart and its openness to Himself and to His grace. But still, all must seek and follow the Light, so far as they can, even to the level of formulation and intellectual discipline.

If the position of the Christian intellectual under the light of faith be such as I have described, then the reality of a philosophy that is Christian as to its state, even though not in its intrinsic nature as specified by a natural formal object, seems evident enough. Gilson has so emphasized this idea of Christian philosophy as an examination of natural objects under a theological inspiration that he even conceives Christian philosophy as the study of the "revealable." [4] Such a formulation runs the risk of confusing philosophy with the theological metaphysics spoken of above, but it does bring out the transfiguration of philosophy that takes place in the light of Christian wisdom. The actual impact of Christian revelation upon the history of philosophy has been traced out by Gilson in his *The Spirit of Medieval Philosophy*.[5]

But perhaps a better exposition of the notion of Christian philosophy

---
[4] *The Christian Philosophy of St. Thomas Aquinas* (New York, 1956), p. 3–25.
[5] New York, 1936.

is to be found in Jacques Maritain's *Essay on Christian Philosophy*.[6] In terms of the distinction between abstract nature and concrete state in a Christian knower, Maritain outlines the effects of Christian wisdom on the inner structure of philosophy. Even apart from the existential orientation of such a philosophy beyond itself, and the subjective helps afforded by divine grace rectifying the weaknesses of fallen nature, in the very line of the object known the ordering and importance, and indeed the very positing of problems for the philosopher is different because he is a Christian. The central problems of God and the nature and end of man occupy the center of the stage, even if in hurrying on to these fundamental questions the philosopher must leave somewhat undeveloped his analysis of many important matters such as the nature of the physical world and that of human language. Also, the very answers to many of the questions are already outlined in a theological light, in this manner facilitating the philosopher's inquiry and search for understanding according to his proper light of human reason. And in the domain of the practical, of moral philosophy, the light afforded by revelation on the actual state of man as elevated, fallen, and redeemed, and on the actual helps which are offered to him, as well as on the concrete character of man's last end, enables the Christian philosopher to arrive at an ethics that is more than purely natural and therefore capable of being an existential norm for man as he actually is in his concrete moral decisions.

Clearly, all that has been said means that there must be a continuing vital interaction between the Christian philosopher and the Christian theologian in the narrower sense. Indeed, for one who knows what is what in this domain it is really necessary for the same man to be both philosopher (and therefore also theologian in the broader sense) and theologian (in the narrower sense). It is not an accident that the greatest of scholastic philosophers have also been theologians, and indeed usually primarily theologians. Gilson assures us that the true scholastic philosophers will always be theologians. Christian philosophy and Christian theology feed each other and flow into each other, and all the more so as Christian wisdom comes to more and more complete dominance in the life of the Christian thinker. There can be mere philosophers among Christian professors (sad to say), but there are no mere philosophers among the Christian saints. And the ages of profound theological understanding of the ontological depths in the revealed dogmas have also been the ages of progress in Christian philosophy. The

[6] New York, 1955.

current emphasis upon positive theology in many circles and the consequent depreciation of the role of philosophy as an instrument in the development of theological understanding may lay some groundwork for a future development of dogmatic theology; but it would seem to promise an even further decline in dogmatic theology in the immediate future, at least in such intellectual circles. One might even wonder whether it is not in fact the decline of ontological understanding in both philosophy and theology that has led to the current emphasis on – or is it retreat to? – positive, chiefly Scriptural, theology.

I hope that all this suffices to make understandable my own personal position – that I could never be merely a philosopher, that Christian philosophy for me is a way, and a very good way, to Christian theology. Theology of course, has other sources of material that transcend all the wisdom of the philosophers; and the Christian philosopher who crosses the threshhold of theology in the more special sense must take account of these materials more than of his philosophy. Yet surely it would be a surrender to human inertia to forego the theological inquiry because of the necessity of learning a few new things about method and a few new sources. The very dynamism of Christian philosophy under the light of Christian wisdom, and the call of God to the Christain philosopher to enter more fully into His light make it impossible for him to stop and rest content with even Christian philosophy. The pagans spoke of the necessity of man to philosophize, but the Christian philosopher must speak of the necessity of man to theologize. So it is that after considerable investigation and writing in the fields of logic, the philosophy of science, the philosophy of nature, metaphysics, and moral philosophy, I feel compelled to push on and set down the theological reflections of a Christian philosopher.

But before concluding this brief essay, I feel it necessary to correct a possible false impression. In bringing out and setting in strong relief the character of the fully Christian intellectual as a theologian in at least the broader sense, I may perhaps seem to have made an unbridgeable gulf between the Christian intellectual and the non-Christian. In a certain sense this is quite true, and yet something else must be said. We saw previously the existence of a basic existential option, through which men can be open under grace to the fullness of being and to the divine ways at a profound level of conscious life even while there is no clear evidence of this at the level of formulated knowledge. Men in this state are in fact already Christian without knowing it, for it is the grace of Christ which brings them into this state. Christian wisdom is already operative in them in secret ways, and they grope toward a greater fullness of the Light. They are already friends of the Word, as St. Justin has pointed out. All who have a truly unreserved dedication to the truth in all its plenitude, to the good wherever it may be found, and a consent to the totality of being and therefore to the divine ways (though they may not understand this latter for what it is), all men of this kind – although who of us can with utter assurance and clear certainty declare himself to be of this number? – whether they be within or outside the visible Church of Christ, are in fact fellow Christians and fellow pilgrims moving toward the fullness of the Light that illumines all men who come into this world.

SOME REMARKS ON THEOLOGICAL METHOD

Every science of the real world must begin with some given data, which are then to be understood in their principles in a systematic way. In theology the data are the revealed truths accepted by divine faith. Prior to the systematic understanding of the principles of the data, ordinarily there is an attempt to systematize the data themselves, according to greater or less generality, clarity, certitude, etc. This too is in its way a "science," but very imperfect in its form. With regard to revealed data, this could be called the science of faith, while theological grasp of the intelligible principles of these revealed data, so far as possible, would be better called the "wisdom" of faith. This first portion of scientific theology is commonly called positive theology.

In fact, positive theology does not exist apart from some achievement in the line of explanatory theology. How could it even be adequately determined that such and such a statement truly deserves the assent of divine faith, unless one had already come to understand in some manner what revelation is, what are the criteria of its recognition, what are the means through which it is proposed? But this is already to go somewhat beyond the historical data in the books of Scripture and in the Tradition of the Church. Still, there is a certain natural priority of positive theology to any other theology; for all explanations must ultimately rest on factual data. It may be that the first acceptance of these factual data is rather confusedly given in a degree of obscurity, and that only later can one clarify to himself what he has done. So it seems to have been in the case of the Apostles, who accepted Christ and His words long before the Spirit came to clarify what they had done. But there could be no clarification unless there was first a simple hearing and acceptance. Therefore, positive theology can rightly be called the foundation of the entire structure of theological science.

The effort to ascertain what has actually been revealed is difficult enough; this revelation has gradually been unfolded at determinate points of space and time in a historical process and has been continually presented in first less and then more developed formulations by the teaching Church, again at determinate points in space and time in words and writings. The positive theologian must search the historical past, particularly through the Scriptures and the Tradition presented by the Fathers and doctors of the Church, and the diverse pronouncements of the magisterium of the Church, in order to determine more and more clearly and solidly what it is that has actually been revealed by God through whatever instruments he has chosen to use. To accomplish this work, he must make use of historical understanding of the spatio-temporal contexts in which the formulations of revelation were made, in order the better to grasp precisely what was meant by formulae appearing in cultural contexts utterly different from our own. So also, linguistics, anthropology, and other human sciences must be brought into play. But positive theology is not simply a purely natural knowledge proceeding according to the natural lights of the historian; it accomplishes its work in the light of an already existent faith, a global assent to the revelation of God which is presented to us through the Church. It is in the light of the analogy of faith that the positive theologian seeks to make more precise and more clear the meaning of authoritative and infallible statements of the revealed truth, and of the testimony of the Fathers and doctors.

Once again then, if positive theology has a certain logical priority in the development of theological science, still it does not accomplish its task without continual light from the already achieved explanatory understanding of faith. In fact, even the presentation of revealed truth in Scripture is found to include something of the effort of theological understanding, so that the revealed data themselves are already more than mere data. One can see this easily enough by comparing the writings of John and Paul to the Synoptic Gospels, although it is also true even of the Synoptics themselves that what is presented is not just fact and word but interpreted fact and interpreted word.

Nor does this mean that we must try to distinguish a "*purely* human" element in the Scripture from a "divine" element. The whole of Scripture is inspired, both the presentation of data and the interpretation of data. This beginning of theology in the full and proper sense was made in the privileged state in which its formulations were protected by the charism of divine inspiration – a state which even today is not lacking insofar as the Church can by its infallible teaching authority canonize certain theological formulations in solemn definitions or even through the agreement of the ordinary teaching of the bishops. But the protective charism is no longer that of inspiration in the proper sense, in which God is truly the author of the very words of the human author, but rather that of divine guidance, in which the teaching authority is guarded by the Holy Spirit from making an error in teaching the contents of revelation and urged on by the Spirit to teach what has actually been revealed.

I do not intend here to discuss the various *loci*, or fonts, in which the revealed truth can be found, and the problems connected with each. The manner of approaching and evaluating the data from Scripture, the Fathers, the theologians, the Councils, the pronouncements of the Pope, the common teaching of the bishops throughout the world, and the common consent of the faithful themselves, may be learned from the various classic and authoritative works on the subject. Here I only wish to dwell upon some problems of special contemporary interest, arising out of the recent growth and progress of studies in Sacred Scripture and positive theology in general. The principal such problem is that of the place of Scripture in the whole of theological science; but a few words will be added concerning the place of the magisterium and the relation of the magisterium to the work of the theologians, both positive and explanatory theologians.

Sacred Scripture does not appear to us as self-evident light but as a mystery into which we can enter ever more deeply. We find ourselves in profound ignorance of such matters as place, date, manner of composition, precise context in the life of the time, as regards the books of the Old and New Testaments. To a certain extent this ignorance is illumined by our hypotheses and by solid scientific achievements in the study of ancient languages and cultures and of the relation of the Bible to these. But in fact much of the knowledge gained in the current movement of Scripture study is still radically hypothetical, frequently resting on methodological canons themselves susceptible to questioning and further refinement. In any event, whatever be the convergence of evidence toward the acceptance of certain hypotheses as the most plausible for the interpretation of Scripture, still such interpretation – ultimately still in the order of the hypothetical and probable – cannot possibly be the norm for the fundamental act of Christian faith.

The content of Christian faith does not appear to us for the first time ready-made and shining out at us from the pages of Scripture. Rather, we read Scripture in the light of an already existing faith and Christian commitment, and then interpret this Scripture under the guidance of the teaching Church and in the light of the analogy of faith. Current assertions that the deposit of faith is in fact entirely contained within the pages of Sacred Scripture are really irrelevant here. Who could find all the elements of the deposit of faith there but the man of faith interpreting this Scripture under the guidance of the Church by the light of the Holy Spirit?

We have already seen that Scripture is theology at a certain level of development – it is not only a set of data but also theological interpretation of these data. And this is so despite the fact that it is neither scientific in its mode of presentation nor even very literary, at least for the most part. Yet Scripture could not be *the* source of all valuable theology, as some would have it; were this so, a careful study of Biblical theology would pretty well exhaust the contents of theological science. But this would fail to take into account the necessary development of dogmatic thought demanded by the very evolution of human intellectual life and therefore of every idea that captivates the mind of man. And yet, Sacred Scripture does still have some kind of normative influence in all subsequent theological speculation, and not only normative in a negative sense but also in the positive sense of inspiring faith and theological reflection and the consequent growth of the science of theology.

Sacred Scripture contains a divinely inspired global presentation of the Christian reality of God saving the world in Christ and through the Spirit. This presentation is mysterious and obscure, and calls for pondering and meditating on the part of those who wish to know the will of the Lord; God extends His hand to us, but He insists that we in turn make a free response to His call, even to the point of demanding that we must reflectively ponder His word in order to understand what it really means. But though this word of God be mysterious and obscure, it still remains divinely inspired and is consequently a standard against which the (human) theological science of every age must stand to be compared and judged, so as to determine its continuity with Scripture as genuine development rather than adulteration or alteration. The comparison itself is frequently difficult enough, because of the obscurity of Scripture. And yet there are general lines of thought which can be discerned even outside the visible Church, even where mere human scholarship and private judgment are set up as the ultimate judges of the meaning of Scripture. For example, the theme of divine election, of the Messiah to come, of the unique claim of Christ, of a new and final dominion of God over all, these and other such themes of Scripture can at least be understood, if not accepted, even by unbelievers. But it is the Church which has the prerogative of being the definitive interpreter of Scripture and teacher of the whole of divine revelation; she alone can make the definitive judgment as to whether or not theological elaborations of later centuries are genuine expressions and developments of the revealed dogmas rather than human interpolations.

But in making such a judgment, even the Church does not ordinarily see fit to define the real meaning of texts of Scripture; these texts themselves are not all-important. It is the faith which is already in the Church and which she brings to the reading of the Scriptures that is the real norm of judgment, just as it was this faith already existing in the Jewish and later the Christian community that produced the Scriptures in the first place. In this light, the comparison of later theological statements with those of Scripture and early Tradition appears as something far beyond the merely linguistic level; it is a comparison of the intelligible content of such statements; and, even more than this, it is a comparison of the realities referred to by such statements, since faith does not rest in statements but in reality itself. The crucial question is whether the less scientific, more "primitive" statements of Scripture and early Tradition actually refer to the same reality as do the more scientific theological elaborations and developments, or whether these later statements of theological science have not turned our attention to a so-called reality quite other than that which was revealed to Israel and to the Apostles. The question is often not an easy one to answer, and we must wait to hear the voice of the Church under the guidance of the Spirit.

But the Church is far from reluctant to accept theological formulations in non-Scriptural terms, even in the solemn definitions of dogmas of the faith by the Popes and by the Councils. She will cite Scriptural texts, but these are ordinarily not in the definitions themselves. She understands that the statements of Semitic minds are not necessarily the clearest and the best incarnations of the revealed truth in linguistic form for men of other cultures and other times. However privileged in virtue of the charism of divine inspiration the Semitic writings are, it is necessary that the revealed truth be brought to all men by whatever means assure clarity and precision in each succeeding age and culture. If the charism of inspiration be lacking to subsequent formulations, there is still the charism of the protective guidance of the Holy Spirit.

It was under this guidance that the great Ecumenical Councils defined the dogmas of the Trinity and the Incarnation, of justification, of the relations between faith and reason, etc. It was under this guidance that the Church gave and still gives staunch support to the effort of scholastic philosophy and theology and yet recognizes the needs of further advances in the Christian synthesis, speaking of *Deus scientiarum Dominus* and of a program of *vetera novis augere*. In all this, while recognizing and insisting upon the power and value of the very inspired texts of Scripture themselves, she never shows that blind hankering after Biblical categories, Biblical idiom, Biblical theology which would disregard all the subsequent doctrinal development as distortion and even falsification.

Sacred Scripture is not, and never will be, something only of the past, over and done with, valuable for its time but now to be set aside in favor of a new form of faith. It is an inspired, though mysterious and even obscure message for men of all ages, with power to evoke a deeper response of faith in the man of faith and even to call for faith in the man of no faith. Out of its mystery shines light of infinite richness, which we shall never be done with seeing in all its facets. But at the same time Scripture never has been and is not the sum total of theology. Even within Scripture the process of dogmatic development clearly begins, and it continues throughout the history of the Church.

Christ and His message endure for all time in the Church, and the Church must seek ever more apt means by which to incarnate His message, even in the frail vessels of merely human language and merely human thought. Such vessels are as infinitely unworthy in themselves of conveying the divine message as a human nature was of showing us the very Person and face of the Word. Yet by the power of God, through the guidance of the Spirit, the Church may dare to make use of the poor human stammerings of theologians and philosophers to formulate and express something of the revealed mysteries. In this manner Christ in the Church speaks not only to the Hebrews in Semitic idiom but to the Greeks in Greek idiom and to all the various cultures in their own idioms. It is only by a strange paradox and misunderstanding that some theologians could oppose the idea of cultural adaptation of the presentation of divine revelation; for the very work of scientific theology is essentially a work of cultural adaptation in a broad sense, a movement from Semitic modes of presentation to more universal modes.

In the light of the foregoing remarks upon the place of Sacred Scripture in the whole of theology, it is perhaps easier to see why theologians say that it is not Scripture but the formulated teaching of the magisterium of the Church that is the *proximate* norm of faith, the immediate criterion by which we judge the genuinity of our faith and of its object. And it would not be correct simply to add that in making its declarations this magisterium simply draws as on an ultimate norm or source from the sayings of Scripture. It is not the words of Scripture as linguistic forms, not the ideas of Scripture as ordered and even conceptualized by the mind of a Semite, but rather the very reality which is described by these words and these ideas, and the very faith which had already attained this reality even before giving itself expression in the words of Scripture, that is the true ultimate norm and criterion for the pronouncements of the magisterium.

But these pronouncements do not simply materialize when needed. The Church here makes use of the formulations of the theological tradition, of words and concepts and propositions which might even have originated in non-Christian philosophical contexts before they were assimilated into Christian theology. Long before the Church could produce its dogmatic formulations, there was need of the efforts of theologians seeking to understand the data of revelation as they encountered them in their own time and place, seeking to penetrate their meaning more profoundly and then to judge, in the light of faith, of the precise value of such understanding as they had achieved. Here would have to begin the much-maligned but necessary business of assigning "theological notes," which specify the noetic value, the certitude, the type of certitude, the degree of probability, of various theological statements. Theology cannot simply "wait on" the magisterium; rather, it is the magisterium that waits on theology. If the process of dogmatic development and adaptation of the presentation of the Christian message to cultures ever more intellectually advanced is to continue, and surely this is necessary if we are to restore all things in Christ, then the theologian could never rest content with pointing to past pronouncements of the magisterium and to the texts of Scripture, the Fathers, and the ancient and medieval and early modern doctors. Always he must seek to understand and to interpret for his contemporaries in the terms they can understand, with the help of a truly growing and developing perennial philosophy (and here so many Thomists have failed Thomism), the contents of the revealed truth. But this call to more than a collection of the data of the past is a call to more than positive theology; it is also a call to more than the history of theological systems and especially the history of Thomism. It is a call to carry on the work of understanding the data of revelation in their inner meaning, their ontological reality; this is the work of metaphysical theology.

The inspired word of God in Scripture and in early Tradition was not presented in a scientific mode, but rather in the medium of common language and common understanding, so that men other than the most learned could readily hear and grasp it. In order that this might be done it was necessary to incarnate the revealed truth in the language, categories, and cultural context of the people who first received this revelation, that is to say, the Semitic people of Israel. Not only because of the native tendency of the human intellect to plumb as deeply as possible whatever mysteries it finds presented to itself, but also because of the need to make the revealed word accessible to all times and all cultures, it was necessary that theological speculation carry the formulation of the revealed word and of its more amplified understanding from the level of common language and common categories and common sense to the level of more fully developed scientific theology with its refined terminology and categories conveying something of the deeper meaning and ontological reality in themselves of the truths of faith.

In this work of theological understanding the same basic method as that of any human scientific knowledge had to be followed. First had to come the sharper analysis of data given at first in confusion, leading for example to the more precise formulation of the relation of Christ to the Uncreated God, and of the nature of the Holy Spirit. Following such clarification it was necessary to seek for the ontological principles of the data, as is exemplified in St. Augustine's attempt to understand something about the mystery of the Trinity, and even more in the great efforts of scholastic theology in the Middle Ages. Even the first task of analysis is really a movement beyond the data of revelation itself, since the new formulations are not themselves to be found in the primitive expressions of revelation and depend upon the human ingenuity of very human theologians for their reality as matter to be assumed by the Church in its dogmatic formulations. But this kind of theological development as a result of human effort is especially manifest in the second task, penetration of the ontological principles of the data of revelation.

In this latter work, the achievements of philosophical analysis, and especially of the analogical intellection of metaphysics, are necessary instruments. The primary truths of revelation concern spiritual realities and the relation of man and of the material world to these spiritual realities. But in order to understand these more deeply we must make use of analogies and conclusions from our philosophical understanding of being, of spiritual reality, of the inner nature even of the material world, of moral truth. Other human knowledges are also of value; but the role of philosophy here – as the handmaiden of theology, to use an old expression which has acquired unfortunate connotations – remains paramount. There are those in every age who decry the use of philosophical ideas by theology, and of course there is such a thing as the abuse called rationalism in theology; such anti-intellectual theologians who would resolutely refuse to philosophy any role at all in the understanding of the revealed truth have some vocation in the Church – but it is not to the work of the theologian. But if philosophy is necessary here, this means especially metaphysics, which is the very heart of philosophical understanding and the primary natural knowledge through which we can come to some understanding of being in general and even of spiritual being in particular. This is why we have called the kind of theology we are considering "metaphysical" theology.

Four diverse modes or levels may be distinguished in metaphysical theology. The first is that refinement in understanding, a translation into more scientific and even metaphysical terminology and concepts, of the real elements of revelation. This is that clarification of the data of which we have spoken. One of the easier cases of this to see is the transition from the Scriptural mode of speaking of the three Persons in the one God to the use of such terms as consubstantiality, person, nature, etc.

At the second level of metaphysical theology there is the attempt to penetrate the ontological principles of given truths of revelation, either by accounts that are certain so far as they go, but inadequate, or by hypothetical accounts, which employ analogies constructed on the basis of natural, usually metaphysical, knowledge. Of the first kind of explanation examples can be seen in the distiction of the three Persons in God by relations of opposition, in the understanding of created grace as supernatural, both a principle and result of the divine indwelling, a participation in the life of God and the beginning of eternal life, and something flowing from the missions of the Son and of the Holy Spirit in time. Examples of the second kind of explanation can be seen in various theories explaining the hypostatic union, the ontological nature of the created supernatural, the processions in God, the structure of the beatific vision, the reality of the sacrament of the Eucharist, etc. I do not wish to suggest that one could never transcend the level of hypothesis in such domains, but in any event these domains have been fertile fields for the generation of such hypotheses.

At the third level of metaphysical theology is the elaboration of a theological metaphysics, metaphysics seen under the light of revelation as grounding the possibility of the revelation we actually have, therefore a metaphysics consistent with the fact of divine revelation itself and with every revealed truth, a metaphysics open to the totality of the supernatural order. Clearly, since revelation does not itself present us with such a metaphysical system, this theology requires as matter the historical reality of philosophy, and particularly of the "perennial philosophy." One must await the formulation of philosophical, metaphysical interpretations of being and then judge of them in the light of revelation – although this does not in any way preclude a genuinely Christian effort to philosophize, or the reality of such a thing as "Christian philosophy."

But these are still distinct tasks: to philosophize even as a Christian and to judge in the light of theology and of the magisterium concerning the relation of philosophical doctrines to revelation and its contents. These two tasks should of course both be performed by the one same Christian philosopher, so that there is in him a kind of continuing dialogue between faith and reason. But the magisterium of the Church is not a philosopher; she waits and observes lines of philosophical speculation and their consequences before she speaks out with a favorable or unfavorable judgment. Yet when she does finally speak, a certain narrowing down of possible positions even in philosophy itself must result for the Christian philosopher; nor should a favoring of one line of philosophizing at the expense of others appear as a total surprise (as it seemingly does to some Christian intellectuals). Some questions that were formerly open do become closed as the thought of the Church develops in time; it would be a sad commentary on the worth of the human intellect were this not so. The Church's recommendation of the scholastic philosophy and especially of Thomism does not mean that the best expression of philosophical truth is for all time found in scholasticism and specifically in Thomism. But it does mean that there is a certain harmony between the truth of revelation and the truth as reason sees it in such philosophy, this itself being a strong confirmation of at least the global truth of the philosophical intuitions of Thomism. Certainly, a number of systems of philosophy, such as materialism, Kantianism, pantheism, have been definitively excluded as regards certain of their fundamental principles on the ground of their incompatibility with the kind of divine revelation we have actually been given. It may well be that revelation and theology do not give us a criterion by which we can eliminate all philosophical alternatives but a uniquely determined one, so that there would be one and only one possible elaboration of theological metaphysics. But in any event, certain general outlines of theological metaphysics can emerge clearly enough, to one who attentively considers the pronouncements of the magisterium. For example, the declaration of Vatican I that we can come to a knowledge of God's existence by natural reason requires a certain confidence in human reason as a means of knowing the real; the insistence of the same Council upon the reasonability of the act of faith tends toward the same confidence in the power of human reason. The very fact of dogmatic formulations binding on the belief of the faithful commits us to confidence in the value of human conceptualization and judgment. Much of natural theology in the scholastic sense is not at all free matter for dispute among Christian thinkers since it pertains in one manner or another to the deposit of faith and to the theological understanding of the deposit of faith. The absolute uniqueness of God and the createdness of absolutely everything other than God, the absolute immutability of God and the radical mutability of every creature, the infinity of God and the radically finite nature of every creature – all these and other such truths come to us through a light of faith higher than any philosophy and foreclose a good deal of philosophical controversy (although of course it remains one thing to believe such truths or conclude to them in the light of faith and quite another thing to come to see the natural evidence for them).

The fourth level of metaphysical theology is that of its sapiential function, which has already been described in the previous essay. This level is outside of what has commonly been regarded as theology in the strict sense, and yet in fact it is in continuity with such theology and indeed proceeds under the same formal light of faith using reason and therefore pertains to the same one science of theology. The wise man orders and directs; so it must be with wisdom itself. If theology is not only science but also the genuine wisdom of faith, which must order and direct the whole of human life in all the spheres of knowing and acting, then its sapiential function is not just something extra-added to the essential but rather the fulfillment of theology in its wisdom-character. Order and direction – what do these mean? It is a matter of assigning to each of the diverse and manifold modes of knowing and loving its place in the total movement of man to God under grace. It is therefore also a matter of judging currents of history, of political, economic, social and cultural life. No sphere of human activity should be allowed to escape evaluation and judgment under the light of faith and theology.

But the exercise of the sapiential function of theology is quite complex and demands greatest care in the avoidance of precipitate and uninformed judgments and in recognizing the conditions for valid judgment, direction, and ordering. Always there is the primary condition of immediate acquaintance before judgment can take place. And since the truth of revelation is generally of an order high above so much of merely human knowing and action, even easily dismissed as irrelevant by those who are either not interested or unwilling to take the pains necessary to bring it to bear in a relevant manner on the concerns of men, it is necessary that faith and theology exercise their sapiential influence through the instrumentality of relatively autonomous intermediary modes of knowledge and of human freedom – human sciences like philosophy and human institutions like the state. The philosophy of science knows better than theology in the narrower sense about the diverse modes of being and of knowing according to which one can distinguish, relate, and integrate the various human achievements in the lines of philosophy and the positive sciences. The state knows better than the theologian how to order the affairs of diplomacy, economic regulation, and the conditions of peaceful exercise of political freedom. If the Christian intellectual and the Christian politician are illuminated by theological wisdom, then their autonomous exercise of their proper tasks is still informed, illuminated, orientated, elevated by a higher light than that of merely human knowledge and prudence; this is quite enough to make this work an instrument of and a participation in theology in its sapiential function. It is far more discerning and prudent of the theologian to allow such intermediaries to do his work than to disregard them and try to issue orders for all things from afar. Such theological imperialism in fact ends in the disregard of the truth of theology which men see as making claims that it cannot possibly fulfill.

In fact, this hierarchy of intermediaries, autonomous but needing supernatural elevation through the overall direction of faith and theology descending through the chain of intermediaries, is not a small and simple hierarchy but a very large and very complex one. The principle of subsidiarity applies not only in the order of political freedom but throughout the entire sphere of human activity both speculative and practical. So it is that the mere enunciation of revealed truth is not sufficient to secure the order and direction of all things in the current of divine life in the world. Each must seek to know his place and to gain a natural knowledge of the context of his work in the totality of human life in order to properly fulfill his role in the earthly beginning of the building up of the city of God. The physicist could not be only a physicist, disregarding all else in the world; nor could he be content with being a Christian physicist referring all he does to a rather generically conceived "glory of God." He must also try to relate his life as a physicist to other domains of human life, to see which of these domains has a special claim upon him, perhaps even in his activity as a physicist. Only in such a manner can his divine call to "glorify God" in all he does take on a fully specific and individual character at every moment of his life. We have had more than enough of Christians who, in all subjective sincerity, pursue in simplicity their little work without regard for its total context in the human life of men; so it is that "holy" Christians can be so oblivious of the social dimensions of what they do, of the need to relate it to the greater and common work of all Christians in the building up of the body of Christ not only in the interior life of grace but also in the exterior "merely" human achievements of knowing and action which form the substratum on which grace must build.

With all this being said about the complexity of the hierarchy of intermediaries through which theology exercises its sapiential function on the whole domain of human existence and action, it remains true that the highest intermediary, the most proximate of merely human sciences to theology, is metaphysics. This is so because metaphysics considers being in its totality and alone can provide an adequate context in which the diverse modes of being and knowing can be placed. In its philosophy of science, metaphysics provides ordering principles governing the speculative life of man in the natural order; in its philosophy of value, metaphysics yields ordering principles for the moral and aesthetic life of man. Still, we must insist on the need of lower intermediaries, for metaphysics stands far above other sciences and modes of human action.

This brief outline of the sapiential function of theology and the mode of its exercise through autonomous intermediaries was necessary in order to show the whole range of metaphysical theology. However, the essays to follow will be confined to what we have called theology in the narrower sense, in an effort to penetrate something of the meaning of various key Christian ideas, either themselves dogmas or at least closely related to the dogmas. I have insisted that the sapiential function of theology is too much neglected by the theologians, but I must proceed by steps. My own theological reflections more properly relevant to such theological direction and judgment of human things must be left to be treated elsewhere.

3

FAITH AND INTERSUBJECTIVITY

I. INTRODUCTION

In the never-ending discussion and output of literature concerning the nature of faith as a response to the revelation of God in the Old and the New Testaments, two sharply opposed concepts of faith have appeared and come to dominate the discussion. The scholastic textbooks of theology have, in their logically precise manner, crystallized the opposition under the names of "trusting faith" (*fides fiducialis*) and "assenting faith" (*fides ut assensus*). In trusting faith, confidence in God holds the first place; dogmatic truth is secondary. This faith is first of all affective, an act of the will, a personal commitment to a person. It is the confidence that we see agian and again in the New Testament, which Our Lord demands *before* He works the miracle.[1]

On the other hand, in assenting faith, intellectual assent to revealed truths expressed in propositions holds the first place. There is an affective component in such faith, since faith is an act of the intellect as moved by the will in the absence of the manifest intrinsic evidence of the truths to be believed. But the affection is in some sense subsidiary. The idea of personal commitment to a person is not utterly eliminated, but it is allowed to recede into the background. Such faith is also found in the New Testament,[2] and the Church has never ceased to insist upon its necessity for every Catholic.[3] Scholastic theologians analyzed this

---

[1] See, for example, Mt 9: 2, 20–22, 27–30; but these are only a few among many. For a detailed study, see Edward D.O'Connor, C.S.C., *Faith in the Synoptic Gospels*, Notre Dame, 1961.

[2] See, for example, Mk 16: 15–16 and Lk 8: 12. Examples of this kind of faith are rarer in the Synoptics. But they are found with great frequency in John and in Acts. See, for example, John 1: 48–50, 2: 22, 3: 32–34, 5: 24, 25, 31–33, etc. and Acts 2: 41, 3: 22–23, 4: 4, 8: 12–14, 35–37, ect.

[3] In the New Testament, see, for example, Rom 10: 9, I Cor 15: 1–17, Phil 2: 11, Hebr 11: 6, John 8: 24, 17: 20–23, 20: 31, I John 4: 15, 5: 5, etc. For early Symbols, see DB 16, 18, 39, 40, etc. Vatican I is quite clear: DB 1789, 1791, 1792, 1814, 1815. (If there be any reader unaware of the meaning of DB, it refers to any of the editions of Denzinger-Barnwart's *Enchiridion symbolorum*.)

kind of faith thoroughly, and in the light of their analyses came to interpret Scriptural faith, the faith of the New Testament, mainly in the light of this idea.[4] This emphasis on faith as intellectual assent only received greater impetus from the reaction in the Church to the Protestant Reformation and its insistence on the idea of trusting faith.[5] Then too the tendency among some Protestants to minimize the power of mere natural reason, and consequently the reasonableness of the faith, evoked in the Church a counter-emphasis upon the reasonableness of the faith and upon apologetics – which could only make the intellectual assent in faith even more prominent and diminish the element of trust in faith even further.

But what is the reality of faith? Is it *only* personal commitment? Is it *only* assent to propositions? In fact, there is a consensus between Catholics and large numbers of Protestants that faith for a Christian does require intellectual assent to some propositions – for example, that Christ is God – that this same faith also contains an element of personal commitment, that the faith of the New Testament is not simply one *or* the other. Pietism and Liberal Protestantism, and the Existentialist anti-dogmatic themes of certain vocal Protestant leaders of today are not in fact adequately representative of Protestant thought. Nor are the pronouncements of ultra-rationalists (at least in appearance if not in intention) on the Catholic side entirely representative of Catholic thought.

Since Vatican I, the sharp opposition between the two ideas of faith has been somewhat broken down in many ways. Aubert has traced carefully the growing emphasis on the role of affective elements, of subjective dispositions, of connaturality in the act of faith.[6] All this, as will be seen in subsequent chapters, leads toward a strong reaffirmation of the elements of personal commitment, trust, affection, in the act of faith. For the present, however, it will be sufficient to note three points

---

[4] This has led theologians to insist on the necessity of an explicit belief in the propositions that God exists and that He rewards and punishes, according to Hebrews 11: 6, as the minimum essential for salvation. Others go further and require an explicit belief – by, if necessary, a special revelation – in the Trinity and in the Incarnation. But it is possible that some distinction can be made between the state of a Christian and the state of a non-Christian; that a non-propositional mode of assent in an adult non-Christian may suffice to replace the propositional mode of assent demanded of an adult Christian. This will be considered in Chapter VII.

[5] See the decree on justification by the Council of Trent (DB 798, 808, 822–825, 837, 838). The emphasis of the Council was especially against trusting faith as carrying with itself an assurance of justification and salvation. But this does not mean that every form of trust is to be excluded from the Catholic conception of faith.

[6] Roger Aubert, *Le problème de l'acte de foi*, 3rd ed., Louvain, 1958, 223–787.

tending to suggest that the opposition of the two kinds of faith has been too sharply drawn. These points appear in a reexamination of the statement of Vatican I concerning faith, in the current reexamination of Scriptural statements on faith, and in a reemphasis of certain aspects of the teaching of St. Thomas concerning faith and the virtue of faith.

Vatican I, in the Constitution *"Dei Filius,"* reaffirms the teaching of the Council of Trent that divine faith enables us to believe that the things revealed by God are true. It is at least at first sight difficult to conceive of this as meaning anything other than assent to revealed propositions. Trent says:

...fidem *ex auditu* concipientes, libere moventur in Deum, credentes, vera esse, quae divinitus revelata et promissa sunt.

Vatican I gives a more explicit formulation:

Hanc vero fidem, quae "humanae salutis initium est," Ecclesia catholica profitetur, virtutem esse supernaturalem, qua, Dei aspirante et adiuvante gratia, ab eo revelata vera esse credimus, non propter intrinsecam rerum veritatem naturali rationis lumini perspectam, sed propter auctoritatem ipsius Dei revelantis, qui nec falli nec fallere potest.[8]

In the corresponding canon, the point is reemphasized:

2. Si quis dixerit, fidem divinam a naturali de Deo et rebus moralibus scientia non distingui, ac propterea ad fidem divinam non requiri, ut revelata veritas propter auctoritatem Dei revelantis credatur: A.S.[9]

Theologians of the scholastic tradition have been quick to interpret these statements as meaning that faith is essentially an intellectual assent to one or more propositions, although it may be more also. However, even this interpretation may well be an unwarranted leap made in the context of a philosophy which recognizes only formulated concepts and propositions as giving real knowledge, which tends to regard any other mode of awareness of the real as illusory or at least in some manner irrelevant. But the danger of operating in such a context has been pointed up by the rise of Existentialism, which at least claims to be concerned with other domains of being beyond those expressed in formulated concepts and propositions. It is only too easy to dismiss such a claim with the

[7] DB 798.
[8] DB 1789.
[9] DB 1811.

observation that one could hardly *talk* or *think* about such domains without the aid of formulated concepts and propositions. Yet this observation misses the point (although certain Existentialists have perhaps made themselves vulnerable by their manner of speaking). It is one thing to *express* reality in formulated knowledge; it is another thing to *merely designate* or *signify* domains of being which cannot be directly expressed in formulated knowledge. We must all use intellectual and linguistic formulations, but their reference to what we know may be quite diverse in, for example, the spheres of phenomena or essences as opposed to the sphere of interpersonal relation or the sphere of the lived existence of the self. In the former, the formulations may well express what we know; in the latter, the formulations can only point to what we know. And it is quite possible for the knowledge, in either case, to exist even prior to the formulation. But assent, at least in the ordinary sense of the term, presupposes formulation of the proposition to which we assent. If we wish to apply the term "assent" to knowledge at this deeper, pre-conceptual and pre-propositional level, we must be prepared for a rather analogical notion of assent. This will become clear especially in the discussion of the faith of pure intersubjectivity.

But despite the above remarks, Vatican I clearly indicates the necessity for the Christian to assent to the truth of certain propositions, the propositions which express the divine revelation. While the door may be left open as regards a more analogical notion of assent to apply to non-Christians to whom the revelation of God has not been preached effectively, Christian tradition is sufficiently clear as to what is expected of members of the Church. From the New Testament through the early Symbols through the Fathers and through the teaching of all orthodox theologians, the necessity for assenting faith in the Christian has been cleary affirmed; and it is in the context of this tradition that Vatican I gave its definition of faith. Yet it is well to bear in mind that both Trent and Vatican I were speaking of Christian faith, faith in the Church, and that they were speaking of it against those who would distort this faith, on the one hand, into a confidence alone or, on the other hand, into a conclusion of reason alone. It is well to keep this context before us, and not to read these decrees in the light of discussions that only began many years after Vatican I. In this light, it is somewhat less than evident that assenting faith *always* for *all* men means an assent to propositions.

But even in those within the Church, the intelligibility of faith is not exhausted, according to the statement of Vatican I, by assenting faith.

Two sentences of the decree are of particular interest here:

> Cum homo a Deo tanquam creatore et Domino suo totus dependeat et ratio creata increatae Veritati penitus subiecta sit, plenum revelanti Deo intellectus et voluntatis obsequium fide praestare tenemur.[10]

> Quare *fides* ipsa in se, etiamsi *per caritatem* non operetur, donum Dei est, et actus eius est opus ad salutem pertinens, quo homo liberam praestat ipsi Deo oboedientiam gratiae eius, cui resistere posset, consentiendo et cooperando.[11]

In the first statement, faith is seen as a personal commitment of man, wholly dependent upon God, to the personal revealing God. It is a service of intellect and will which is due to God as Creator and Lord, for created reason is by right completely subject to Uncreated Truth. The commitment is a free obedience to God Himself, again therefore an affair between persons and not simply a matter of assent to propositions, as is clear in the second statement. But such free acceptance of divine revelations by one who is by nature subject to the revealer is a kind of trust and supposes at least the beginnings of affection. Why else would it, even in one without charity, nevertheless exist only as the result of a free obedience?

In order to grasp more fully the richness of the idea of faith presented by the Vatican I statement, it is also well to dwell on the thoroughly religious context in which this act of faith is elicited. This is pointed out by various phrases in the above statements and in those quoted earlier. The phrases *"penitus subiecta," "intellectus et voluntatis obsequium," "salutis initium," "Dei aspirante et adiuvante gratia," "propter auctoritatem ipsius Dei revelantis"* – all these phrases contribute to the conception of faith as an interpersonal reality, an interpersonal relation between a created "I" and an infinite, eternal "Thou," and not simply a relation of the human intellect to the truth to which it assents. Faith then is presented to us by Vatican I as much more than assenting faith; it is also commitment-faith, interpersonal faith, trusting faith. If certain theologians did indeed appear to put forth a more limited conception of faith, the fault was in their rationalism and not in the Catholic tradition, summed up in this statement of Vatican I.[12]

Similarly, the reexamination of Scriptural texts concerning faith leads to the same conclusion. It has long recognized that the New

---

[10] DB 1789.
[11] DB 1791.
[12] In this regard, see also Chapter I, n. 5 of the *Dogmatic Constitution on Divine Revelation* of Vatican II.

Testament contains three sets of texts, some favoring the idea of confidence-faith, others the idea of assenting faith, and still others which are ambiguous.[13] Catholic scholars have long taken special pains to discover all the texts which can in any way be construed as favoring assenting faith as requisite for a Christian, and such texts are not lacking.[14] But in the Synoptics there are far more texts which refer to confidence-faith. The New Testament seems as a whole to use the word "faith" as connoting confidence almost as often as connoting an assent. One may well ask whether the ideas of confidence and commitment are ever completely absent in the New Testament idea of faith. It would seem that even when the idea of assent is in some manner primary, the idea of confidence and commitment is at least implicitly present.

Finally, if we look back at the treatment of faith in the writings of St. Thomas, we find that, while faith is for him an assent,[15] it is at the same time utterly dependent on the will and its desire for the good.[16] The reasons that can be given for believing (motives of credibility) are not sufficient to cause the act of faith; there is necessarily an infused instinct inclining toward this assent.[17] Faith goes beyond reason, to rest upon the authority of God revealing, the *veritas prima loquens*.[18] But this is a personal commitment again, a trusting faith, in response to the revelation which is itself first of all of a personal God.[19] Nor should we allow the abstract name of *"Prima Veritas,"* which St. Thomas uses so often to designate the motive of faith,[20] obscure the fact that this is the Uncreated, Infinite, *Personal* God of whom St. Thomas speaks, here designated under the most appropriate of His eternal names as the source of revelation, as the revealer.

All these points serve to point out more clearly that assenting faith is not the fullness of Christian faith. In some sense, faith must be at least two-dimensional: it connotes assent (however analogically this term may have to be taken in some cases of possible faith which will be seen later), but it also connotes a personal affective relation of trust

---

[13] See notes 1 and 2.
[14] See note 2.
[15] *Summa theologiae* (ST), II–II, q. 2, a. 1; 6, 1, c. (Standard abbreviations will be employed in references to the works of St. Thomas.) *De veritate*, q. 14, a. 1; *III Sent.*, d. 23, q. 2, a. 2, qla 1; *ad Hebr.*, c. 11, lect. 1; etc.
[16] ST II–II, 2, 1, ad 3; 2, c.; 9, c., etc.
[17] ST II–II, 6, 1, c.; 4, 4, ad 3; 5, 4, ad 3, etc. For the use of the term *"instinctus,"* see *In Ioan*, c. 6, lect. 4, n. 7, lect 5, n. 3, *In Ioan*, c. 15, lect. 5, n. 4, In Rom, c. 8. lect. 6, and Quodl. II, a. 6, ad 3.
[18] ST II–II, 1, 1, c. 2, 2, c.; 5, 1, c.; *Contra errores graecorum*, I, c. 30, etc.
[19] ST II–II, 1, 1, c.; 11, 1 c.; *De veritate*, q. 14, a. 8.
[20] ST II–II, 1, 1, c., 2, 2, c., 5, 1, c.

and commitment. The need for such a two-dimensional concept of faith will emerge anew in a rather striking way in the course of the following discussion – the theme of this essay – of the problem of the manner in which we attain the formal motive of the act of faith as the ground of this act.

The formal motive of the act of faith, that on account of which we believe, was described in that phrase already quoted above from Vatican I:

> ...non propter intrinsecam rerum veritatem naturali rationis lumine perspectam, sed propter auctoritatem ipsius Dei revelantis, qui nec falli nec fallere potest.[21]

Only this motive of divine authority can ground the absolute certitude of faith,[22] a ceritude which is therefore more firm than that of any merely human knowledge.[23] So great is this certitude that:

> 6. Si quis dixerit, parem esse conditionem fidelium atque eorum, qui ad fidem unice veram nondum pervenerunt, ita ut catholici iustam causam habere possint fidem, quam sub Ecclesiae magisterio iam susceperunt, assensu suspenso in dubium vocandi, donec demonstrationem scientificam credabilitatis et veritatis fidei suae absolverint: A. S.[24]

But this formal motive of faith is attained only by a supernatural act of a supernatural virtue, under the inspiration and help of grace.

> Hanc vero fidem...virtutem esse supernaturalem, qua, Dei aspirante et adiuvante gratia,...credimus.[25]

Faith is an eminently reasonable act:

> Ut nihilominus fidei nostrae *obsequium rationi consentaneum* esset.[26]

> Licet autem fidei assensus nequaquam sit motus animi caecus.[27]

Yet at the same time faith is a free act:

---

[21] DB 1789.

[22] *De veritate*, 14, 8, c.: Sicut autem esse creatum, quantum est de se, vanum est et defectibile, nisi contineatur ab ente increato; ita omnis creata veritas defectibilis est, nisi quatenus per veritatem increatam rectificatur. Unde neque hominis neque angeli testimonio assentire infallibiliter in veritatem duceret, nisi quantum in eis loquentis Dei testimonium consideratur.

[23] ST II–II, 4, 8; *De veritate*, 14, 1, ad 7; 10, 12, ad 6 in cont.

[24] DB 1815.

[25] DB 1789. See also DB 1791.

[26] DB 1790.

[27] DB 1791. See also DB 1812, 1813.

... fides... donum Dei est, et actus eius est opus ad salutem pertinens, quo homo liberam praestat ipsi Deo obedientiam gratiae eius, cui resistere posset, consentiendo et cooperando.[28]

5. Si quis dixerit, assensum fidei christianae non esse liberum, sed argumentis humanae rationis necessario produci: A.S.[29]

The act of faith, then, is reasonable but free, certain but supernatural. This raises the most crucial difficulties concerning the relation of faith to reason, of grace to nature, in the genesis and continuation of faith. This problem of the *analysis fidei* has received two generic solutions, with a considerable diversity of further specification within each school. One may say that the two generic solutions result from a fundamental divergence concerning the manner in which the life of grace is present in us.

The Thomists insist that the motive of divine faith is the *Prima Veritas* cognitively attained, however obscurely, in itself. This means that the supernatural must in some obscure manner enter into the field of human consciousness, into the psychological order. Belief of course presupposes natural reasons for believing; but it goes beyond these reasons for a truly supernatural motive, following an interior instinct given by grace. But such belief, however certain, remains the result of a free decision; for the motive is only present in an obscure manner, not with the clarity which could necessitate belief.

On the other hand, the post-Reformation rationalist scholasticism argued that the formal motive of the act of faith in the intellectual order is the authority of God revealing as it becomes known naturally through reason. But the act of faith itself nevertheless is not a merely natural act, for it is elevated and strengthened by a supernatural grace in the will; this grace makes the assent, commanded by the will, to be the firmest of all assents. In the field of consciousness, belief is grounded only in the natural reason; but they are reasons which in themselves suffice for a true natural certitude. Yet faith remains intrinsically free; for, the propositions of faith lacking intrinsic evidence for us, these propositions cannot by themselves determine the intellect to assent. It is necessary that the will intervene, moved by the natural evidence of credibility yielding a natural evidence of the authority of the revealing God as backing up these propositions to be believed. It is this kind of *analysis fidei* which has come to be known to many as the

---

[28] DB 1791.
[29] DB 1814.

"traditional" doctrine, although it represents a tradition which was rather late in starting. It will be considered in more detail in the next chapter.

The mere outline presentation just given of the two solutions of the problem of *analysis fidei* serves to point out more clearly the difficulties. If the act of faith is really reasonable – in the sense that the natural evidence of credibility says to us, "Believe!" – then this act does not seem to be a supernatural act at all, or at least it need not be. Conversely, if the act of faith is truly free, then it seems that a consideration of the reasons for believing is not to be conclusive; but in this case it is difficult to see how the act of faith is entirely reasonable. The problem may be put even more concisely: If the assent of faith goes beyond the natural evidence, then it is not reasonable; if this assent is entirely reasonable, then what need is there of supernatural grace and in what sense can the act be said to be really free?

In fact, speculation before Vatican I did tend in some cases toward one or other of these extremes. Hermes so insisted upon the reasonableness of the faith that he ended by diminishing unduly the role of grace.[30] Bautain and Bonnetty, on the other hand, tended toward fideism.[31] Both tendencies met with authoritative denunciation even before Vatican I,[32] but the rationalists were especially denounced.[33] The same preoccupation with the rationalists is to be noted in Vatican I itself.

But Vatican I presented a doctrine concerning faith which was neither rationalist nor fideist. It held both the reasonableness and certitude of the faith, together with the freedom and supernaturality of the faith. But it did not explain how these diverse, and apparently irreconcilable, attributes of faith were to be reconciled. One may consider post-Vatican I speculation as a long effort to resolve this problem in a more satisfactory manner than that in which the post-Reformation rationalist scholasticism did. If there is any common trait of the greater part of this speculation, it is that it manifests in some manner a reaction to the former rationalism. But the new solution has not been easy to find, for one ordinarily ends by unduly diminishing the reasonableness of the faith. Some of the especially important moments of this speculative inquiry will be considered in Chapter III. In fact, out of all this speculation some new lines of thought for a scholastic analysis of faith do emerge, as we shall see.

[30] Aubert, *Le problème de l'acte de foi*, 103–112.
[31] *Ibid.*, 113–127.
[32] *Ibid.*
[33] *Ibid.*, 127–130.

II. THE SO-CALLED "TRADITIONAL" DOCTRINE AND ITS DIFFICULTIES

The diversity in theological tradition concerning the problem of the formal motive and analysis of faith was suggested in the last chapter. It does not seem particularly helpful for the purposes of the present essay to detail the names and schools of thought.[34] It is sufficient to recall here the generic distinction between the Thomist doctrine and the so-called "traditional" doctrine.

The Thomist doctrine was in the background in the nineteenth century, although it was of course preserved among the Dominicans. It is only for this reason that the so-called "traditional" doctrine is thus called. But the Thomist view is in fact coming to the fore again in the Church's theology.[35] It will become more and more apparent that it is this view that underlies the present essay.

The "traditional" doctrine arose in reaction to some ideas of the Reformation concerning reason, concerning religious experience, and concerning the role of the will. If the Reformers would minimize the power of reason, and therefore the reasonableness of the faith, Catholic theologians had to emphasize the power of reason even in this matter of faith.[36] If the Reformers greatly exaggerated the role of religious experience, even asserting that through it one could be certain of one's justification and predestination, then Catholic theologians must emphasize the obscurity of the supernatural life in the soul.[37] If the Reformers would go so far as to deny that human freedom had anything to do with grace, that grace in its workings was in any way conditioned by nature, Catholic theologians must insist on the role of

---

[34] See S. Harent, S.J., *Dictionnaire de théologie catholique* (DTC), t. VI, coll. 98–122, 469–512, and Aubert, *op. cit*. Although there is some overlapping, Aubert supplements the historical treatment by Harent and brings it nearly up to date.

[35] John L. Murphy, in "Two Theories of Faith," *The American Ecclesiastical Review*, CXLVII, 1962, 31, points out this turning toward the Thomist view, at least as regards the essential point of the psychological effect of divine faith, and gives a few recent references (1948–1960) as supporting evidence. It is particularly interesting to note that this trend exists among Jesuits. The names of De la Taille, Hocedez, Malavez, De Broglie, Alfaro, and Vignon need only be mentioned in this connection.

The decline of the "traditional" doctrine has several aspects. Besides the current special interest in the theology of St. Thomas, under the impetus of a line of authoritative declarations from the Holy See, one can see, as will become more evident in the following chapter, tendencies to emphasize the supernaturality of faith, its affective character, its entry into the psychological order in one manner or another, its discontinuity with reason, and also the weakness of reason even in the domain of the motives of credibility.

[36] But this emphasis also derives from the rationalism of recent centuries.

[37] DB 802, 805, 822–826.

human freedom and of preparatory human acts – themselves inspired, of course, by grace.[38]

At the risk of over-simplification, the "traditional" doctrine, despite divergences among its proponents, may be described through nine fundamental principles.[39] Afterwards, the modifications of these principles introduced by Billot will be seen.

First, in this view there is no supernatural experiential or otherwise noetic component in faith-knowledge.[40] The supernatural life of grace, the infused virtues, and the gifts is an ontological reality in the soul; but it does not manifest its presence in the psychological order in any manner at all.

Second, as a consequence of the first principle, supernatural faith is for us noetically indistinguishable from a natural faith based on the authority of the revealing God.[41] This authority must be attained by natural reason in either case, and it is the divine authority precisely as naturally attained by discursive reason meditating on the motives of credibility that truly specifies or gives an objective determination to the act of divine faith. As a result, the supernaturality of the act of faith is not really a substantial supernaturality at all (arising in virtue of the very object of the act) but only a modal supernaturality, a supernaturality in the mode of assent in so far as this assent is dependent on the will.

Third, the grace of faith, then, is most properly a grace in the will, which elevates the act of the will in so far as the will is determining the intellect to assent to the object of an otherwise natural faith.

Fourth, and this is implicit in the second principle, the formal object of supernatural faith is exactly the same as the formal object of natural faith.[42]

Fifth, the evidence of natural credibility, that is, the natural evidence of the authority of the revealing God, is required as a directly influencing cause (not merely as a condition) of the assent of faith.[43]

---

[38] DB 797–798, 814–817, 819.

[39] There are many sources to draw from to see this doctrine. It seems unnecessary to give a wealth of references. One can consult Harent's *"Foi"* in the DTC, t. VI, coll. 55–514; Straub's *De analys ifidei*, Innsbruck, 1922, and Aubert's *Le Problème de l'acte de foi* for a general view. Here it will be sufficient to point out only some instances.

[40] Aubert, *Le problème*, 234, n. 14; Murphy, "Two Theories of Faith," 27; Harent, "Foi," DTC, VI, 142–144.

[41] Aubert, *Ibid.*, 232; Murphy, *loc. cit.*

[42] Aubert, *Ibid.*, 233; L. Molina, *Concordia*, q. 14, a. 13, disp. 38, ad 3.

[43] Ludovicus Lercher, S.J. – F. Schlagenhaufen, S.J. *Institutiones theologiae dogmaticae*, 5th ed., Barcelona, 1951, I, 399; F. Stentrup, *Praelectiones dogmiticae: de fide*, Innsbruck, 1890, 143–145, 205–225; etc., etc.

This evidence need not necessarily be sufficient for absolute certitude of credibility; it is enough that the evidence be sufficient for relative certitude (a certitude grounded on objectively insufficient reasons which nevertheless suffice at least for the moment for the person in question). Note that this evidence of credibility, while an influencing cause, is not to be the complete and adequate cause of the assent of divine faith; for grace does enter to elevate this assent as regards its modality, so that the assent is indeed more firm and certain than any assent due to natural reason alone.

Sixth, all the knowledge connected with the assent of faith, whether it be knowledge of credibility or faith-knowledge itself, is formulated, conceptual, and propositional knowledge, whether implicit or explicit. If divine faith does involve adherence to the *personal* God, this adherence is entirely a matter of the will and in no manner enters into the noetic order as any manner of conscious communion. In fact, the interpersonal element in faith does not seem to be really essential to faith in this view; this interpersonal relation seems to be only concomitant, at the most only a property flowing from faith and not central to the very constitution of faith.

Seventh, since both the motive of faith and the fact of revelation can be evidently known to natural reason itself, the essential obscurity of faith is not to be found in these areas but only in the absence of intrinsic evidence in the material object of faith, that is, in the very propositions which are to be believed. There is, of course, another obscurity associated with faith, the obscurity in the psychological order of the workings of grace, an obscurity which is really a total absence of any psychological manifestation, so far as the so-called "traditional" doctrine is concerned. But this point was touched upon in the first principle; the seventh principle concerns only the obscurity with which the actual noetic elements of the act of faith are grasped. These noetic elements are three – which in fact reduce to two, since the fact of revelation really is part of the motive of faith – the motive of faith, the fact of revelation, and the propositions to be believed. The fact of revelation here cannot be the active testimony of God, which pertains to the uncreated supernatural; for the uncreated supernatural could not become evidently known, or indeed even obscurely known, in any manner to natural reason alone. This fact of revelation is therefore the passive testimony of God, the created effect of the active testimony, known by most certain signs (miracles, prophecies, etc. – and here the traditional apologetics can unfold itself) to have proceeded from God. In the "traditional" view, this passive testimony could become evidently known to natural reason, as also could the other elements of the authority of the revealing God (the knowledge and veracity of God). The sole noetic obscurity of faith which could not become clear in this life is the obscurity of the articles of faith themselves. This does not mean that the natural evidence of the divine authority and of the fact of revelation is luminously clear to all; but it does mean that all can (and indeed must, if they are to make an act of faith) have sufficient evidence to ground a certitude of natural reason (be this certitude absolute or only relative) in these matters.

Eighth, despite the evidence of the motive of faith and of the fact of revelation, the act of faith remains a free act, one which a man may consent to elicit or refuse to elicit.[44] For once the intellect has achieved a speculative certitude of the motive of faith and of the fact of revelation (and therefore that the revealed propositions are believable), it is still necessary for the will to determine the intellect to the ultimate practical judgment – "*I* must *here and now* believe these revealed propositions." The propositions to be believed cannot themselves compel the assent of the intellect since they lack intrinsic evidence, while the evidence of the motive of faith and the fact of revelation are themselves not evidence of the propositions but rather evidence that the propositions should be *believed*. The intellect itself remains undetermined as regards belief at this point, nor does the will intervene to determine the intellect to believe unless the will itself is determined, in the order of formal causality, by the ultimate practical judgment of the intellect. But this ultimate practical judgment is itself ultimate and practical only because the will freely makes it so. Ultimately, then, the assent of faith is freely commanded by the will. But the resultant act of faith may be either natural or supernatural. That this faith be true supernatural faith, a special grace is necessary, first in the will (but also in the intellect – elevating but not illuminating the assent), to elevate the mode of assent so that it be more firm than all other assents. But this grace, being purely ontological and in no manner manifested in consciousness, does not enable the believer himself to say with certitude whether he has only natural or supernatural faith. At this point, it is well to note that while, if there is to be genuine supernatural faith, grace must enter in at least in the commanded judgment of faith itself, all agree that the

---

[44] Explanations differ regarding this freedom of the act of faith (see Aubert, *Le problème*, 239–241). But the point must be maintained at all costs, in accordance with the decree of Vatican I.

purely natural process leading up to this point may well be found frequently, if not practically always, to be stimulated and guided by helping graces. It is difficult to see how the "traditional" doctrine can consistently insist on the necessity of grace even in the practical judgment of credibility, since the faith which follows is specified by a natural formal object, the authority of the revealing God as known to reason.[45]

Ninth, this faith is essentially a purely assenting faith; any element of trust pertaining to such faith follows as a property (because of some of the truths revealed) and does not in any way constitute such faith. For trust is a personal act in regard to a person, but for this kind of faith it is sufficient to regard God as a source of truth, not altogether unlike an infallible computing machine.

Cardinal Billot has modified some of the principles just enunciated[46] in order to remove some obvious difficulties, and his views have gained wide acceptance.[47] The fourth principle, that "the formal object of supernatural faith is exactly the same as the formal object of natural faith," will now be: while in the noetic order there is only one (natural) formal object, in the ontological order there are really two, the second being the supernatural authority of the revealing God; this supernatural authority is, however, not affirmed; nor is it an immediate object of knowledge, in the act of supernatural faith.[48] Note that this revision still affirms the absence of any psychological effect of the grace of faith: the causality of the supernatural motive is entirely ontological.

Since it is the supernatural authority that really grounds the act of faith, Billot does not make the evidence of natural credibility an influencing cause in the very motive of faith. The fifth principle then is modified to: the evidence of natural credibility is required only as a condition and in no way as a directly influencing cause of the assent of faith.[49]

The clarity and obscurity of the noetic elements of faith remain the same for Bollit as in the common "traditional" doctrine. But, in fact, since beyond all these elements there is a higher supernatural motive

---

[45] I have passed over the role of the judgment of credentity (of the moral obligation to believe) in this brief account. It seems to introduce an unnecessary complication at this point. Let it suffice to say that this judgment of credentity *should* not require grace in the system which is being considered, since it can still lead to an act of merely natural faith. It will require grace in the Thomist system, since it there refers, not to a faith specified by the same formal object as natural faith, but to a faith supernaturally specified by the *Prima Veritas* as such.

[46] Ludovicus Billot, *De virtutibus infusis*, 4th ed., Rome, 1928; see also Aubert, *Le problème*, 241–255.

[47] Aubert, *Ibid.*, 241.

[48] Billot, *De virtutibus infusis*, Thesis XVI.

[49] Aubert, *Le problème*, 244–245; Billot, *De virt. inf.*, Th. XVI–XVII.

exercising an ontological causality even while it remains unknown as such, the seventh principle can only be somewhat misleading as a description of Billot's doctrine.

The location of the real objective motive of supernatural faith in an unknown ontological formal object rather than in an evident natural credibility means that the freedom of the supernatural act of faith is clearer in Billot's system than in the preceding, and the necessity of grace is more obvious in order that the assent take place. The eighth principle may be somewhat modified in order to better express the thought of Billot: despite the natural evidence of the motive of faith and of the fact of revelation, the act of faith remains a free act; moreover, the assent of supernatural faith in no way rests on this natural evidence but rather on the entirely non-evident supernatural motive of the authority of God revealing.[50] Such a faith is called "authoritative faith," as opposed to the "scientific faith" that would be grounded in the natural evidence of the motive of faith and of the fact of revelation. Yet it must be pointed out that this difference in motive of faith does not mean any psychological difference at all; it would be possible for one to make a natural act even of "authoritative faith." The role of the grace of faith here is therefore analogous to that in the earlier system.

It will be noted that this "authoritative faith" is essentially not only an assenting faith but also a trusting faith. Thus the ninth principle is simply contradicted in this view of faith. One may perhaps question the manner in which this trust is manifested; but to set aside the natural evidence of the motive of faith and of the fact of revelation and freely to rely upon the unknown supernatural motive of faith, the supernatural authority of the revealing God, is certainly to make some kind of act of trust in God.

But in fact Cardinal Billot does not really escape serious difficulties in his revised treatment of the act of faith. Both the "traditional" doctrine and his modification are full of difficulty in almost every one of the principles enunciated. We may now turn to a critical commentary upon each of the principles, taking into account whatever modifications have been introduced by Billot, beginning with the ninth and going back to the first principle.

It does not seem necessary to dwell on the ninth principle itself, the inadequacies of which were seen in the first chapter from a consideration of the statements of Vatican I, of Scripture, and of St. Thomas Aquinas. But again it must be pointed out that Cardinal Billot's position

[50] Aubert, *Ibid.*, 247, n. 17; Billot, *Ibid.*, Th. XVI.

at least does not share these difficulties, since in it there is very definitely a place for trusting faith.

The eighth principle, concerning the freedom of the faith even in the face of the natural evidence of the motive of faith and of the fact of revelation, as this principle is understood in the "traditional" doctrine, presents serious problems. It is difficult to see why the will must intervene in order to determine the intellect to assent to the propositions as guaranteed by the naturally known authority of the revealing God. If one really knows that God always speaks the truth (the divine authority) and that He has in fact spoken (the fact of revelation), then assent to the revealed propositions is logically necessary. But for the intellect to follow a logical necessity no special intervention of the will is necessary. A further intervention of the will to stimulate the intellect to pursue the inquiry more zealously and to hold to the conclusion more firmly is of course possible, but it is not necessary for the assent of faith. Some have in fact been led to deny that there is real freedom at the moment of assent but rather place it only in the course of the inquiry which leads to the moment of assent.[51] But such a position simply does not leave room for the intervention of grace at all; for the inquiry can be carried on by reason alone, and if the inquiry is successful it must lead to a logically necessary (for *natural* reason) assent. The only sense in which such an assent can be called an assent of *faith* is that the assent is to propositions which do not appear intrinsically evident. But, after all, may not the same be said of propositions which are known as conclusions of scientific demonstration? Such a faith is well-named when it is called "scientific faith." But it is difficult to see how it can be called Christian faith, the faith of the Vatican Council.

In the light of the above remarks, it is perhaps easy to understand why Billot thought it necessary to distinguish between such "scientific faith" and an "authoritative faith" which is necessary for a Christian. But this "authoritative faith" for Billot rests on no *known* motive. It is indeed a free assent; but since it is made in complete abstraction from the natural evidence, on the basis of a motive which is in no way psychologically manifested to the believer, indeed on the basis of a motive which is not even in any way affirmed, it seems that freedom has been preserved only at the price of reasonableness and of any psychologically sufficient reason for the assent to be made. Nor must one minimize the importance of such a psychological ground for the assent; for the assent is not a mere objective reality, adequately ac-

[51] Aubert, *Ibid.*, 240, n. 34.

counted for in terms of its objective, ontological, formal object, but rather a subjective reality in the mind of the believer. Such an assent cannot be postulated in defiance of psycholocigal laws; it demands a psychological ground as well as an ontological ground.

In the light of the criticism of the eighth principle, the comment on the seventh principle is perhaps too obvious. Since the natural evidence of credibility that is here postulated seems to really necessitate the assent of faith, either such natural evidence is not really given at all or the act of faith does not finally rest on this evidence in any way but rather on something else (but not Billot's unknown supernatural authority). In fact, both of these alternatives turn out to be true in some manner; the first is partially true, while the second is wholly true. The first point will be considered in the criticism of the fifth principle; the second will be considered in the criticism of the fourth principle.

The sixth principle, that the only knowledge to be considered in the problem of faith is formulated conceptual or propositional knowledge, explicit or implicit, appears very much weakened by the advent of modern Existentialism. All belief seems to be based on a relation of persons in some kind of conscious communion, and this communion is not simply reducible to conceptual and propositional knowledge. This point will be considered in detail in later chapters.

The fifth principle, requiring the natural evidence of the authority of the revealing God as a directly influencing cause of the assent of faith, or, at least for Billot, as a necessary condition of this assent, has several difficulties. Real evidence of the authority of the revealing God requires a knowledge of the existence and nature of God, matters subject to continual dispute even among professional philosophers, and also a knowledge of the historical evidence for the intervention and revelation of God in history, a matter subject to continual discussion and argument among the most learned historians. Let it be granted that the common sense knowledge of the existence and nature of God, however obscure this be, sufices in place of philosophical knowledge for many men; and let it be granted that a certain moral certitude of belief in persons one generally deems trustworthy (e.g. the ecclesiastical hierarchy) suffices in place of scientific historical study for many men. Still, does not the spectacle of heretical sects following their own leaders in good faith make one pause to wonder about the value of his own "common sense" evidence? And how compelling, objectively, is the natural evidence of credibility possessed by children who learn the Christian doctrine from their parents? Do they perhaps not yet have the faith? But this cannot be so. And what of the adult who now comes to examine his previously uncriticized common sense assumptions? As he puts aside certain ideas hastily accepted without sufficient evidence at some time in the past, may he not wonder also about the assumptions of his Christian faith? Is it necessary for him to become a philosopher and an historian in order to set aside these fears? But if the faith truly depends upon this natural evidence in the way described, it seems that he must; for the evidence he seeks is not accessible except to the philosopher and historian. And what is to become of the faith of one undergoing one of those well-known trials of faith in which all natural evidence of credibility seems to disappear and one is left with pure faith alone? And if one should seek to evade such difficulties by the doctrine of relative certitude, certitude founded on a motive objectively insufficient but sufficient for the person in question here and now, further problems arise. This doctrine does not really seem to resolve the problem of the man undergoing a trial of faith; but even apart from that, other problems present themselves. Assent on the basis of objectively insufficient evidence is erroneous assent, even if *per accidens* it may turn out to be right. Such an assent would be sinful if one knew what he was doing. But this error is a necessary condition in order that relative certitude be possible. That divine faith should in so many cases presuppose as a necessary condition a certain ignorance and error very much invites a few *I told you so*'s from unbelievers. And the difficulty is really even more serious than it appears at first sight. After all, how many men are there in the world who can actually understand the probative force of the historical evidence for the fact of revelation? How many men are there in the world who can fully understand the philosophical demonstrations concerning the existence and the nature of God? But unless they can do these things, their certitude of the credibility of the faith is only a relative certitude. And even if they can do these things, can the fragility of such hard-won natural knowledge about such difficult questions really underly, either as a directly influencing cause or as a necessary condition, the assent of faith, that assent which is firmer than all other assents and on which, as on a rock, is built the firm hope of our salvation and the self-sacrificing love that is stronger even than death?

All this criticism of the requirement of natural evidence of the authority of the revealing God does not mean that such evidence as can be gained in this matter is unimportant. Later it will be seen that this evidence, even if inadequate for a "scientific faith," may be quite adequate as a sign leading one to "personal faith"; indeed, some degree of such natural evidence with its sign-value seems to be a necessary condition for such personal faith.

The fourth principle stated that the formal object of supernatural faith is exactly the same as the formal object of natural faith, or at least that it is the same formal object that is noetically attained, whether the act be one of natural or of supernatural "authoritative faith" (Billot). This is in many ways at the heart of the difficulty with the "traditional" doctrine. What it means is that two specifically distinct intellectual acts, one of natural faith and the other of supernatural faith, may have one and the same formal object. Thomists have always insisted that this is impossible, for the specific difference of acts results precisely from the specific difference of their formal objects. An act is essentially a tendency toward something; an intellectual act is essentially a tendency toward something to be known. Its whole intelligibility as such an act is derived from the object of the tendency, not just the material object (the being which is known) but rather the formal object (the being precisely under the aspect under which it is known). This is only to say that the formal object of an act specifies the act, and that where there is only one formal object there cannot be any specific diversity of acts. The formal object of supernatural faith, as an act of the intellect, must be the divine authority as attained supernaturally;[52] the motive of supernatural faith is the infallible authority of God and not our fallible natural knowledge of this authority.[53] In this manner the assent of faith can truly become firmer than all other assents, for it rests on a motive in itself independent of our fallible natural knowledge. This manner of understanding the formal motive of faith succeeds in avoiding the difficulties already seen above concerning any faith which presupposes as a directly influencing cause the natural evidence of credibility, assuring at once a better founded certitude (because of the infallible authority) and a freer assent (assuming, as is really obvious, that this supernatural motive is known at best only obscurely).

Since the term of an intellectual act is knowledge, it follows that the formal object of any intellectual act must be in some manner, however obscurely, known. This eliminates at once Billot's concept of an "authoritative faith" grounded in an unknown formal motive and the third principle of the "traditional" doctrine. This principle stated that the

[52] ST II–II, 1, 1, c.; 2, 2, c,; 5, 1, c.; *Contra errores graecorum*, I, c. 30, etc.
[53] *De veritate*, 14, 8, c.

grace of faith is most properly in the will (though secondarily in the intellect, insofar as it is moved by the will). This principle meant that the grace merely strengthened the will-determined assent of the intellect without giving any illumination to the intellect itself. But in fact there is some obscure illumination given in the grace of faith, since the intellectual act of faith has a supernatural formal object, and not a merely natural formal object.

But if the above is true, then the second principle, that supernatural faith is for us noetically indistinguishable from a natural faith, must likewise be denied. The noetic distinction may be difficult to see and even impossible to isolate through introspective analysis, but it is nevertheless present as a psychological reality, perhaps capable of being isolated through an analysis in the light of scholastic philosophical psychology. Such an effort of analysis will be attempted later.

After all this, there can be no question concerning the first principle. There is in some manner an experiential or otherwise noetic supernatural component in faith-knowledge, although it is very obscure. But this does not mean that it will be sufficient simply to restate the Thomist account of the act of faith. At least one new dimension has appeared, one new aspect of the act of faith, in the course of the discussion above. Faith is an interpersonal act, and we may well suspect that the obscure noetic component in the supernatural order is somehow bound up with this interpersonal structure of the act of faith. Such a unification would succeed in integrating assenting faith and trusting faith into much closer unity and would therefore perhaps better correspond to the sense of the statements of Vatican I, the sense of Scripture, and the fuller meaning of the idea of St. Thomas that faith is first of all assent to a person.[54] The brief summary in the next chapter of speculation since Vatican I will suggest still other aspects of faith to be considered in an integral account, but it will especially confirm the suggestion just made.

III. SOME POST-VATICAN I TENDENCIES

The purpose of this chapter is threefold: to trace out in a very summary way some of the important moments in the speculation con-

---

[54] ST II–II, 11, 1, c.: Quia vero quicumque credit alicuius dicto assentit, principale videtur esse, et quasi finis, in unaquaque credulitate ille cuius dicto assentitur: quasi autem secundaria sunt ea quae quis tenendo vult alicui assentire. Sic igitur qui recte fidem Christianam habet sua voluntate assentit Christo in his quae vere ad eius doctrinam pertinent.

cerning the nature of the act of faith following upon the Vatican Council, to draw out some suggestions on the basis of this speculation, and to draw up a list of questions to guide the remainder of this inquiry.

A common denominator of the speculation following Vatican I has been its reaction against the extreme rationalism which preceded the Council and which in many quarters is still with us in the name of "tradition." This speculation has tended to lessen the role of the evidence of credibility preceding the act of faith, although in most instances this evidence still plays a not unimportant role either in the process leading up to the act of faith, or concomitantly with the act of faith, or at least consequent upon the act of faith. A much greater importance has been attributed to affective life in the genesis of faith — the ideas of need, inclination, and connaturality appear and reappear. Faith is regarded as an act of the whole person and not merely of the intellect. The role of religious experience in the act of faith, even of "intuition," is stressed.

Some of these themes obviously call for comment and criticism, but my intention here is not to criticize but simply to present them in order to better get some suggestions for the present inquiry concerning the formal motive and analysis of faith. The detailed work of exposition and criticism has already been well done by Aubert.[55] It will be enough here simply to summarize his exposition.

Cardinal Billot's attempt to emphasize more the role of the will and of grace by his distinction between "scientific faith" and "authoritative faith" was already considered in the previous chapter. Essentially, it was an attempt to patch up the rationalist theory so as to meet its obvious difficulties. But it seems to have gained a good deal more acceptance than it really deserves.

Lest it appear as if an oversight has been committed, the influence of Newman upon speculation since the Vatican Council should be mentioned. But this seems to focus more around the problem of credibility than around the problem of the formal motive. Cardinal Newman was not himself much of a metaphysical theologian. But the problem of the formal motive and of the analysis of faith is a problem of metaphysical theology.

Blondel [56] called attention to the irrelevance of apologetics until men have come first to understand their need of and the possibility of a

[55] Aubert, *Le problème*, 223-644.
[56] Maurice Blondel, *L'Action*, Paris, 1893.

divine revelation. Indeed, he depreciated the value of a good deal of the traditional apologetic anyway. To waken men to their need of the divine revelation, Blondel proposed his method of Immanence, an attempt to show the exigencies of existential man for the supernatural. The real proof of the rightness of faith was to be found in action; if one saw the need of faith, but did not yet have it, it was necessary for him to act as if he had it so that its truth could be seen in the truth of such action. Despite certain accusations against Blondel that he breaks down the distinction between nature and grace and makes the supernatural a mere projection of man's own natural needs, he seems rather to be speaking always of concrete man, in whom grace operates to produce the experienced need and exigency for the supernatural. From this perspective, then, Blondel stresses not only the importance of the will in faith but also the importance of grace. But the distinction between a concrete nature permeated with impulses of grace and a concrete nature demanding as a natural complement what had previously been called the supernatural is not always an easy one to see, and the Modernists failed to see it.

Gardeil,[57] working in the Thomist tradition, attempted to incorporate the new emphasis on the importance of subjective dispositions in the genesis of the act of faith into an elaborate Thomist theory of faith. He distinguished natural and supernatural faith, and three kinds of credibility. As a good Thomist he insisted on the logical independence of supernatural faith with respect to any natural faith and to the credibility of the faith. But he was original in insisting on three distinct ways of reaching the credibility of the faith. The first is by way of scientific demonstration (so much he inherited from the nineteenth century rationalism), but this is reserved for only a few men. The second is by way of a moral certitude, a prudential estimation founded on probable arguments. Here, what is speculatively only probable can become practically certain, as in many other areas of moral choice. Where necessary, this movement from speculative probability to practical certitude can be facilitated by "subjective helps" of the affective order. This gives the third kind of credibility, a conviction less than moral certitude but converted to moral certitude by the aid of such affective, and perhaps supernatural, dispositions. Gardeil also drew attention to the role of a supernaturally inspired right intention toward the good, and therefore also toward the faith, the *intentio fidei*, as such a subjective and affective aid.

[57] P. Ambrose Gardeil, O.P., *La crédibilité et l'apologétique*, 2nd ed., Paris, 1912.

Rousselot,[58] contrary to Gardeil, denied the possibility of a purely natural faith, and declared that miracles could not be known as such without the help of supernatural faith itself. A kind of reciprocal causality obtains between faith and the miracle. The very grace-inspired affective disposition which makes one to believe also makes one to see by connaturality the miraculous intervention of God in the signs which give a rational ground for the faith. It is this new insight through connaturality or sympathy which gives rise to the expression, "les yeux de foi." But the manner in which this new seeing takes place was not explained by Rousselot.

The ideas of Scheler [59] provided inspiration for thought in Germany between the two wars. Scheler considered that the domain of values is not accessible to ordinary intellectual analysis but is known by emotional intuition, or sentiment. The intuitive grasp of the highest value — the Sacred — is religious knowledge. Through this means the personal God reveals himself to us, to Whom we as persons may now enter into relation.

Karl Adam [60] followed up this idea and postulated a special "mystical" intuition at the base of supernatural faith. This presence of the revealing God and of the supernatural in our lives can exist in a manner that is scarcely conscious at all. But Adam does not deny the value of the arguments for the rational credibility of the faith. He says that they may be used by the believer after his act of faith, to justify the reasonableness of faith. But without such faith, a satisfactory knowledge of credibility is impossible in the concrete order of things. Yet such knowledge of credibility is in fact not necessary, for faith rests on the intuitive perception of the divine testimony. While faith can be said to be non-rational, it is not a mere leap in the dark.

In response to such modern currents, and in reaction to the rationalist conception of the act of faith, various Dominican and Jesuit Thomists [6] have come to elaborate a conception of the act of faith as resting on a knowledge through affective connaturality, not according to Rousselot's idea of a connaturality-knowledge interpreting the signs of credibility, but rather a connaturality-knowledge making us see that the revelation *ought* to be believed. This is the *instinctus interior* of St. Thomas. The

---

[58] Pierre Rousselot, S.J., "Les yeux de la foi," *Recherches de science réligieuse*, I, 1910, 241–259, 444–475.
[59] Max Scheler, *Der Formalismus in der Ethik und die materiale Wertethik*, Halle, 1916, and *Vom Ewigen im Menschen*, Leipzig, 1921.
[60] Karl Adam, *Glaube und Glaubenswissenschaft im Katholizismus*, Rottenburg, 1923.
[61] This "school" of theologians is described in Aubert's *Le problème*, 585–615.

judgment of faith is here a judgment according to tendency or inclination, the inclination being obscurely perceived as of divine origin and perhaps giving a true experimental knowledge of the First Truth.

Finally, Mouroux,[62] following the development of Existentialist thought, has treated the existential structure of faith as an organic ensemble of personal relations. Beyond the communication of abstract ideas, there is a concrete and mysterious experience of persons in spiritual contact or communion. At this point it is not a question of mere knowledge apart from love; here both love and knowledge conspire together and compenetrate each other. Such an interpersonal relation of communion exists between the believer and God. There are signs to manifest the person of God testifying to us, but these signs should be used as means for communion with a person and not as a basis for a demonstration of credibility. Such a demonstration in fact cannot be had; it is only possible to show that the affirmation of belief founded upon such signs violates no scientific procedure.

These are not the only moments of great importance in the progress of the discussion concerning the act of faith. But they are sufficient themselves to suggest a number of points for further reflection. One point which has continually recurred is that the evidence of credibility is in reality a set of signs that revelation is from a trustworthy source, not a set of premises which conclude logically to an act of at least natural faith. Such signs do not necessitate faith, but they are at least understandable as signs, whether before, concomitantly with, or after the act of faith. Perhaps the understanding of their sign-value can be present at all three moments, but in different ways.

Another suggestion is that belief itself involves an I-Thou relation of personal commitment. Such an I-Thou relation would completely transcend the evidence of signs, and yet it might well in some manner presuppose this evidence — as person-to-person relations among men transcend mere signs of trustworthiness and yet in some manner or other presuppose such signs.

A third suggestion, or set of suggestions, is that affective connaturality may well be the means by which the I-Thou relation comes into being, that through this affective connaturality a certain experimental interpersonal communion of an obscurely conscious kind may arise, that this affective connaturality and communion may well provide a special stimulus to integrate and relate more fully the evidence of signs to the trustworthiness of the person to Whom they refer.

[62] Jean Mouroux, *I believe*, trans. by Michiel Turner, New York, 1959.

In the light of these suggestions, a list of five questions may be drawn up to guide the course of the inquiry. Each question will be the concern of a separate chapter.

(1) Can affective connaturality be the means of an intersubjective I-Thou relation? (Chapter IV).

(2) What role does an I-Thou relation play in ordinary human belief? (Chapter V).

(3) How can the *locutio increata*, as revealing the truths of Christian faith, become present in such an I-Thou relation? (Chapter VI).

(4) Could the *locutio increata* become present without such propositionally formulated truths, and could this truly be called faith? (Chapter VII).

(5) How does the conception of intersubjective faith correspond to New Testament faith? (Appendix).

IV. AFFECTIVE CONNATURALITY AND INTERSUBJECTIVITY

Can affective connaturality be the means of an intersubjective I-Thou relation? I have already treated this question elsewhere,[63] but it is necessary to make here rather detailed analysis in order to carry on the inquiry concerning the act of faith. To come to an understanding of intersubjective presence it is useful to begin with a general discussion of presence and awareness, and the diverse modes of presence and awareness. In fact, among these diverse modes is to be found intersubjective presence through the medium of love.

Consciousness, awareness, and presence are correlative – a simultaneous triad. Consciousness, as the subjective state of one who is conscious, is always consciousness-of-some-thing. Awareness designates this consciousness precisely as consciousness-of-some-thing, and refers us beyond itself to that of which we are aware. That of which we are aware, in so far as we are aware of it, is said to be present. We of course exclude here those lesser modes of presence that are not correlative with consciousness and awareness – such as the mutual presence of any efficient cause and its effect.

Presence always includes two terms, the present and that to which it is present (a human existent), and a relation between these two terms. Even in self-presence there is a duality between what is present

---

[63] See my *Inquiry Into Being*, Chicago, 1965, 149–154, and *The Christian Intellect and the Mystery of Being*, The Hague, 1966, 74–90.

and that to which it is present. But presence is transcendence of such duality in union, without destroying the duality and with conscious recognition of it as remaining. The being that is present may be a real being or only a construction of the mind thought of as having some reality, at least for the mind. Presence to a human existent is a union of some being as other with a human existent.

Consciousness and awareness are divided into diverse modes according to the diverse modes of presence, for they are essentially relative to what is present as such. Presence itself is divided into non-objective presence and objective presence. In objective presence, the other (or self) becomes present as other, but not in its otherness (or selfness). The subjectivity of the other (or self) – its being as a subject of existence and activity outside any knower and as an incommunicable whole, as a *subiectum* or *suppositum* – is not present, but rather various objective aspects or facets appear to the knower. Objects in fact are always only aspects of subjects – the subject alone exists and manifests itself, through its various objective aspects, to the knower.[64] And yet subjectivity itself could never be objectively known, since that would be to transfer it to the plane of objectivity.[65]

Since the term "knowledge" is primarily applied to the objective modes of awareness and presence, these objective modes may be termed "knowledge through knowing." There are many such modes, but it is unnecessary to dwell on them here.

In non-objective presence, the very otherness of the other (or the selfness of the self) becomes present, perhaps even in its own subjectivity. There are in fact many such modes of non-objective awareness and presence. For the moment only those modes which arise simply as lived awareness of existence and of activity will be considered. Knowledge here may appropriately be called "knowledge through living." This is always an intellectual knowledge, for only a spiritual being is capable of such awareness. The most obvious examples of such knowledge are in one's lived experience of one's own existence and of one's own activity; and these modes ground the possibility of other modes of "knowing through living." The special activity which is intellectual consciousness is in itself a reflexive act, being not only consciousness-of-some-thing but also consciousness-of-itself. In all these modes of knowledge, one contemplates some mode of being not as an object, across a gulf, as

---

[64] Jacques Maritain, *Existence and the Existent*, trans. by G. Phelan and L. Galantière, Garden City, 1956, 74.
[65] *Ibid.*, 77.

"there and then," but rather as of oneself, as "here and now," in lived immediacy. In a similar manner, the existence and activity of other things is known in a kind of lived resonance in the human knower. There is even an obscure, natural awareness of the primary causal influx and existence of the Infinite Being, an awareness "lived" in the living of one's own existence and activity and of the existence and activity of other things in so far as these resonate in us. But a detailed treatment of such modes of awareness and presence seems unnecessary here.

Mere awareness of actually exercised existence and activity is only awareness of non-objective aspects of subject-things. The awareness of actual existence and activity *as exercised* is awareness of the *subjectivity* of subject-things, awareness of the *subject as subject*. Are there such modes of awareness of the subject as subject, of that which nor merely possesses but actually exercises [66] existence and activity?

Immediate awareness of one's own existence and activity is immediate awareness of oneself exercising these existential acts – their whole being is to be not merely possessed but also exercised. In this privileged case there is immediate non-objective awareness of the subject as subject. But one does not live the exercise of existence and activity of other things, or so it would seem. While one can indeed become non-objectively aware of the actual existence and activity of other things in the manner already suggested, it is quite another thing to become aware of their actual exercise of existence and of activity, of their very subjectivity.

Still, one of the facts of human life is intersubjectivity. And poets, mystics, and children will testify even to the intersubjective relationship of human existents to non-human reality. If such intersubjectivity cannot be accounted for in terms of "knowledge by knowing" and "knowledge by living," then there must be some other kind of knowledge, or awareness and presence. At this point we must turn to consider the reality of another type of non-objective awareness, itself found in many diverse modes, that is, "knowledge by loving," or knowledge through affective connaturality.

The fact of union through love, of "knowing by loving," is especially pointed out by Gabriel Marcel and Erich Fromm. Marcel distinguishes two domains of reality and knowledge: the domain of the "problem" and that of the "mystery," [67] of the problematic and the meta-problem-

---

[66] Maritain, *The Degrees of Knowledge*, trans. directed by G. Phelan, New York, 1959, 436–439.

[67] See, for example, *Position et approches concrètes du mystère ontologique*, Paris, 1949, 57–62; *The Mystery of Being*, Chicago, 1951, I, 197–219; *Man Against Mass Society*, Chicago, 1952, 67f.

atic, of objectivity and existence.[68] The object, the domain of the problematic, is "wholly apart from me and in front of me,"[69] the object of thought, in our sense of the objective aspect of the thing itself. But since being itself in not merely an object,[70] philosophical insight does not concern "something whose reality, by definition, lies completely outside our own." [71] Philosophy is concerned with mystery as opposed to problem.[72]

What are the marks of the meta-problematic? "A mystery is something in which I myself am involved, and it can therefore only be thought of as 'a sphere where the distinction between what is in me and what is before me loses its meaning and its initial validity.'" [73] This is the field of intersubjective, interpersonal relations,[74] of the virtues such as fidelity,[75] of the non-objective awareness of personal subject as subject. *And one can only enter this sphere of the meta-problematic through love.*[76]

Erich Fromm's *The Art of Loving* emphasizes the importance for man of the knowledge that arises in love. The deepest need of men, to overcome their separateness and isolation,[77] cannot be met unless they learn to love.[78] "The act of love... is a daring plunge into the experience of union." [79] "The knowledge which is an aspect of love is one which does not stay at the periphery, but penetrates to the core." [80] "Love is active penetration of the other person...." [81] And yet it is even more than this. "In the act of loving, of giving myself, in the act of penetrating the other person, I find myself, I discover myself, I discover us both, I discover man." [82]

This same kind of knowledge is an essential component of the "I-Thou relations" of Martin Buber. But the idea of knowledge arising through the formal medium of love is not new; it is in fact a commonplace in

---

[68] See, for the first, *Journal métaphysique*, Paris, 1935, 328 and *Position et approches*, 56–59; and for the second see *Journal métaphysique*, 315f. and *Position et approches*, 56f.
[69] *Man Against Mass Society*, 67.
[70] *Metaphysical Journal*, Chicago, 1952, Author's Preface to the English Edition, p. viii; *Journal métaphysique*, 315f.; *Position et approches*, 56f.
[71] *The Mystery of Being*, I, 216.
[72] *Ibid.*, 211; *Position et approches*, 59.
[73] *The Mystery of Being*, I, 211.
[74] *Ibid.*, II, 106f.
[75] *Position et approches*, 77ff.
[76] *Ibid.*, 59.
[77] *The Art of Loving*, New Yotk, 1956 8 f.
[78] *Ibid.*, 9, 18.
[79] *Ibid.*, 31.
[80] *Ibid.*, 29.
[81] *Ibid.*, 30.
[82] *Ibid.*, 31.

Christian ascetical and mystical tradition. St. John of the Cross regards love as the formal means of supernatural mystical union.[83] John of St. Thomas [84] and Jacques Maritain,[85] among others, have developed this idea. Maritain has ranged far beyond the problems of mysticism and sees a much wider scope for intersubjective communion through affective connaturality. But even his investigations are only the beginning in this domain that has to a great extent eluded the concern of scholasic thought for so long.

Experienced union through love with other persons is assumed in what follows. There are various types of such awareness, revealing both the subjectivity of the knower himself and something of the subjectivity of the *other*. It is on the latter revelation that we are focusing at present.

It does not seem necessary here to repeat the considerations already developed elsewhere [86] of the grounds in the Thomist tradition for an explanation of the fact of intersubjective communion through affective connaturality. We shall here omit the textual references and proceed directly to a brief metaphysical-psychological explanation of the fact.[87]

The will is moved by knowledge of present reality to the spontaneous passion of love (*amor*), and the intellect is itself aware of this movement of the will and of its own role in causing this movement. The manner in which the will is thus moved by the intellect is a matter of dispute among Thomists, with Cajetan defending an efficient causality of the intellect upon the will and John of St. Thomas defending a "metaphorical motion." At first sight the view of Cajetan seems promising, since efficient causality is at least easier to understand and since we must account for a real intentional modification of the will. But in fact this view is full of difficulties. The passion of love is produced by knowledge, but it is also produced by the will itself. Moreover, in some manner it must be produced by the thing itself even more than by the knowledge, since this love is a love for the thing itself and not merely for the knowledge of the thing. Moreover, the influence of the thing itself upon the will is not an influence of efficient causality but one of final causality. Even if one were willing to accept a mysterious trans-

---

[83] See *The Spiritual Canticle*, first redaction, XI, 6 in *The Complete Works of Saint John of the Cross*, transl. by E. A. Peers, London, 1953, II, 65.
[84] Cursus Theologicus, I–II, qq. 68–70, disp. 18, *passim*.
[85] *The Degrees of Knowledge*, cc. 6–9.
[86] See n. 1.
[87] The matter of the following pages has been drawn principally from my *Inquiry Into Being*, 152–154, with the permission of Loyola University Press, Chicago.

formation of the final causality of the thing itself into an efficient causality of the act of knowledge of the thing upon the will, still, on this hypothesis, it would seem that is it not so much the thing as the knowledge of the thing which moves the will. But, to go even further, one may well ask what has become of the distinctive character of final causality, if it is to be reduced, even in the intellectual order, to an efficient causality of knowledge upon the will. And beyond all this there is still the problem of understanding how the intentional form of knowledge in the intellect can efficiently produce anything at all so real as the passion of the will.

In the face of these difficulties, it seems well to consider the view of John of Saint Thomas that the influence of knowledge upon the will is a "metaphorical motion," a motion of final causality itself. This causality is more a causality by the known thing than by the knowledge of the thing, but it cannot exist apart from knowledge. And yet this causality cannot be simply located in knowledge; for it is a causality which influences the will, not simply producing the passion in the will, but in some manner by *being* this passion. This passion, considered precisely as in dependence ultimately upon the loved thing, is the final causality of the final cause. This same passion, considered as flowing from the will itself as from an efficient cause, is also the effect of the final causality of the known thing. These are, of course, only two ways of looking at what is really identical, namely, the passion of love itself. The passion of love is an induced activity in the will; but the influence which induces this activity, though dependent on something other than the will, is not distinct from the very activity itself.

Why is it necessary that the causality of the final cause not be in knowledge alone but in the very passion produced in the will? If this causality consisted in knowledge alone or some aspect of knowledge, then everything would be desired precisely in so far as it were known. The final cause is a cause of desire, not so much by *producing* desire as by *being desired*. This is why the motion of final causality is only a metaphorical motion.

But if this causality of the final cause is in the passion of the will, as the causality of the final cause it must somehow be exercised by the final cause itself. This exercise of influence is in the thing as representatively present in the intellect, and consists in the contact between the intellectual representation and the will. The contact, therefore, is not entitative or physical but merely representative, and arises in virtue of the spiritual compenetration of intellect and will.

The exercise of such contact, formally by the intentional representation of the thing and fundamentally therefore by the thing which is represented, is both the "attraction" (final causality) and the specification (formal) of the act of the will. The will itself acts as an efficient cause under such contact (which is an existential state of the will), in virtue of the natural dynamism of the will with respect to the good.

Through the intentionality of the passion of love that has been induced in and produced by the will, the will tends toward the real thing itself through the medium of its intentional representation in the intellect. It is the intentionality of knowledge which guarantees the continuity of the intentionality of the will all the way to the real thing itself. But this tendency of the will is a tendency toward the very subjectivity of things, and therefore presupposes in some manner a cognitive attainment of the subjectivity of things. This cognitive attainment has still not been explained.

The affective connaturality of the will with the loved thing consists in the tendency of the will. But presupposed to the connaturality itself is the connaturalization of the will by the "metaphorical motion." This metaphorical motion of final causality is exercised fundamentally by the thing itself in so far as the thing exercises its existence and activity; this constitutes the real attractiveness of the thing, for it is existential act to which all things tend. But the metaphorical motion is exercised formally in the representative contact already spoken of. Clearly, this formal exercise of final causality in representative contact is ultimately dependent upon, grounded in, the fundamental exercise of final causality which is the exercise of existential act in the real thing itself. The thing as represented, therefore, is vicarious with reference to the real subjectivity of the thing, so far as the exercise of final causality is concerned. It may even be said that the subjectivity of the thing is now vicariously present in the intellect, exercising final causality in the formal sense. But it is present only in so far as the object in the intellect is actually connaturalizing the will by the metaphorical motion which induces the passion of love in the will. Thus, the subjectivity of the other is known in the very moment of the affective connaturalization of the will. (This moment, of course, endures so long as the other is being regarded with a degree of affectivity.)

The will then, in tending toward the subjectivity of things, is not making any blind existential leap. It is not only true that the intellect understands *that* there are subjects, from the evidence of the activity of things as exercised act. The intellect also understands, in a vicarious manner, the very subjectivity of things at the moment of the connaturalization of the will. Moreover, this vicarious subjectivity is referred to the real thing itself through the prior knowledge of the intellect *that* the thing is a subject. Therefore, as connaturalized, the will tends toward a subjectivity which already revealed itself as subjectivity in the very connaturalization of the will.

Through even the affective connaturality arising in the first spontaneous movement of the will are revealed the *ratio boni* of whatever presents itself, the tendencies of the human subject, and the subjectivity of the other that is the object of the appetitive movement. In this awareness of the subjectivity of the other, indeed constitutive of it, there is a loving "taste" in the will. In the passage from the spontaneous movement of the will to the free love of the other for itself, the loved thing connaturalizes the will to a far greater degree and much more stably than before. One willingly "suffers" the being of the other, enduring the weight by which it pulls him away from his own concerns, a weight now much heavier than before. As this weight increases, so also knowing penetration and loving taste of the subjectivity of the other deepens. But this penetration is still a "dark knowledge"; for it remains non-objective. And the taste is only vicarious; the subjectivity of the other is tasted only in its "resonance" in me.

It is in this manner that the subjectivity of other persons, and even things, is encountered in intersubjective union. Affective connaturality is thus the principle of a wide variety of modes of "knowing by loving." Some of these special modes of such knowing were pointed out in my *The Christian Intellect and the Mystery of Being*,[88] ranging from the heights of mystical union to ordinary human intersubjective awareness, from the most primitive grasp of very general aspects of the natural moral law to the moral sensitivity of the saint. We must now consider the role of such knowledge in ordinary belief, in order the better to see its place in the act of divine faith.

V. INTERSUBJECTIVITY AND HUMAN BELIEF

Belief in the word of another is a personal act in regard to the testimony of another person; it involves an interpersonal relation, in some manner an I-Thou relation. It is necessary to consider the role that such an I-Thou relation may play in ordinary human belief, more easily

[88] pp. 86–89.

known to us, before going on to consider its role in the act of divine faith.

Since belief is the acceptance of testimony, all belief in some manner presupposes dialogue. Belief, in fact, is totally immersed in dialogue; the interpersonal relation of belief is the interpersonal relation of dialogue. It will be seen in the analysis of the general conditions of human dialogue that in fact dialogue presupposes belief just as belief presupposes dialogue. This means that belief exists at two distinct levels, one in complete subordination to the other.

Finite being, and therefore the finite human person, is at once both generous and indigent. Being is diffusive of itself in action; this is the dynamic generosity of being. It will communicate something of itself in transitive action, will lend itself as a subject for a new, intentional mode of being of others in sensation, will give itself in human love. At the same time finite being is indigent; it is imperfect and needs to be perfected, even tends toward being perfected in its manner. And as each human person begins the long development of his spiritual life of knowledge and love, he seeks to communicate something of the treasure he has gained to other men and also to be enriched by the truth, beauty, and goodness which others have to offer him. This mutual communication is human dialogue.

The dialogue cannot begin until one person encounters another as a person; only then does each appear to the other as a real center of human values from whom to profit and to whom to communicate one's own goods. This encounter, as was pointed out in the last chapter, takes place in virtue of affective connaturality, in virtue of a certain at least minimum love or interest in *the other*. This minimum of love or interest is in its way natural. It presupposes a natural simplicity prompting one to give what one has and a natural openness prompting one to receive what is offered, and it gives rise to a free (though still quasi-natural because it is so spontaneous) simplicity and openness. It is the free simplicity and openness which leads one to say what is in him and to listen to what is in others; and it is this speaking and listening which is dialogue.

More than just ideas are communicated in the dialogue; the persons engaged will communicate something of their very selves, of their personalities, of their depths of subjectivity and lived existential attitudes.

This simple, spontaneous dialogue, of course, also presupposes that common inheritance of mutual trust which is part of ordinary human common – sense life. Such trust is founded upon certain genuine insights about people, at first present only obscurely – but perhaps gradually clarifying. An example of such an insight is expressed in the moral and psychological principle that no one lies without a reason ("Nemo gratis mendax").

But such insight and consequent mutual trust finds itself challenged by the facts of human error and human deception, leading to disappointment and caution in accepting what others say. The problem now is: When to believe? For belief is free; we may accept or reject what others say, and we must ultimately ourselves be responsible for such acceptance or rejection. Belief is now seen to be not only a personal relation but also a personal problem of personal commitment.

Sometimes the aspect of personal commitment in belief does not appear very strongly by reason of the common and universal nature of the questions and of the answers. The testimony in favor of the existence of Australia is so great that my belief in it does not appear as very much a matter of personal commitment. It is similar in the case of my acceptance of the universality of the fact of death.

But in many important and more difficult matters, belief appears much more obviously as a personal commitment to a person. For example, since one must begin to learn complex matters by first believing someone, a teacher, one must look about to find someone whom he deems worthy of such trust. One must find a teacher, perhaps a philosopher or a theologian, who can guide one into the inner sanctum of truth behind all the conflicts, schools, confusions, etc. To take someone as a teacher in philosophy or theology, and at least to some extent in any other area as well, is truly a matter of personal commitment. Here we can see how much belief is first of all belief in a person! For this reason, belief always connotes some slight minimum, at least, of humility, of willingness to forego the myth of the complete autonomy of the finite person.

But how is one to find another whom he may believe? This is not a matter of knowing whether so-and-so speaks the truth in this particular case. Such an inquiry, establishing the knowledge and veracity of the one who has testified, as well as the fact of the testimony, is in fact impossible to carry through very frequently, except in very controlled scientific studies like sientific history. The problem is ordinarily rather to know if such a person is trustworthy, whether we may with assurance and security allow him to lead us into the night in which we cannot, at least as yet, see. We are looking not for the credibility of a testimony but for the credibility of a person. This is to look for signs of goodness and truth in the person who speaks, for signs that he *has* and *lives* the truth.

Trustworthiness is a moral matter, a moral quality; for to seek, to know, and to express the truth is a moral concern. It is the good man who is open to the truth, because he knows his limitations and need of the truth. It is the good man who is docile to the truth, because he knows his dependence and acknowledges it in his life. It is the good man who is truthful, because he is determined to be true to himself and his nature, to know and speak the truth.

Trustworthiness is more than veracity; it also involves knowledge itself. For if a man is morally trustworthy and speaking, then this can only be because he knows, because he has sought out the truth. Ultimately then it is the quality of the person in the moral order that is decisive as regards both his credibility as a person and also our belief in him which is itself first of all commitment to him as a person.

Yet men can be deceived about trustworthiness. Always one must scrutinize the signs. These signs are the signs of moral quality, of the virtues, and in particular of the virtues which pertain more closely to the search for truth and its communication to others: docility, humility, openness, generosity, exactness, diligence, sense of order and proportion, reverence for things, love of truth, reverence and respect for the *other* as such, sincerity, control of passions, disinterestedness, etc. And what are the signs of such things? They may be a thousand or a million little things, of the kind that do in fact determine every day whether we are to accept or reject something of another man and what he says or does.

Still, one may point out that this is a very dangerous way to proceed. So it is. We can indeed be deceived, and sometimes are; but sometimes we think this impossible. There are times when we are very sure indeed, and then we have a special kind of so-called moral certitude. This is not the "moral certitude" of a "scientific faith," but something at once better and not as good. It is much less analytic than such "scientific faith," and yet the intuitions on which it is based may be much firmer than the often somewhat tenuous lines of argument by which we establish knowledge, veracity, and the fact of the testimony in a scientific manner. Of course such intuitions, if they are to be truly valid, presuppose some moral dispositions in the believer too; otherwise how is he to recognize the true signs of trustworthiness?

There are, of course, times when the consensus of testimony can give even more than the special kind of moral certitude just mentioned. It is possible that the unanimity of testimony from diverse persons may enable one to apply the metaphysical principle of sufficient reason and reach a real metaphysical certitude about matters of which one hears only through testimony. In fact, our belief in the existence of Australia or in the occurrence of the Second World War (for those of us who did not actually see the fighting) does indeed rise to this level of metaphysical certitude. And yet there are times when a consensus can be deceptive. For example, the prejudices of a nation or of a region may well lead one to accept as indisputable fact what is only the result of collective prejudice.

But if I do finally think that I have found trustworthiness in someone, then I can enter into at least a minimum of friendship and complicity with him. His acts, at least in one domain and perhaps in more or even in all (though this last is too much when there is question of mere men) domains, are accepted as mine. I can therefore make his knowledge my own by belief. The formal motive of such belief is his "authority," which is precisely the trustworthiness of which we have been speaking. As has been indicated, this is much more than mere competence. Frequently, it is competence alone of which the believer explicitly thinks; but even confidence in the competence of another is more a matter of trust than of deduction – unless one is very uncritical indeed and makes an inference with large gaps. Thus, there is an "I believe" even before the man again speaks. Now there may be real dialogue, no longer the simple, spontaneous dialogue spoken of much earlier, but now the dialogue of mature persons. Such dialogue, to be mutual, rests on mutual, mature, responsible, and free self-commitment; if it is all this it is already the beginning of real friendship.

The structure of dialogue may now be briefly summarized. At the base is the love between persons, at first natural and spontaneous, then free. The affective connaturality arising from such love grounds an I-Thou relation of union of ontological cores and centers of value. For fully mature dialogue, personal encounter and communion must result from free and responsible commitment following some discernment of the moral signs of trustworthiness. This encounter through commitment is itself already belief in a person; such encounter and communion can themselves then be called "belief." Bacause of it, the acts of the other, his acts of knowledge and love, in so far as they are manifested and communicated, are now made one's own. To accept the propositions of another on faith, which is what is ordinarily called belief, is therefore grounded in the primary form of belief which is belief in a person. So-called "scientific faith" is belief only in a secondary sense. In fact the assent of scientific faith is not really free. Such a knowledge is called belief only because the truth of the proposition to which one is assenting is not intrinsically evident. But it remains that the proposition is accepted for an extrinsic reason known scientifically to be an adequately valid reason. This may not be an Aristotelian demonstration, but it is just as rigorous in its own way and just as thoroughly removes any opportunity or necessity for the free intervention of the will.

And now it is necessary to face the special problems of Christian faith as belief in God and acceptance of what He has said. We have seen that there is some supernatural noetic component in divine faith, that it somehow refers to the uncreated authority of God the revealer. Now that we have seen the manner in which interpersonal communion is at the heart of human belief, is it possible to find a parallel explanation for the supernatural noetic component of divine faith? Can the *locutio increata*[89] become present in an I-Thou relation of obscurely conscious communion, as the psychological ground of the act of faith? If so, how can one's attention be ordinarly called to it that it may exercise its psychological influence? How in fact does God "speak" in the soul? What is the role of the Church in all this?

VI. INTERSUBJECTIVITY AND DIVINE REVELATION

In II, the necessity of a psychological and not merely an ontological ground for the act of faith was pointed out. This consists in some kind of supernatural noetic content, not precisely in the propositions to be believed, but rather in the formal light under which they are believed. This formal light is the authority of the revealing God, not as attainable by the natural light of reason reflecting upon miraculous signs, but rather as attainable supernaturally in itself, with the help of grace. This authority of the revealing God is nothing else but the very *locutio increata*, identical with the pure truth that is God, and obscurely manifest in the soul of the believer. Such a conscious relation to the *locutio increata* is a personal conscious relation to a personal God known as trustworthy in the very *locutio* itself; it is the result of a personal commitment and trust. Since faith as a relation to the *locutio increata*

[89] ST, II-II, 11, 1, c.

is a conscious interpersonal relation, an intersubjective communion, it must be analogous to the belief in a person that was described in the last chapter. But because this faith in divine revelation is a relation to an entirely new, supernatural order, it is necessary to consider more closely the structure of such faith. While it may be likened to ordinary human belief in a person, it also has some significant peculiarities of its own.

The Modes of Intersubjective Communion Between Man and God

Before coming to focus upon the special mode of intersubjective communion that is divine faith, it is worth noting that in fact there is more than one mode of such communion given to man. In distinguishing these modes we shall be in a better position to focus upon the special mode that is involved in divine faith.

All these modes are above and beyond the ways of the discursive intellect in its approach to God, both the ways of "common sense" and the ways of philosophy. In order to understand them, it is necessary to reflect upon the spiritual nature of the intellect, the will, and the soul of man. Spirituality is the root of intelligibility, and what is in a spirit is always more than simply potentially intelligible. There is always an obscure actual intelligibility of every spiritual substance to itself; and this obscure actual intelligibility extends even to all that is in this spiritual substance – powers, habits, existence, action. Such a substance, and such is the soul of man even while it is united to the body, is *aware* of itself, its powers, habits, existence, and action; and this awareness is always obscurely actual.

And now note still another point. Existence and action, as existential act, bear in themselves a likeness to the Pure Act of Existence who is God. Moreover, at every instant, existence and action in creatures derive all their actuality from a divine causal influx and depend immediately upon, refer immediately to, the divine Pure Act of Existence. But such likeness to and immediate dependence upon and reference to this Pure Act, and not simply to the Pure Act as distant but rather to the Pure Act as more present to the finite existent than this existent is to itself, must lead to an intentional union with the Pure Act. And in a spiritual creature, such as the soul of man, this intentional union must be obscurely conscious; for here the created existence and action which are the principles of the intentional union are themselves obscurely present to consciousness.

Can this obscure presence of God to the soul through the intentional medium of the existence and activity that are in the soul be truly called an intersubjective presence, and the union between man and God thus achieved an intersubjective union or communion? It seems so, for God is here attained precisely as exercising His power in the creature. But to attain the divine activity as exercised is in some manner to attain the divine subjectivity.

In a similar manner, the "resonance" of the existence and activity of others in the self (in sensible and intellectual knowledge taken together) can be a means to the same intersubjective communion with the divine being; for again the conditions of intentionality and of conscious intentionality are met. Even the resonance of the existence and activity of other things is itself immediately dependent upon, relative to, and like the Pure Act of Existence.

It might be well for Thomists to reflect upon the Indian distinction between Brahma and Brahman in this connection, to see whether or not the distinction between the Pure Act of Existence in itself and the Pure Act of Existence as obscurely present to the soul in its own existence and activity and also in the resonance in it of the existence and activity of other things might not be parallel to, and even a fruitful interpretation of, the distinction between Brahma and Brahman.

These four modes of intersubjective communion between man and God just described are all in the natural order of things. Two others in the natural order may also be considered here. The first four all referred to God as exercising in some manner or other His efficient causality in creatures. But intersubjective communion between creatures was seen in Chapter IV to be grounded in the exercise of final causality. In fact, God also exercises His final causality in the mind and will of man, even more than do creatures. But He does this in two manners. First, and most obviously, He does this under the sign of the idea of God, attracting man to Himself as the known Infinite Good. But second, He may also do this under the sign of the known created *bonum honestum*, the absolute goodness and above all the moral goodness of the created order (indeed, the absolute goodness of the created order is itself a moral good since it calls for, makes a demand for, the "consent" of man). In this second case, one may have no idea of God at all, or at best a falsified and distorted idea of God leading to the rejection of the God conceived in such a manner. But the very dynamism of the will toward the good, the unlimited commitment to the *bonum honestum*, contains in itself in an implicitly actual manner a commitment to God

Himself, a genuine love of God above all things. In both the first and the second instances of the exercise of final causality by God in the mind and will of man, through affective connaturality arises a new presence of God as subject and not merely as object, that is to say, there are new modes of intersubjective communion between man and God. The second mode will be of special interest in the next chapter, when it is considered as elevated by grace and giving rise to the faith of pure intersubjectivity.

The six modes of intersubjective communion between man and God in the natural order that have just been considered can all be said to pertain to the order of natural mysticism. The first four are obviously present in every man since they arise in virtue of the very nature of man and his intellectual operation. But their presence is obscure and they do not engage the attention of most men. It requires a considerable ascetical effort to suppress all that distracts from them, which means the rest of human conscious life, in order that they may appear more distinctly – though always enshrouded in darkness. This much the Indian mystics of the *Upanishads* seemingly succeeded in doing. But it also requires a considerable intellectual effort to interpret the content of such natural mysticism correctly and to avoid the temptations of pantheism. This the Indian mystics of the *Upanishads* failed to do.

The preceding analysis of natural modes of intersubjective communion between man and God should lead one also to expect that there are supernatural modes of such intersubjective communion. In the line of the exercised efficient causality of God, we expect such modes in virtue of the presence of sanctifying grace and of the infused virtues and gifts and of their acts. In the line of final causality, we expect a mode of intersubjective communion between man and God to arise wherever an act is directed toward God under the inspiration of grace, wherever there is an act of supernatural love of God, whether it be the fullness of love that is charity or even the mere beginnings of love that are required in faith and hope.

Clearly, several of these modes are relevant to the act of faith. But it will be well to focus upon the mode which is most proper to the act of faith as a free commitment to the authority of God, and upon the mode of intersubjective communion in which the very *locutio increata* itself is attained. In fact, the free commitment and the hearing of the *locutio increata* are most intimately bound up together, although not simply to be identified.

The Analysis of the Act of Faith

The analysis which follows, of the diverse moments leading up to and including the act of faith, is not meant as a universal description of every act of faith. The following chapter will consider a "faith of pure intersubjectivity" which does not quite follow the course to be described here. But this analysis may well be taken as a description of the genesis of faith in an adult who, in his search for the meaning of life, actually comes upon the Church presenting the message of Christian revelation, a set of propositions to be believed as the testimony of a personal God revealing and desiring to communicate Himself more fully to men. But even after making this limitation in the scope of the analysis, one must finally admit the freedom of the divine action in leading men to faith. Grace may intervene at any of the moments in its own ways, or all along the way. But at least one may hope that the analysis will convey some idea of the overall metaphysical and psychological structure of the act of faith.

Twelve moments may be distinguished. They will first be presented in outline form and then discussed in more detail.

(1) Natural desire of the intellect to know the truth.

(2) Desire of the will for the good.

(3) Knowledge of a hierarchy of truths and goods.

(4) Desire for good according to the hierarchy of good, and quest for the ultimate good of human life.

(5) Intellectual inquiry, finally encountering the signs of credibility of the divine revelation concerning the ultimate good of human life.

(6) Judgment of credibility of the divine revelation, made by reason itself as a natural judgment (with or without the help of grace), based upon the evidence of signs.

(7) Indeliberate affection and connaturalization of the will in relation to the supernatural end of man, caused by an impulse of grace in the will in the face of the intellectual presentation of the supernatural end.

(8) Complex of awareness and judgment based on this affective connaturality, leading to the supernatural practical judgment, "God here revealing should be believed."

(9) Inclination of the will to believe, and deeper connaturalization of the will.

(10) Intensified intellectual awareness of the motive of belief and firmness in the practical judgment leading to the actual decision.

(11) Deliberate choice of the will to move the intellect to the act of faith, to free commitment to God and therefore to the truths He reveals.

(12) The willed intellectual assent of faith, or act of faith, formally specified by the intellectual awareness (in intersubjective communion) of the motive of faith, and specifying the act of the will in so far as this intellectual act still contains virtually the practical judgment mentioned in (10).

In this outline there is a see-sawing back and forth between the acts of the intellect and the acts of the will. Frequently the priority and posteriority is therefore only logical and not temporal, but it enables us to make a clearer consideration of the process.

The first four steps do not require any particular comment. They constitute the necessary ground for the act of faith, since out of them come the fundamental need for and capacity for faith, the stimulus for inquiry concerning revelation, the natural judgment of credibility. Already included in these first steps are at least the first four modes of natural intersubjective communion with God, and perhaps the last two as well. Already there is ordinarily some manner of "common sense" discursive intellectual approach to God, and perhaps a philosophical one as well. Thus, even before the confrontation of man with the revelation of God, God already is drawing him in natural ways toward Himself. There may even already be a true divine faith of pure intersubjectivity, of the kind that will be described in the following chapter.

Steps five and six concern the evidence of credibility which is accessible to natural reason. This evidence is an evidence of signs, analogous to the signs that lead us to accept another human person as worthy of belief, signs which collectively tell us that it is Truth that speaks here and Goodness that calls us, or that "God is here," or something similar. The logical process involved ordinarily if not always, is not one that leads from signs to a "scientific faith" in the truth of the testimony, but rather one that leads from signs to a "personal faith" in the truth of the testifier, in the trustworthiness of the testifier. Perhaps it is better to see it as more intuitive than discursive – presupposing the gathering evidence of signs.

The signs which convince will vary from one man to another. Guardini has pointed out the wide diversity of ways in which God can call men to faith.[90] The contemplation of miracles and prophecies,[91] in

[90] Romano Guardini, *The Life of Faith*, transl. by John Chapin, Westminister, 1961, 11–22.
[91] Denz. 1790: Ut nihilominus fidei nostrae *Obsequim rationi consentaneum* esset, voluit Deus cum internis Spiritus Sancti auxiliis externa iungi revelationis suae argumenta, facta scilicet divina, atque imprimis miracula et prophetias, quae cum Dei omnipotentiam et

the context of the wonderful life of the Church,[92] and of the human needs which can only be met by revelation,[93] may come about in different manners; but the signs are accomodated to the understanding of all and are most certain. They can lead one to a true natural assent to revelation, based on a natural trust in the revealer. But such a natural assent based on such a natural trust would be rather precarious; the signs are not such as to force themselves upon us or to monopolize our attention. And of course such an assent and trust would not be Christian faith. What is demanded is an absolute, irrevocable commitment founded upon the solid rock of the divine testimony itself and not merely upon the collected evidence of signs brought together with such difficulty and so easily dissipated, a commitment made possible only by grace.[94]

While such a natural assent and trust may perhaps be found in some few cases, perhaps as an intermediate stage before the grace of supernatural faith is given, ordinarily one moves from the natural evidence (at least "sufficient," but not necessarily compelling) of signs directly to the supernatural act of faith through the intervention of grace. The manner in which grace intervenes is the concern of the last six points of our analysis.

Once one has become acquainted, at least in a general way, with the claims and content of revelation and with its credibility, and now contemplates in some manner or other the proposed supernatural end of man (by a contemplation of natural reason itself), a spontaneous, indeliberate affection must arise in the will, just as it does when any good is presented through the intellect. But while a natural affection of this kind is possible, it would of itself be insufficient, non-proportionate,

---

infinitam scientiam loculenter commonstrent, divinae revelationis signa sunt certissima et omnium intelligentiae accommodata.

[92] Denz. 1794: Ad solam enim catholicam Ecclesiam ea pertinent omnia, quae ad evidentem fidei christianae credibilitatem tam multa et tam mira divinitus sunt disposita. Quin etiam Ecclesia per se ipsa, ob suam nempe admirabilem propagationem, eximiam sanctitatem et inexhaustam in omnibus banis foecunditatem, ob catholicam unitatem invictamque stabilitatem magnum quoddam et perpetuum est motivum credibilitatis et divinae suae legationis testimonium irrefragabile.

Quo fit, ut ipsa veluti *signum levatum in nationes* et ad se invitet, qui nondum crediderunt, et filios suos certiores faciat, firmissimo niti fundamento fidem, quam profitentur.

[93] Denz. 1795: ...praeter ea, ad quae naturalis ratio pertingere potest, credenda nobis proponuntur mysteria in Deo abscondita, quae, nisi revelata divinitus, innotescere non possunt.

Denz. 1799: ...fides vero rationem ab erroribus liberet ac tueatur eamque multiplici cognitione instruat.

[94] Denz. 1791: ...nemo tamen "evangelicae praedicationi consentire" potest, sicut oportet ad salutem consequendam, "absque illuminatione et inspiratione Spiritus Sancti, qui dat omnibus suavitatem in consentiendo et credendo veritati."

and finally unfruitful in relation to the proposed supernatural good. While it could lead to the precarious natural act of faith described above, it could not lead to the firm and irrevocable (that is, irrevocable in itself, though revocable through sin) commitment which is Christian faith; so also, it could not eventually fructify into charity but only into an inefficacious desire for the supernatural end. It is necessary for the genesis of Christian faith that such a natural affection either give way to, or be preempted by, a supernatural, grace-inspired affection for the supernatural end of life in God; at this point the intervention of grace becomes absolutely essential. The grace-inspired affection just mentioned gives an incipient inclination toward and connaturalization to the supernatural end. And such inclination and connaturalization have several noetic effects in the intellect, which are summed up in (8).

The intellectual awareness of one's grace-inspired connaturality with the supernatural end has a triple significance. First, through such connaturality one enters into an obscure intersubjective communion with the Infinite Good, the Infinite Subject Who is also Infinite Truth. Thus there is present in an intuitive, non-conceptualizable manner the very trustworthiness of God, the divine authority, the *locutio increata*, now testifying through this very inclination which He inspired toward Himself and toward the revealed propositions which are seen as means toward this supernatural end. The inclination toward personal commitment to a person here grounds, or even includes, the inclination toward assent to the revealed propositions, even while this same inclination is the formal means through which is attained the fundamental trustworthiness of the person who "reveals" these propositions or thus "testifies" to their truth. More will be said of the relation between the belief in the person and the belief in the proposition later.

One must note that the supernatural intersubjective communion just described in fact has as its conditions the evidence of signs and some kind of natural judgment of credibility. In this sense, such intersubjective communion could be said to come about "in" and "through" the signs. And yet, under these conditions, there is an intersubjective communion and *locutio increata* which is in itself independent of these conditions. Thus the formal motive of the act of faith, which is precisely this *locutio increata*, completely transcends all the natural evidence for it. One can at least conceive of an act of faith depending on a formal motive attained without any of these conditions, without exterior signs and perhaps even without formulated propositions to which to assent, a faith which is a pure faith in a person with no more than a willingness to assent to propositions revealed by Him if they were known. Such a faith would be the faith of pure intersubjectivity to be seen in the next chapter.

The second significance found in the intellectual awareness of one's grace-inspired connaturality with the supernatural end is that one is conscious of the inclination to "believe in" this end, to adhere to it, to assent also to the propositions belief in which is seen as a means to this end. Thus arises a practical judgment grounded in connaturality, a grace-inspired, supernatural judgment: "It is good for me to believe in the Revealer and in in His revelation." Here belief is seen as "fitting" one's being, not his natural being but rather his being as subject to this impulse of grace. When this consciousness of the inclination to believe is taken together with the already described obscure intersubjective communion with and attainment of the *locutio increata*, the judgment becomes even more determinate: "God here revealing *is* to be believed." It is no longer a question of goodness for me in my particular state, but rather of the goodness of the act of belief as grounded in the order of things and in the true relation of an indigent creature to Pure Truth condescending to speak to him. This is not just a matter of "it is good for me," but rather of "I am morally bound." This brings us much closer to faith itself; here already appears also the possibility of infidelity.

The third significance of intellectual awareness of grace-inspired connaturality with the supernatural end and with supernatural revelation is that one has an impulse to order intellectually such natural sign-knowledge of credibility as he has and even to seek more such sign-knowledge, that the natural reasonableness of the act of faith may appear more clearly to the intellect. It is at this point that one may locate Rousselot's "eyes of faith," though obviously in a more qualified sense.

All these happenings in the intellect in virtue of the first grace-inspired affection and connaturality in the will must now lead to a second moment of indeliberate affection in the will, a stronger inclination actually to believe and a fuller connaturalization with the supernatural end and the means to it. This is moment (9).

Following upon the second moment of indeliberate affection must come an intensification of the authoritatively revealing presence of God in obscurity in the soul, of the awareness of the inclination to believe, and of the firmness of the practical judgment: "I ought to believe." This intensification will lead on to the actual decision to believe, unless the will should intervene to break off the consideration and to refuse consent. It is at this point that the sin of infidelity can actually take place in a formal sense; this would be a rejection of the divine offer even in the face of the obscurely (but sufficiently) manifested authority of God – making a liar out of God and refusing to Him the submission which we owe to Him as indigent creatures before the Light who can supply our need.

But if the will does not intervene in such a negative manner, it follows up the immediatly practical judgment ("I ought to believe" or "Believe!") by its own deliberate choice and motion, moving the intellect to the act of faith. The will thus makes the immediately practical judgment ("Believe!") to be also the ultimately practical judgment, which is assumed in a virtual manner into the :ugdment of faith itself.

At this moment of the judgment of faith, a complex reciprocal causality can be discerned. The now deliberate affection of the will, as a connaturality, is the formal means through which the intellect attains, in intersubjective communion, the formal motive of the act of faith which is the *locutio increata testificans*. The judgment of faith itself specifies the act of the will, and as specifying the act of the will must be said to contain virtually the ultimate imperative to believe; but this same judgment is itself produced under the motion of the will. And the motion, and before it, the affection of the will, while specified in some manner by the judgment of faith, are in fact more properly specified by the very presence of God in intersubjective communion, a presence which the judgment of faith necessarily expresses only in a most inadequate way. Perhaps it would be permissible to say that there are two quite distinct levels of "specification" and reciprocity of intellect and will. At the level of formulated knowledge, the judgment of faith specifies the motion of the will and at the same time is produced under this motion. But this level is only the superficial level of the dynamism of faith. At a deeper level, the judgment of faith must itself be seen as an inadequate formulation of the obscurely present *locutio increata testificans*, the First Truth Itself; and the motion of the will must be seen as a consequence or aspect of the lived affection which is at once "specified" by the intersubjectively present Infinite Good and at the same time itself the formal medium through which this intersubjective presence comes to be at all. In this way, the assent of faith, assent to propositions, can be seen to arise out of a deeper commitment and trust, an obscurely conscious relation of person to Person.

It is still necessary to explain in a little more detail how it is that this relation of person to Person is bound up with assent to the set of revealed propositions. This will be considered later. But first, a few words are in order concerning the psychological manifestation of the authoritatively revealing presence of God; for, after all, it was the necessity for a supernatural noetic and psychological reality in the act of faith that led us into the reflections of this chapter.

Supernatural Consciousness in the Act of Faith

Whenever supernatural consciousness has been mentioned, it has been emphasized that this consciousness is obscure. It is so obscure that it cannot be isolated as an object apart from the natural components of consciousness. Indeed, it suffers from a double obscurity. All knowledge arising through affective connaturality has a generic obscurity about it, especially that knowledge which has been called intersubjective communion. So true is this that despite ages of testimony of poets, mystics, and other reflective spirits, there are still innumerable philosophers who deny the very existence of such knowledge. (But if one were deterred by the disagreement of many philosophers, the search for truth would nearly come to a halt.) And besides this generic obscurity, there is another which arises from the impossibility of distinguishing in the concrete between impulses of nature and of grace in our affective lives.

And it does not alleviate the problem a great deal to point out that while grace is not itself an object of knowledge, it is still a means of knowledge of objects and itself noetically present in virtue of the obscure reflexivity of spirit. The problem is that the supernatural object of faith, the *locutio increata testificans*, is still itself only obscurely present, unable to be clearly distinguished from what is present in virtue of natural intersubjective communion. And the noetic presence of grace in virtue of the obscure reflexivity of spirit leaves matters very much the same as they were.

For more clarity it is necessary to look in another direction. Even in the investigation of the principles of natural knowledge, we find it necessary to begin, not with ontological (metaphysically psychological) principles of such knowledge, but rather with the fact of such knowledge. In order to account for it, we find it necessary to affirm other more obscure forms of knowledge, such as "complete reflection" in the act of intellectual judgment. It is not that the intellect must await this affirmation before it goes ahead and makes judgments; the intellect already knows what it is doing in an obscure, but sufficient manner before any analysis and consequent affirmation take place. So it is also in the act of faith. We do not await the results of the analysis of the act of faith before making the act of faith. The obscure perceptions of the intellect, however obscure they may be, are nevertheless sufficient to ground the commitment and assent of faith. That they are thus sufficient is manifested by the security of the act of Christian faith.

But if it is possible to point to indirect psychological manifestations of the ontologico-psychological substructure of natural knowledge (for example, attributes of a judgment that is founded upon complete reflection), then one may well hope to point out similar indirect psychological manifestations of the ontologico-psychological substructure of the act of faith. Such manifestations do in fact exist, both in the moments before the act of faith in which infidelity is still possible and in the very act of faith itself.

The authoritatively revealing presence of God *before the act of faith* is psychologically manifested indirectly by the experience of the moral obligation to believe, which can be only intelligible in the obscurely perceived dependence of the two indeliberate affections upon God Himself, and in the correlative intersubjective and obscure awareness of God as testifying (through affective connaturality). This authoritatively revealing presence of God *in faith itself* is further indirectly manifested psychologically by the unconditioned firmness of the assent and commitment, despite the obscurity of the object and motive; such unconditioned firmness is again intelligible only in virtue of the same obscurely perceived dependence, this time of the deliberate affective, upon God Himself, and of the correlative awareness through affective connaturality of this authoritatively revealing presence of God.

Personal Belief in God and Belief in Propositions

Two kinds of belief have been distinguished: belief in the person and belief in the truths communicated by this person. Belief in the truths communicated is consequent upon belief in the person and presupposes this belief, at least logically. The manner in which belief in the person takes place in divine faith has been perhaps sufficiently explained. But the manner in which belief in the propositions of faith is related to and derives from belief in the person revealing in this case of divine faith still deserves further explanation. It is one thing to understand how the *locutio increata testificans* is attained as a formal motive of faith and quite another to understand how the special revealed propositions are themselves seen as guaranteed by this *locutio increata testificans*.

In ordinary human belief in the word of another, sign-knowledge first leads one to belief in the person as trustworthy; from this one moves to the believing assent to the propositions the trustworthy person communicates to him. But in divine faith it cannot be this way. Unless belief in the divine person and the hearing of the *locutio increata testificans* somehow take place in the very act of believing assent to the propositions revealed, it does not seem possible to relate in any necessary manner this particular set of propositions to the *locutio increata*. This means that the very revealed propositions themselves are the primary signs calling one's attention to the *locutio increata*. The grace-given inclination toward both the supernatural end and the revealed propositions (as means to the supernatural end) itself renders the divine person obscurely present through affective connaturality (and indeed as the first efficient cause of this inclination as well), present as "testifying" in this manner. The believing assent to the revealed propositions thus appears to the believer, however obscurely, as at the same time and necessarily a loving adherence to the revealing Person. In other words, the reception of the revealed "good news" of salvation appears as a *necessary* means in this adherence to the revealing Person who is supernatural end and Salvation; for it is precisely in the inclination to the "good news" that there is found the inclination toward and obscure presence of the revealer who is also Salvation itself. To refuse the good news of salvation is at the same time to refuse Salvation and the Saviour: it is to withdraw oneself from the light that is offered as a foretaste of the clear light of heaven, and consequently to abandon oneself to an aimless wandering in the darkness.

But the grace-given inclination to accept the good news of salvation can ordinarily only be given and bear fruit when the message is presented *as the good news of salvation,* not as going counter to all that man could value, but rather as fulfilling in a higher way all human desires. Only in this way, unless there be question of a most extraordinary grace, could one freely respond by belief and commitment. If the Christian message is presented in a distorted way, more to repel than to attract, perhaps by reason of the peculiar background of the hearer, then there is hardly any chance that it will be accepted; for the obscure workings of grace can hardly fructify in total opposition to everything in nature. In such a situation, one can only hope that, despite natural repugnance, some sympathetic chord will be struck, that some almost hidden appeal of revelation will make itself felt despite obvious aversion. And if even this is out of the question, then there is only hope that despite rejection of the Christian revelation at the level of formulated concepts and propositions, there may still exist the more obscure and profound faith of pure intersubjectivity, to be considered soon.

If the revealed propositions themselves are the primary signs which call one's attention to the *locutio increata testificans*, in which this *locutio* is attained, it is nevertheless true that the sign-value of these propositions becomes even more apparent in the context of miracles, prophecies, and the wonderful life of the Church – as was indicated in the decree of Vatican I. All these are further signs, and it is the total complex of such signs that adequately disposes one to listen to, hear, and heed the *locutio increata*. The sum total of signs, however, does not by itself in any way constitute this *locutio* with its sovereign claims. By them one is only brought to the door of faith; internal grace alone can help one freely to enter.

All the signs taken together, the revealed propositions and their total context in the Church which teaches them, can constitute a compelling call to listen. Together they can manifest much of the goodness and truth that is in (and behind) the Church which testifies to the truth of the revelation. Could the fullness of human truth and goodness which is offered to us in the treasury of the Church exist in a liar? Would not the lie deny the real truth and goodness which we cannot deny to be there? But if the Church falsely claims to be the infallible mother and teacher of men, the divinely protected custodian of the deposit of revealed truth, then she is a liar, a hypocrite, a usurper of the place of God. But if all the signs are taken together – the miracles, the prophecies, the wonderful life of the Church, the teaching itself, etc. – can one still call the Church such a liar, hypocrite, and usurper? Even leaving aside the dominion of God, which could not permit a contradiction (indeed, God would have to do more than merely permit it anyway if it actually existed), is it conceivable that such a moral chimera could ever exist, offering such riches of goodness and truth to men and at the same time at very bottom a liar? Indeed, if goodness and truth are to be fully attained anywhere in all the world, it must be finally in the Church. Such reflections constitute, to say the least, a very compelling case, a call to the nations to listen and to hear the voice of God. Finally, however, whether such evidence of credibility in the natural order can be attained with scientific moral certitude, with reductively metaphysical certitude, or only with the special kind of moral certitude we have been considering (certitude through moral signs apprehended by one who is rightly disposed to apprehend them), the actual assent of divine faith and the personal commitment involved in it utterly transcend this evidence of credibility and require a free act under the impulse of grace. It is only under the impulse of grace in the will that the sovereign authority of the *locutio increata testificans* obscurely manifests itself and that one is enabled freely to adhere immediately to this *locutio* in the act of faith.

Finally, before turning to the question of faith of pure intersubjectivity, a few words may be added about the possibility of arriving at a true divine faith, not only in the Person of God but also in at least some of His revealed propositions, through signs outside the visible Church – perhaps through the teaching even of non-Christian religions or through the testimony of "sages." It does not seem impossible that one could be disposed to listen for and to hear the *locutio increata* through such signs, that the mercy of God might confer the necessary graces leading to true divine faith in God and in some of the propositions of revelation, at least the essential ones that God exists and rewards and punishes, even outside the visible Christian economy. Still more can this be true of separated Christians. But even if a given soul, or a great number of souls, are so untouched by religious ideas that even this minimum of propositional knowledge is denied them, there still remains another way, the minimum possibility for divine faith, the faith of pure intersubjectivity.

VII. THE FAITH OF PURE INTERSUBJECTIVITY

Is it possible that an act of divine faith could take place as pure faith in a Person (faith of trust and commitment) without any element of assent to revealed propositions? One could not, of course, even answer such a question by a simple appeal to empirical data or to psychological introspection. But certain testimony may lead one to suspect the existence of such faith. However, it may be possible to conclude to the possibility of such faith, and even to its actuality, by a metaphysical analysis conducted under the light of revealed truths. The proper point at which to focus such an analysis has already been marked out by St. Thomas. It is the point at which the infant, even unbaptized and totally ignorant of revelation, reaches the "use of reason" and must make his first moral choice. Here St. Thomas appears to require just such a non-propositional act of divine faith.

Let us consider the doctrine presented by St. Thomas in the *Summa Theologiae*, I–II, q. 89, a. 6, with some of its difficulties and their solutions. This article of St. Thomas concerns the unbaptized infant reaching the use of reason and the implications of his first moral decision. The analysis can, however, be extended *mutatis mutandis* to anyone reaching the use of reason, whether baptized or unbaptized. See Maritain's remarks on this point in *The Range of Reason* (Scribner's, 1952), p. 75. The doctrine has been the subject of continuing discussion both within and outside of the Thomist school for hundreds of years. However, recent developments within the Thomist school hold out some promise of a satisfactory solution of the problems presented by this doctrine.

There are six parts in this consideration:

(1) Presentation of the doctrine of St. Thomas and of some objections to the doctrine.

(2) Isolation of the special problem concerning justification at the first moment of moral life and some remarks on the contemporary significance of this problem.

(3) The relevance of diverse metaphysical perspectives to the present problem.

(4) Intersubjective faith.

(5) The impact of the metaphysics of the existential subject upon the other objections against the doctrine of St. Thomas.

(6) A final question: Is the necessary grace actually given at the first instant of moral life?

It is well to begin with the very words of St. Thomas himself in the article cited:

Cum vero usum rationis habere inceperit, non omnino excusatur a culpa venialis et mortalis peccati. Sed primum quod tunc homini cogitandum occurrit, est deliberare de seipso. Et si quidem seipsum ordinaverit ad debitum finem, per gratiam consequetur remissionem originalis peccati. Si vero non ordinet seipsum ad debitum finem, secundum quod in illa aetate est capax discretionis, peccabit mortaliter, non faciens quod in se est. Et ex tunc non erit in eo peccatum veniale sine mortali, nisi postquam totum fuerit sibi per gratiam remissum.

Three fundamental points are made in this text:

(1) There is a grace precept of ordering oneself to God as last end upon reaching the use of reason.

(2) Either justification (and remission of original sin) or mortal sin immediately follows.

(3) There cannot be venial sin in anyone in the state of original sin alone.

All three of these points have been the source of much discussion among scholastic theologians. Beraza cannot be said to be well disposed toward them. He says: "Haec tria quae in hoc articulo continentur, intellectu haud facile capi possunt. Ideo doctores catholici de hac doctrina varie loquuntur. Plures enim, clausis mentis oculis, toto corde illam amplectuntur; alii suis commentariis illam obscurare videntur; alii ei aperte contradicunt; alii denique, quos et nos sequimur, summa cum reverentia suo auctori illam relinquunt." [95]

Harent, in his article "Infidèles," in the DTC, Vol. VII, coll. 1863–1894, is in general rather unsympathetic with the view of St. Thomas. He directs us to Suarez and Schiffini as presenting strong arguments against the Thomist position (1887–1891). Lombardi [96] calls attention especially to the treatment by Suarez.

But the treatment given by Suarez [97] does not live up to this advance billing. The treatment is rather diffuse, and shows a lack of understanding of the metaphysics of finality. He interprets the last end in question as pertaining to the order of nature alone, and cites Cajetan and some others in support. However, no mention is made of any Thomists on the other side, who maintain that there is question here of the supernatural end. In the present-day discussions of the problem among Thomists, it is assumed that this end is a supernatural end. Schiffini, whatever is to be said of the validity of his arguments against the doctrine of St. Thomas, at least is very clear about the supernaturality of this conversion to the last end. He says: "Unum tamen apud me est indubitatum, conversionem illam in debitum finem, de qua hic loquitur Angelicus, non esse talem, ex mente S. Doctoris, quae sine motione gratiae salutaris fiat, adeoque ex unis viribus naturalibus liberi arbitrii. Constat aperte ex ipsius verbis, quae ante exscripsimus p. 546: *Hoc ipsum quod aliqui* (infideles) *faciunt quod in se est, convertendo se scilicet ad Deum, ex Deo est movente corda ipsorum ad bonum:* (Thren. 5, 21) *Converte nos, Domine, ad te et convertemur.*" [98]

Schiffini uses fundamentally the same argumentation as does Suarez, but presents it in much more concise and clear form.[99] His arguments are directed against the three points of St. Thomas noted above. If it be

---

[95] B. Beraza, S.J., *De gratia Christi*, Bilbao, 1929, n. 434.
[96] R. Lombardi, S.J., *The Salvation of the Unbeliever*, London, 1956, 240.
[97] *De Gratia* II, Lib, IV, c. XV; *De peccatis*, disp. 2, sect. 8.
[98] Schiffini, *De gratia Divina*, Friburg, 1901, 549, n. citation from St. Thomas, *Ad Rom.*, c. 10, lect. 3. See also I–II, 112, 2, c.
[99] *Ibid.*, pp. 548–549, n.

permitted to put into the form of enthymemes what are already quite concise arguments, Schiffini argues as follows:

(1) ...Non est credibile, Deum obligasse hominem, cum primum ad annos discretionis pervenerit, ad difficillimum praeceptum statim implendum, qualis est amor Dei super omnia, eo vel maxime quod cognitio Dei multa eget disciplina, ut comparari possit, praecipue in iis, qui versantur inter homines veram Dei fidem non habentes.

In response to Cajetan's comment that one need not have God explicitly in mind at this moment but only the *bonum honestum in communi*, Schiffini adds:

Neque enim constat de hac obligatione. Nam tale propositum generale, quo quis totam suam vitam ordinet ad bonum honestum, non est per se necessarium ad rectitudinem operationis; siquidem potest quis honeste operari aliquando, tametsi illus generale propositum non conceperit.

(2) ...etiam posita praedicta obligatione, utrovis modo explicetur, illus praeterea difficile intelligitur, cur in ea adimplenda nequeat subrepere negligentia aliqua leviter culpabilis, etiamsi homo per aetatem capax sit peccati mortalis.

(3) ...ad iustificationem adultorum infidelium necessaria est necessitate medii fides, proprie sumpta, eaque explicita in Deum remuneratorem, ... Quis autem umquam probaverit, omnibus pueris infidedelibus, vix ad usum rationis pervenerint nec mortaliter peccaverint, statim affulgere lumen divinae revelationis, ut eam fidem concipere possint?

As I have indicated above, I believe that the first two arguments rest on a lack of understanding of the metaphysics of finality. However, in fairness to such eminent scholars it must be said that until recently the *manner* in which the Thomist metaphysics of finality could be preserved in this domain was rather difficult to understand, and indeed still has a certain obscurity about it. But it is not a desirable method to sacrifice metaphysical principles in the face of difficulties. These two arguments will be briefly reconsidered later.

In the third argument the fundamental problem for St. Thomas is brought into the light. Even if we suppose that actual grace has intervened in the dynamism of the first free moral act, to say that justification follows must also mean that faith makes its appearance in the agent. But this would seem at least unlikely; it seems that, at least in many instances, if not most, there is not even a ripple on the surface of consciousness to indicate the presence of supernatural faith, however much we restrict the contents of the act of faith. The problem may be put more generally: How can faith and charity enter into the dynamism of human acts without any apparent manifestation at the level of objective consciousness, of formulated concepts and propositions? Here it will be most instructive to follow the consequences of two diverse "Thomisms" in the understanding of the act of faith, and to see the diverse conclusions to which they can lead as regards the explanation of the text of St. Thomas which we are considering.

Since "Thomism" here means first of all metaphysics of being, three principal "Thomisms" appear, depending upon how being is considered. Happily, the day has now passed when serious scholars could contend that St. Thomas thought of being as essence, as if existence were only an aspect of essence. The scholarship of the twentieth century has made this view simply untenable. Contemporary Thomism recognizes the presence of both essence and existence in distinction in every finite being, and emphasizes (although here there is not unanimity) that existence is ultimately primary in being.

But at this point, a fundamental divergence appears among Thomists, one of greatest importance for our present problem. It is one thing to see the world as a world of existent essences and quite another thing to see the world as a world of existent subjects. An essence is composed entirely of communicable elements, matter and formal intelligibility. Every element of formal intelligibility is characterized by discreteness; it is enclosed within determinate limits and sharply distinct from other formal intelligibility, "atomized," we may say. Such a world of existent essence is a world of intelligible atoms interrelated in diverse manners. The Cartesian ideal of clarity and distinctness well befits knowledge of such a world. All knowledge of such a world (except perhaps the knowledge of existence itself) can be adequately expressed in terms of concepts and propositions. Anything less than clarity is not much better than ignorance. Thomism which sees the world in such a manner frequently prides itself on the name of "Thomist existentialism"; but this existentialism is far removed from the metaphysics of the existential subject, which has been set into sharp relief by the efforts of many non-scholastic Existentialists.

But there is a Thomism (of what is still a minority party in Thomist circles) of the existent subject. A subject is not simply the sum total of its essential components; it is a subject in virtue of its incommunicable exercise of existence and activity as dynamic acts. A subject affirms itself in existence against nothingness, and in activity (though not without dependence, utter dependence, upon divine influxes and activations). Because a subject is more than essence, more than a synthesis of essential components, because it is ultimately incommunicable in its being as a subject, its intelligibility cannot be exhausted in concepts and propositions; this can be expressed by saying that the subject is not simply an objective reality but a transobjective reality. The being of the subject, as more existential than essential, is not enclosed within the determinate limits of form but shares in the richness, the superabundance, the overflow of the act of existence itself. The noetic alternatives are no longer simply clarity or practical ignorance. Being can be known with some clarity in its essential principles, but there must always remain for us in this life an obscure mystery in being, which cannot be directly expressed in concepts and propositions, although it is attained in diverse manners in the "I-Thou" relation of interpersonal communion, especially in dialogue, and in poetic intuition, mysticism, moral and prudential intuition, etc. While even such experience of the mysterious depths of subjectivity may be indirectly approached at the level of concepts and propositions, there is no substitute here below for such experience and it may be of considerably greater value than much formulated knowledge.

In fact, the divergence between the two forms of Thomism just presented, while fundamental as regards its consequences, is not altogether insurmountable. It is possible to move from Thomist existentialism to the Thomism of the existential subject through reflection upon the relation of essence to existence. Yet the divergence does exist and results in two distinct lines of approach to the interpretation of our text.

If the world is a world of existent essences, and the only really significant knowledge about it that expressed in concepts and propositions, then the act of faith required for justification is indeed difficult to find in the infant reaching the use of reason. Some Thomists living in such a world have adopted the notion of an *"intentio fidei,"* a tendency toward faith which is not yet faith but which suffices in place of faith. The theory, first presented by Gardeil,[100] has been subsequently discussed by other Thomists, such as Labourdette and Nicholas [101]

---

[100] A. Gardeil, O. P., *La crédibilité et l'apologetique*, Paris, 1912.
[101] M. M. Labourdette and M. J. Nicholas, O. P., "Théologie de l'apostolat missionaire," *Revue Thomiste* 46, 1946, 575–602. These authors, however, take note of the ideas of Maritain which will be considered below, and suggest what I hope to show, that Maritain here has achieved a significant development in Thomist thought on his problem.

and Congar.[102] Congar has expressed the supernaturality of this *intentio fidei* in a few concise words:

> And it is supernatural because that last end is, in fact, supernatural, because it is ordered from the first to a supernatural outcome, namely the act of faith itself, and lastly because it is entirely animated and sustained by the assistance of grace.[103]

But if the world is a world of existent subjects, and intersubjective awareness is given which cannot itself be expressed directly in concepts or propositions, then perhaps some counterpart of propositionally expressed faith can be found at the level of intersubjective presence. It is this line of thought which has been followed up by Maritain and, after him, by Journet. Congar at times seems also to be more inclined toward this view than toward the simple *intentio fidei*.[104] Indeed, it is possible to regard the non-propositional faith of Maritain and Journet as the same as the *intentio fidei*, except that the full richness of the *intentio fidei* as a medium even of intersubjective presence is now better seen in the perspective of the metaphysics of the existential subject. From this viewpoint, however interesting it might be to make a more prolonged consideration of the simple *intentio fidei* doctrine, it seems better to proceed immediately to the view of Maritain and Journet. For the present purpose, it will be sufficient to outline some of the main points of Maritain's essay on "The Immanent Dialectic of the First Act of Freedom." [105] Since Journet merely reproduces the doctrine of Maritain,[106] it will not be necessary to consider his treatment separately.[107]

Maritain begins by analyzing the implications of the first act of freedom in the moral agent. When one is first confronted with the possibility of accepting or rejecting the *bonum honestum* in the moral order, now for the first time seen as such, his choice of this *bonum honestum*, in however small a matter, has three immediate implications. First, the distinction between moral good and moral evil has been made. Second, the idea of a *bonum honestum*, quite independent of the subjectivity of the agent and transcending the purely empirical measures of pleasure and pain, contains the idea of a law transcending the empi-

---

[102] Y. Congar, O.P., "Salvation of the non-Catholic." *Blackfriars* 38, 1957, 290–300.
[103] Y. Congar, *op. cit.*, 292–293.
[104] *Op. cit.*, 292.
[105] Maritain, *The Range of Reason*, New York, 1952, 66–85.
[106] C. Journet, *l'Église du verbe incarné*, Paris, 1951, II, 792–795.
[107] One should also note the most interesting presentation by P. A. Liege, O. P., "Le salut des autres," *Lumiere et Vie* 18, 1954, 741–769, similar in many respects to those of Maritain and Journet.

rical order and therefore refers also to some Separate Good to which this law is relative. If the law is greater than I, it is because the law is relative to some good greater than the good of myself or of other men. Third, therefore in the choice of this *bonum honestum*, there is a tendency beyond the immediate object to God as the Separate Good. But it is not that one tendency is here only virtually contained in another, as certain concepts and propositions may be virtually contained in other concepts and propositions. It is the same tendency, which does not receive an adequate finalization by the particular *bonum honestum* in question, which receives an adequate finalization by the Separate Good which is God. This tendency, then, is directed toward God in an actual and formal manner, and not merely virtually. But since the knowledge which prompts this tendency is not itself formally a knowledge of God, the tendency is Godward only in its lived actuality (*in actu exercito*) and not in its expressed formal specification (*in actu signato*).

This Godward tendency of the will in fact gives rise to a vital and non-conceptual knowledge of God. Maritain explains that the will carries the intellect along with itself beyond the immediately conscious and explicit knowledge of the moral good to the true term of the first act of freedom. The intellect here knows without concepts and below the level of reflective consciousness, through the very impulse of the will itself. Here there arises a natural knowledge of God, not speculative but practical, grasping what is full of metaphysical content but not grasped as such. Such a "knowledge" could even be compatible with a theoretical ignorance of God.[108]

But the analysis is still altogether insufficient. So far, we have been speaking of natural acts; it still remains to be seen how grace intervenes in the process. More specifically, the more easily soluble problem of actual graces in the will may be set aside in order to focus attention on the central problem: how is it possible that faith and the light of faith enter into this natural dynamism?

Maritain himself has stated the problem quite clearly. The faith in the first truth could not be only implicit, for something must be believed explicitly before one can believe what is implicitly contained in it. But here no explicit faith is possible – the child does not really know (explicitly) that he believes in God, nor does he even understand the concept of the ultimate end.[109]

Maritain offers the following explanation in answer to the difficulty.

[108] Maritain, *Ibid.*, p. 70.
[109] *Ibid.*, p. 76.

With the aid of grace the moral good appears to the intellect as – more than just "what is right" – the good which will *save*, which will deliver one from all evil and through which one will be in some mysterious way safe. Here one adheres to God as Savior by means of the "volitional knowledge" already described above, and in this knowledge is attained one of the essentially supernatural attributes of God.[110]

But even now with grace, this knowledge remains most obscure, nonconceptual, at the bare threshold of consciousness. The movement of will which brings it about is itself still very obscure, without the illumination of the higher degrees of spiritual life.[111]

A few observations may be added to these ideas of Maritain. First, since for us in our fallen state, it is impossible efficaciously to choose the unqualified *bonum honestum* (and therefore God as our true last end) without the help of grace, since indeed, such a choice seems beyond the existential possibilities of merely human life here below in its present state, the unqualified *bonum honestum* must assume for us the role of deliverer from our miserable and limited condition. This is to say that the unqualified *bonum honestum* must have for us also the aspect of a *bonum salutare*. That it should appear as a *bonum salutare* which is really possible for us to choose cannot but be the work of grace, the grace of the *pius affectus ad credulitatem*, the light of faith, the assent of faith, and the consequent act of charity. But there is a complex mutual causality here. The *pius affectus* gives a volitional knowledge of the *bonum salutare*, which knowledge is here the light of faith. The assent of faith here is not a judgmental, formulated assent, but rather the adherence of the will in an act of charity to this *bonum salutare*, together with the volitional knowledge consequent upon this act. This free adherence to the *bonum salutare*, known with the obscure volitional knowledge already described, is itself an adequate surrogate under such circumstances, for the formulated judgment of faith (although it must of course *tend* toward such judgment, to be made if and when circumstances such as education, environment, experience, etc. make it possible). The only formulated judgment at this moment of choice is that which bears on the *bonum honestum* in the moral order, such as it might appear to natural reason alone. All the workings of grace take place in the obscurity of a preconceptual and prejudgmental night.

But the question still remains, Is this faith in any sense explicit enough to satisfy the requirements of St. Paul? As Maritain says, both

[110] *Ibid.*, p. 77.
[111] *Ibid.*, p. 78.

of these words, "implicit" and explicit," refer properly to conceptually formulated knowledge. It would be better to say that there is no question here of explicit or implicit conceptual knowledge, but rather of a knowledge which is formal and actual, although preconscious.[112]

The categories of "implicit" and "explicit" are transcended in intersubjective presence. Mere objective presence (revealing essences) is always partial presence; and here one may ask whether a given intelligible content is present explicitly, implicitly, or not at all. But intersubjective presence is the actual presence of the whole subject to another subject. It is this kind of presence which we are considering at present. In the immanent dialectic of the free act, we find that the infinite subject who is God is made present in obscurity in virtue of the tendency toward the *bonum honestum*, and that under the influence of illuminating and helping grace it is the Savior-God who here offers Himself to the believer. But we cannot say that faith here is implicit or explicit; these are categories applicable only to another kind of presence.

If the above analysis in regard to the faith of the infant reaching the use of reason is correct, it suggests that, even for older persons, the formulated denial of God (based on a false concept of God) is quite compatible with a real affirmation and with real faith at a level of intersubjective relation which is far deeper than the level of conceptual and propositional formulations. This in turn may shed some light upon the problem of "good" atheists, agnostics, and pagans, and upon the problem of the divine salvific will in the face of the millions of men through hundreds of thousands of years who have never heard of the revelations of the Old and New Testaments.

It is now possible to return briefly to the other arguments against the doctrine of St. Thomas in I–II, 89, 6 on the infant reaching the use of reason and his first moral decision. The first objection of Fr. Schiffini perhaps embraces three points: (1) the choice of the last end of moral action at the very outset of moral life is too much to ask of the child; (2) this choice is in fact impossible, because of the insufficient knowledge of the child; (3) there is no clear precept obliging the child to make this choice.

All the objections are in fact removed by the simple necessity, imposed by the very metaphysics of finality (the end must somehow be first in the intention), for such an initial determination of one's ultimate end, as well as by the analysis of the immanent dialectic of the first

[112] *Ibid.*, pp. 80–81.

free act which we have just considered. More particularly, the first and second points may be answered by reflecting that, while such a choice at the level of conceptually and propositionally formulated knowledge would indeed be difficult, if not impossible, for such a child, it is in fact spontaneously made at the deeper level we have considered. The third point would be valid if precepts were only known in objective propositional formulae. But in fact the spontaneous moral knowledge of all men first arises at a deeper level, in an awareness of one's deepest inclinations, in a knowledge through connaturality. The precept here is promulgated and known in the existential inclination of man to set an ultimate goal in his free action. In general, the distinction between mere propositional knowledge and knowledge through love and connaturality, between a knowledge which itself is merely "of the head" and knowledge which is also "of the heart" enables one to understand both the fact of the obligation and the manner of its fulfillment.

Neither does the obscurity in which this choice is made prevent this choice from determining the eternal destiny of the one who makes it. God sees into the heart of man far more deeply than does man himself. And even St. Paul must say that he does not know whether he is worthy of love or hatred, that he is not conscious of sin but is not thereby justified. We are all more or less obscure to ourselves, and must throw ourselves on the mercy of God who "knows what is in man" rather than rely on our own righteousness.

Fr. Schiffini objected, in the second place, that one could not rule out the possibility of a slight fault being committed before a mortal sin. This objection, again, rests on a misunderstanding of the metaphysics of finality. There is a confusion here between an imaginable empirical sequence and the metaphysical order. In the metaphysical order, the first moral choice must refer to one's end; and this is surely a grave matter.

Another objection frequently met with against the doctrine of St. Thomas deserves at least brief mention. The young child going to confession should seemingly be obliged to confess so serious a sin as would be the basic option against the unqualified *bonum honestum*. But he scarcely can do so since he is hardly even obscurely conscious of this option. In answer to this objection, it must be pointed out that the obligation to confess concerns sins only in so far as they are known with sufficient clarity at the level of formulated knowledge. But the sin here is not known with such clarity at all. Here the objector may well suggest that mortal sin requires the three elements of grave matter, sufficient reflection, and full consent; but at least the second seems to be lacking here. However, one must distinguish between ordinary sinful action known at the level of formulated knowledge and the more fundamental sinful basic option. This latter, even though not known at the level of formulated knowledge, is nevertheless *sufficiently* known to be a mortal sin. The gravity of the matter (the ultimate end of action) and the wilfullness of the decision (the basic option of the end, only relative to which other choices can take place) are so great that even the obscurity of unformulated knowledge suffices as the third element constituting the sinful act. Note that the problems of confession and of the three elements of mortal sin in fact exist even as regards the basic moral option of the mature adult. Always this option is made in obscurity and remains obscure. But the answers to the difficulties are the same for the adult as for the child in its first moral act.

Two more points should be noted concerning this first moral choice of the child. One must always take care to avoid confusion between the first explicit, objective, and empirically evident psychological decision and the deeper, obscure, transobjective and existential orientation to one's last end. It is not true to say that the first commission by the child of a conscious moral fault in some slight matter is a mortal sin by itself. The mortal sin is here at a deeper level, in the free attitude assumed, in at least an obscure manner, toward one's last end.

Second, one may suspect – for his consolation – that ordinarily the choice at this first instant of moral life is the good one. Reversal would come later, perhaps in a crisis of adolescence or of young manhood. There seems to be a certain accordance of the offered salvation through the moral good with the actual desires, the innocence, and the incipient idealism of the child. May we not think of this itself as an ordinary way in the workings of grace in our world?

Finally, one may object against this entire presentation that it all rests upon the hypothesis that grace will be given at this first moment of moral life, that we have only elaborated a theory to account for *how* one might come to be justified at this first moment of moral life, without at all showing that in fact such grace leading to such justification is given. But if one understands that the choice of one's last end is in fact forced upon him at this first moment of moral life, that the choice of the unqualified *bonum honestum* (and therefore also of God as last end) in fact cannot be made without grace, that in fact this unqualified *bonum honestum* cannot but appear as a *bonum salutare* to man in his present existential state, that the appearance as an attainable *bonum salutare* is itself a grace of illumination (the light of faith), that adherence to this *bonum salutare* can only be through a helping grace in the order of charity, that in fact sufficient illuminating and helping graces must be given at this moment of decision regarding one's last end (since the salvific will of God cannot permit such a man to be tried beyond his strength), the truth of the doctrine of St. Thomas that this first moral act must result in either mortal sin or justification seems clear.[113]

This discussion of the Thomist doctrine concerning the infant reaching the use of reason makes it sufficiently clear that the faith of pure intersubjectivity is not only a possibility but a reality in at least this one case. May we not hope that it has been and is to be found in multitudes of men who have apparently no chance to hear of divine revelation or who hear of it only in a manner so distorted and in a context so unfavorable as to preclude serious consideration? When such men finally do come upon the Christian revelation presented for what it really is and understood by them as such, they will welcome it with warmth; for they already believe in their heart of hearts. One might here recall the words of St. Justin, describing his own encounter with the Christian message as the climax of a long search for the truth of God: "But straightway a flame was kindled in my soul; and a love of the prophets, and of those men who are friends of Christ, possessed me; and whilst revolving his words in my mind, I found this philosophy alone to be safe and profitable." [114]

---

[113] A similar view has recently been expressed by Fr. M. Eminyan, S. J., in *The Theology of Salvation*, Boston, 1960, 197–204.

[114] *Dialogue with Trypho*, chapter 8. Translation from *The Ante-Nicene Fathers*, Edinburgh, I, 198.

APPENDIX

The New Testament and Interpersonal Faith

That the account of the act of faith elaborated in the preceding essay meets the general requirements of the decree of Vatican I should be sufficiently clear from the frequent references to that Council. Perhaps the most serious objection concerns the sense in which faith is an *assensus*. The Council uses this very word in speaking of the act of faith. There is no difficulty concerning the faith of Christians, since this faith of itself involves assent to propositions. But what of the faith of pure intersubjectivity that was described in the preceding chapter? Can such faith be truly called an *assensus*?

It seems possible to meet the difficulty in either of two ways. One might argue that the Council was speaking of the faith of Christians, and simply did not have in mind the case envisioned in the preceding chapter. On the other hand, it is possible to understand the term *"assensus"* in an analogical manner. In the cases of its use in the decree,[115] it is emphasized that the assent is free. There is a genuine grasp of being (*fides terminatur non ad enuntiabile sed ad rem*), and this grasp is through a *free* act. Now in fact the same is true in the case of the faith of pure intersubjectivity, although the manner is different. Of course, it is hardly likely that the Fathers of the Council could have had such an analogical notion of *assensus* in mind at the time; but, on the other hand, it seems equally unlikely that they could have intended to exclude it or to exclude the faith of pure intersubjectivity. It is not clear that the Council intended to pronounce on the nature of every act of divine faith, even one elicited by someone who had never heard of the Church or its claims. Each of the cases in which *"assensus"* is used contains some reference to the more limited context of an encounter with revealed propositions. In DB 1791 there is question of consenting to the

---
[115] DB 1791, 1814, 1815.

evangelical preaching; DB 1814 concerns the assent of Christian faith; DB 1815 refers to the assent of faith given by a Catholic.

In view of these facts, the efforts of recent theologians, referred to in the previous chapter, to describe a faith which is not expressed in propositions, do not seem to be in any manner at variance with the teaching of Vatican I.

To Thomists who object that St. Thomas has no treatment of interpersonal faith, at least not in the developed manner in which it has been treated in the present essay, the remarks of the preceding chapter seem especially pertinent, concerning the two kinds of Thomism and their approaches to the act of faith. It should by now be unnecessary to defend the idea that Thomism itself is capable of organic growth, both in the line of insight and in the line of systematization. Yet the growth suggested here is in fact very much grounded in the explicit teaching of St. Thomas himself. The *Prima Secundae* of the *Summa Theologiae* has numerous references to knowledge through affective connaturality,[116] not only moral knowledge but also presence of the *other* in virtue of love.[117] Intersubjective communion with God, even prior to affective connaturality, is understood by St. Thomas;[118] nor does the apparent change in his position on this point necessarily indicate a real change of doctrine so much as a change of perspective in consideration.[119] But a full treatment of the ground in St. Thomas for the work of this essay would demand another essay just about as long.

What is of special interest now is the Scriptural foundation for the notion of faith here presented. I do not intend here to offer a scientific study of the pertinent texts of the New Testament, but only a brief outline and a collection of texts which may suggest some further directions of research.

The basic facts concerning the notion of faith in the New Testament are clear enough. In the Synoptics, it is the notion of faith as trust that is predominant, while the Acts seem to put assenting faith in the foreground. There is a good deal of ambiguity in the notion of faith in the Epistles, although the idea of assenting faith is clearly enough present throughout. The Fourth Gospel commonly presents a notion of faith in which assent and trust are very much wedded together,[120] although it

---

[116] For example, see ST, I–II, 1, 7; 6, 4, ad 3; 25, 2, ad 2; 28, 2, ad 1; 34, 4; 65, 1, 2. See also I, 1, 6, ad 3; II–II, 45, 2; 51, 3, ad 1; 60, 1, c., ad 1, ad 2; etc.
[117] See ST, I–II, 15, 1, c., ad 2; 66, 6, c.; 69, 2, ad 3. See also II–II, 97, 2, ad 2; 183, 4; etc.
[118] *In I Sent.*, d. 3, q. 4, a. 5, c.
[119] ST, I, 93, 7, ad 4.
[120] Jn 2: 11; 3: 2, 14–18, 32–36; 4: 39–42, 48–54; 5: 31–47; 6: 29, 35–40, 68–70, etc.

also utilizes the idea of simple assenting faith.[121] All in all, it is the conception of the Fourth Gospel that best corresponds to the theological notion of faith presented in this essay, of faith that is at once both assenting and trusting. This perhaps reflects the greater theological penetration into the meaning of faith by the end of the first century.

To be singled out for special consideration here are three sets of texts which bear on special aspects of the notion of faith we have presented. This faith contains a component of supernatural knowledge; it is interpersonal; and it can exist even as a faith of pure intersubjectivity.

I. Texts suggesting a supernatural noetic component in faith.[122]

From St. John:

And as for you, let the annointing which you have received from him dwell in you, and you have no need that anyone teach you. But as his annointing teaches you concerning all things, and is true and is no lie, even as it has taught you, abide in him. I John 2: 27.

This is he who came in water and in blood, Jesus Christ; not in the water only, but in the water and in the blood. And it is the Spirit that bears witness that Christ is the truth. ... If we receive the testimony of men, the testimony of God is greater; for this is the testimony of God which is greater, that he has borne witness concerning his Son. He who believes in the Son of God has the testimony of God in himself. He who does not believe the Son, makes him a liar; because he does not believe the witness that God has borne concerning his Son. I John 5:6, 9–10.

And we know that the Son of God has come and has given us understanding, that we may know the true God and may be in his true Son. I John 5:20.

No one can come to me unless the Father who sent me draw him, and I will raise him up on the last day. It is written in the Prophets, "And they all shall be taught of God." Everyone who has listened to the Father, and has learned, comes to me; not that anyone has seen the Father except him who is from God, he has seen the Father. John 6:44–46.

But he who enters by the door is shepherd of the sheep. To this man the gatekeeper opens, and the sheep hear his voice, and he calls his own sheep by name and leads them forth. And when he has let out his own sheep, he goes before them; and the sheep follow him because they know his voice. But a stranger they will not follow, but will flee from him, because they do not know the voice of strangers. John 10:2–5.

From St. Paul:

The Spirit himself gives testimony to our spirit that we are sons of God. Romans 8:16.

---

[121] Jn 2: 22; 5: 24; 17: 14; 20: 8, 27–29.
[122] I have taken the translations from the Confraternity of Christian Doctrine translaion.

For God, who commanded light to shine out of darkness, has shone in our hearts, to give enlightenment concerning the knowledge of the glory of God, shining on the face of Christ Jesus. II Corinthians 4:6.

Now we have received not the spirit of the world, but the spirit that is from God, that we may know the things that have been given us by God. These things we also speak, not in words taught by human wisdom, but in the learning of the Spirit, combining spiritual with spiritual. But the sensual man does not perceive the things that are of the Spirit of God, for it is foolishness to him and he cannot understand, because it is examined spiritually. But the spiritual man judges all things, and he himself is judged by no man. For "who has known the mind of the Lord, that he might instruct him?" But we have the mind of Christ. I Corinthians 2:12–16.

...that the God of our Lord Jesus Christ, the Father of glory, may grant you the spirit of wisdom and revelation in deep knowledge of him: the eyes of your mind being enlightened,... Ephesians 1:17–18.

From Synoptics:

The lamp of the body is the eye. If the eye be sound, thy whole body will be full of light. But if thy eye be evil, thy whole body will be full of darkness. Therefore if the light that is in thee is darkness, how great is the darkness itself! Matthew 6:22–23.

At that time Jesus spoke and said, "I praise thee, Father, Lord of heaven and earth, that thou didst hide these things from the wise and prudent, and didst reveal them to little ones. Yes, Father, for such was thy good pleasure. All things have been delivered to me by my Father; and no one knows the Son except the Father; nor does anyone know the Father except the Son, and him to whom the Son chooses to reveal him." Matthew 11:25–27 (See also Luke 10:21–22).

The lamp of the body is thy eye. If thy eye be sound, thy whole body will be full of light. But if it be evil, thy body also will be full of darkness. Take care, therefore, that the light that is in thee is not darkness. If, then, thy body is full of light, having no part in darkness, it will all be illumined, as when a bright lamp illumines thee. Luke 11:34–35.

II. Texts suggesting interpersonal communion in the act of faith.

Note that any reference to a union of assenting faith and trusting faith necessarily refers to faith as an interpersonal relation. But here we look for texts which suggest that this interpersonal relation is also itself conscious, that it is *communion*.

It is written in the Prophets, "And they all shall be taught of God." Everyone who has listened to the Father, and has learned, comes to me. John 6:45.

All things have been delivered to me by my Father; and no one knows who the Son is except the Father, and who the Father is except the Son, and him to whom the Son chooses to reveal him. Luke 10:22 (See also Matthew 11:27).

The Spirit himself gives testimony to our spirit that we are sons of God. Romans 8:16.

III. Texts suggesting the faith of pure intersubjectivity.

Then the king will say to those on his right hand, "Come, blessed of my Father, take possession of the kingdom prepared for you from the foundation of the world; for I was hungry and you gave me to eat; I was thirsty and you give me to drink; I was a stranger and you took me in; naked and you covered me; sick and you visited me; I was in prison and you came to me." Then the just will answer him, saying, "Lord, when did we see thee hungry, and feed thee; or thirsty, and give thee drink? And when did we see thee a stranger, and take thee in; or naked, and clothe thee? Or when did we see thee sick, or in prison, and come to thee?" And answering, the king will say to them, "Amen I say to you, as long as you did it for one of these, the least of my brethren, you did it for me."

Then he will say to those on his left hand, "Depart from me, accursed ones, into the everlasting fire which was prepared for the devil and his angels. For I was hungry, and you did not give me to eat; I was thirsty, and you gave me no drink; I was a stranger, and you did not take me in; naked, and you did not clothe me; sick, and in prison, and you did not visit me." Then they also will answer and say, "Lord, when did we see thee hungry, or thirsty, or a stranger, or naked, or sick ,or in prison, and did not minister to thee?" Then he will answer them, saying, "Amen I say to you, as long as you did not do it for one of these least ones, you did not do it for me." And these will go into everlasting punishment, but the just into everlasting life. Matthew 25:34–46.

...God our Savior, who wishes all men to be saved and to come to the knowledge of the truth. I Timothy 2:4.

He who believes and is baptized shall be saved, but he who does not believe shall be condemned. Mark 16:16.

...without faith it is impossible to please God. For he who comes to God must believe that God exists and is a rewarder to those who seek him. Hebrews 11:6.

4

THE TRINITY

I. THREE PERSONS — ONE NATURE

The Christian conception of the Triune God, as even the most passing acquaintance with the history of dogma reveals, did not appear fully developed in the actual teaching of Christ or in the Apostolic Age. It took three hundred and fifty years of meditation and controversy to achieve the dogmatic formulations of Nicea and Constantinople on the divinity of the Son and of the Holy Spirit. This of course does not mean that the truths then formulated were ever absent from the treasury of revelation communicated to the apostles, but instead of such a precise formulation as "three Persons in one nature" there was at the beginning a more obscure and even enigmatic expression of the Trinity in Unity.

Far from speaking in such ontological categories as those of person and nature, Sacred Scripture prefers to focus on the actions and attributes and properties of the Three, whom it also affirms to be One.[1] The three distinct names — Father, Son, and Holy Spirit — are used to designate diverse subjects of predication, clearly diverse because of the diverse and incompatible predicates which each receives. The Son proceeds from the Father,[2] is sent by the Father,[3] asks the Father,[4] along with the Father sends the Spirit,[5] has all things from the Father,[6] and is the only-begotten Son of the Father.[7] So also, the Spirit proceeds from the Father,[8] and also from the Son insofar as He receives from the Son [9]

---

[1] I Cor 8, 6; Mk 12, 29; Deut 6, 4.
[2] Jn 16, 28.
[3] Jn 17, 3; 18.
[4] Jn 17.
[5] Jn 14, 16, 26; 15, 26.
[6] Mt 11, 27.
[7] Jn 3, 16, 18; I Jn 4, 9.
[8] Jn 15, 26.
[9] Jn 16, 14f.

and is sent by the Son,[10] indeed will only be sent by the Son after the Son departs from this world.[11]

All this and much more reveals, or in many cases at least hints at, the distinction between diverse subjects of predication, all of whom are named distinctly and coequally in the baptismal formula of Mt 28, 19, and all of whom are therefore surely God,[12] and indeed one God. The Trinity in Unity then is in fact presented in Sacred Scripture, though not with any metaphysical attempt to speak of the inner being of the Trinity, except perhaps that which may be hinted at in the Prologue of the Gospel of St. John.

But if the metaphysical categories derived from a consideration of creatures are inadequate to express anything about the Trinity, still they are of some use and soon began to be used, in at least a general way, to speak of the Persons and the nature. Much of the intellectual effort of the first half of the Patristic age was occupied with clarifying and refining the manner of speaking about the three Persons and the one nature. Tertullian crystallized the terminology in speaking of the unity of substance and the Trinity of Persons. It is not necessary for us to consider in detail the actual evolution of thought leading up to the formulations of the Councils, both Ecumenical and local. Rather, we will meditate upon the meaning of the finished expression on which Catholic theology has settled, the affirmation that the Holy Trinity is Three Persons in one divine nature.

Three names of three distinct subjects of predication mean three supposits, in the terminology of the scholastics. But these three radically distinct subjects or supposits are endowed with a special dignity, since they are intellectually conscious and free – this dignity is connoted, St. Thomas tells us,[13] by the term "person." Persons are intelligent and free, and exist as incommunicable wholes, not as parts of anything else. They are each an interior universe unto itself, in virtue of the reflexivity of spiritual being, even while being open to the *other*, to all being, and to communion with other persons. We frequently speak of the dignity of the human person, which is grounded in the spirituality of the human soul. With how much more reason should we speak of the dignity of these three divine Subjects, and give them also the name of Persons!

---

[10] Jn 15, 26.
[11] Jn 16, 7.
[12] Jn 3, 16; 1, 1.
[13] *Summ. Theol.*, I, 29, 3, ad 2.

Some refuse to speak of persons and of personality in God, because they consider the meaning of these terms according to their finite referents. But in fact this difficulty would be found with any term of human language, if we overlook the place of analogical conceptualization and predication. No doubt God is more unlike human persons, and each of the members of the Trinity more unlike human persons, than like them; but this point has not gone unnoticed in traditional theology. The Fourth Lateran Council declared that no similitude, however great, could be noted between the creator and the creature, without an even greater dissimilitude to be noted between them.[14] Nevertheless there is a genuine similitude in the lines of knowledge, freedom, incommunicability, interiority, and dignity that has caused orthodox theologians to have no qualms about employing the term "person" in regard to the divine Three.

But if such theologians speak of three Persons, they also insist that there is only one God having numerically only one divine nature, or one divine substance. It was not enough to Nicaea that one should say that the Father and the Son were of similar natures; rather, the Council insisted upon their sameness of nature, their consubstantiality, which has meant to the Church not specific sameness but numerical sameness.

Nature, substance, essence – all these terms have different nuances of meaning to the metaphysician; but for our present purposes we may consider them as synonymous, as referring to the same reality in God and designating that by which God is God, that by which He is *what* He is. In our created world we come upon many individuals having the same specific nature, the same essence, giving the same answer to the question, "What is it?" There are many individual men, many individual atoms of hydrogen, etc. But there is only one God, and there neither is nor can be any other; for His essence is the pure and infinite act of existence which can only be one, since it already includes in itself all the perfection of being that any other such infinite act of existence could possibly have.

Philosophers show that this one pure act of existence must be utterly and simply one, that it cannot have parts of any kind. At this point the basic mystery of the Trinity appears, before which all our explanations must appear as the stammerings of children. How can there be three distinct and incommunicable wholes existing in the one pure act of existence? Yet the history of Christian theology and the en-

[14] DB 432.

couragement even of the magisterium tell us not to give up hope of reaching some degree of understanding, however inadequate, of this mystery.

The problem is aggravated by the fact that in the world of creatures one never finds more than one person for one intellectual nature and never more than one intellectual nature for one person. Indeed, before the advent of the Christian revelation there was no thought of any such distinction as that between person and nature; at most the ancients distinguished between the common, specific nature and the individual nature which was also the ultimate subject of predication (that which we call the supposit). It was the revelation of the Incarnation and the hypostatic union that showed that an individual nature might still not be the ultimate subject of predication, the supposit, the person. The mystery of the Trinity eventually made it clear that the perfection of personality could not simply be identified with that of an individual nature, since here the most simple, unitary nature of all is communicated to three Persons.

It is necessary then to meditate upon the distinction and relation between person and nature, or more generally, between supposit (or subject) and nature. This is in itself a philosophical problem, although some with less insight have suggested that it really ought to be called a theological problem since it would never exist were it not for the revelation of the mysteries of the Trinity and of the Incarnation. As a matter of fact, I do hope to show later on that this problem can be raised entirely outside the context of these revealed truths, and indeed in such a way as to hold out greater promise for the eventual illumination of the revealed truths themselves than is the case with those treatments of the problem which have been developed only within the context of these revealed truths. We seek some illumination of the mysteries of the faith; but if it is necessary to employ such philosophical analysis as a tool, we must not hestitate to do so. There is a certain theological humility which insists on our inability to know anything about the revealed mysteries with the aid of reason as an instrument of faith; but this kind of humility is a false humility, more like the pride of one who would be utterly independent no matter what the cost and consequently refuses the helps, however feeble, offered him by his inferiors.

St. Thomas Aquinas, though aware of the distinction between person and individual nature, and offering us many texts shedding light on this distinction, still failed to make an explicit treatment of the problem in a formal manner. In this perhaps he showed some awareness of the limitations of his conceptual tools to deal with the problem. In any event later scholastics did not show the same hesitancy and clearly posed the problem of the nature of *subsistence*, or that by which an individual substantial nature is constituted as a supposit or person. They conceived subsistence as a further intelligible note to be added to the intelligibility of essence in some manner or other. A wide diversity of solutions to the problem of subsistence has been offered, most of them revealing a tendency to conceive subsistence simply as a special kind of essence to be added to substantial essence. The very diversity of solutions, together with the difficulties that can be urged against them, tends to discourage one. Here we will consider only the five best-known classical positions, before going on to the rather new approach of the later Maritain and to a further development of this idea. In the earlier positions, of course, the entire problem is ordinarily viewed from the perspective of the theological problems of the Trinity and the Incarnation rather than from a purely metaphysical standpoint.

Indeed, it would seem that it is the Incarnation that is generally foremost in the minds of those who consider this question. The theories that have been elaborated for the most part seem rather irrelevant to the problem of person and nature in the Trinity, as will be evident enough in running through a few of them; but there are also a number of difficulties to be urged against them even as regards their explanation of the Incarnation.

The five classic positions on the relationship between nature and person may be "tagged" by the names of Scotus, Tiphanus, Suarez, Cajetan, and Capreolus. Let us look briefly at each of these. Scotus considered that the finite person or finite supposit added to the notes of the individual nature a double negation of dependence on any other being. Such a person or supposit was an individual nature which neither is nor can be communicated to any other being as some kind of part of that being. This is, of course, a rather negative way of speaking about the incommunicability and wholeness unto itself of the person. But even if we were to endow the formulation of Scotus with as much positive significance as possible, it would still remain true that the attributes of the person and supposit that are here hinted at are more descriptive than explanatory. It still remains to point out the metaphysical root of the attributes of incommunicability and wholeness unto itself, which metaphysical root would be the formal constitutive note of the supposit – subsistence. Scotus appears to skirt the problem by merely describing a fact about persons and supposits, namely that they are incommunicable wholes unto themselves; and he does this in a particularly indirect and negative manner. His notion of the relation of person and nature can be applied to the hypostatic union, and it can even be applied to the Trinity; but this is possible because this notion is simply descriptive and not explanatory – it does not shed light on the mysteries.

Similar observations might be made about the opinion of Tiphanus that person and supposit add to the nature the note of wholeness. This is only the more positive formulation of the idea of Scotus that was described in the preceding paragraph, with the modification that only a single negation is here thought to be added to the individual nature, namely that this individual nature is not in fact communicated to a divine person (though it could be). Of course, such a person or supposit *could not* be communicated to any other finite being as a part – at least here the idea of a double negation is preserved; but are we not here perhaps only asserting that any given finite individual nature is irreducibly distinct from any other finite individual nature?

Suarez, limited in his approach to the problem by his inability to see the real distinction between essence and existence, nevertheless did think it necessary to posit a special metaphysical principle of subsistence, a substantial mode outside of and added to the order of essence in the individual thing. This mode has sometimes been described as being in the line of existence, as opposed to Cajetan's mode in the line of essence (which will be seen next). But this does not really seem to be an accurate description, for Suarez could not really think of this mode in terms of the essence-existence distinction. But in any event this mode was thought to be a true ontological and intelligible principle in the finite supposit and person, although there was no real evidence for its existence other than the fact that in the hypostatic union there was in fact an individual human nature which was not itself a human person, but which belonged to a divine person. It was therefore necessary to posit some way in which this individual human nature could differ from those individual human natures which are also persons. Yet such an explanation, by the simple addition of such a postulate, is reminiscent of the attempts to explain physicals effects of all kinds in the middle ages by the simple position of "forces," which were not so much explanations as substitutes for explanations. We want to know more about this mode, about why the construction of the substantial existent calls for it to be added to the completeness of its nature, and why it is that it can be missing in the one instance of the human nature of Christ. Of course, if essence and existence are indeed distinct as Thomists say, then the hypothesis of Suarez is out of the question anyway since it is posited in a totally different philosophical context. But in any event the hypothesis seems irrelevant in the case of the Trinity. The metaphysical principle of personality in the Persons of the Trinity cannot be any such substantial mode added to the divine nature; one would have to explain how there could be more than one such mode in the Trinity, and one would also have explain how to preserve the divine simplicity in the face of such modes.

Cajetan, in the context of the real distinction between essence and existence, postulated an ingenious construction, a substantial mode in the line of essence which terminates the essence in the line of essence as a point terminates a line. This mode then is distinct from the essence in the manner in which the end-point of the line is distinct from the line. It closes off the essence to further perfection in the substantial order and to being assimilated as a part of any other being, constituting this essence as an immediate subject of substantial existence, as *that which is* in the proper sense of the term. Apart from this mode the essence is only a principle *by which* the thing is; with the mode it becomes *what is*, the substantial existent. In his earlier days, Jacques Maritain, following Cajetan, spoke of the essence as being individuated by subsistence with respect to the order of existence and "leaving the line of nature to face up to something altogether different." [15] Through subsistence the essence can appropriate as its own the existence it receives, as its own proper act.[16] In this manner the reality and intelligibility of this essence become reality and intelligibility for itself and not merely reality and intelligibility to be possessed by another.[17]

Clearly, there is here an attempt to enter a little more deeply than in the previous positions into the metaphysical constitution of the supposit and the person. The mode that is here postulated appears as a little more than a mere *ad hoc* hypothesis in the face of the mysteries of the Trinity and of the Incarnation, in that it coheres with other metaphysical principles in the constitution of finite being, playing a plausible mediating role between the substantial nature and its existence. And yet this mode is difficult to comprehend as a real principle of real being. Just how does one distinguish the termination of a line from the

---

[15] *The Degrees of Knowledge*, 433.
[16] *Loc cit.*
[17] *Ibid.*

line? Can one really conceive of a finite line without such a terminating point? How then is the finite human nature of Christ to be conceived as lacking such a termination? Such questions make the postulated mode appear again to be radically an *ad hoc* hypothesis, and indeed as one which is particularly difficult to comprehend. Moreover, such a theory of the composition of the finite person may do well enough, metaphysical problems aside for the moment, at giving a reason for Christ's human nature not being a person while other individual human natures are persons; but this theory does not enable us to achieve a unified notion of person which would be relevant in the conceptualization of the Trinity as well as in the conceptualization of the hypostatic union and of finite persons. If we are going to speak of three Persons in the Trinity, then there ought to be some manner in which one's explanation of the metaphysical constitution of the person is applicable to the Trinity as well as to the other cases. But while one could conceivably speak of the termination of a finite essence, it is difficult to see what a termination of the infinite essence of God would be, and how there could be three such terminations all distinct from each other.

Capreolus pursued a distinctly Thomist line of thought and looked for the ultimate formal constitutive note of the person and suppositum in existence itself. There were no modes between essence and existence, only an existential actuation which of itself made the essence to be an existent. One could not then speak of *that which is*, or the subject of existence, apart from existence itself. Cajetan Thomists have objected that on this hypothesis there could be no such thing as a possible person; but one might retort that while there is no possible person in the line of essence there is in fact the possibility of a person to be found there, in so far as one finds individual intellectual natures which could be recipients of the act of existence. If the person is constituted as such through substantial existence, then the reason why Christ's individual human nature is not a human person is that it lacks a human substantial existence and exists with the existence and subsistence of the Word. Such an explanation of the hypostatic union has been accepted by many Thomists, and is today especially associated with the name of Cardinal Billot.

But is it really conceivable that the infinite act of existence of God be itself the immediate actuation of the finite individual human nature of Christ? And even if it be so, is it possible to distinguish this actuation as that of the Word as opposed to the other Persons of the Trinity?

This in turn raises again the problem of the relevance of such an explanation of subsistence and personality to the distinction of the three Persons in the Trinity. If they are truly to be called Persons, then the metaphysical explanation of the constitution of the person ought to be somehow applicable to the Trinity. But if the person is constituted as such by substantial existence, and if there is only one pure and simple act of existence in God, how can one speak of three distinct Persons in God?

The problems of postulating an immediate actuation of the individual human nature of Christ by the infinite existence of God have led De la Taille to speak of a created actuation by Uncreated Act,[18] an actuation of the creature by God through the medium of a created and supernatural act, an existential act of the obediential potency of the human nature of Christ, which replaces (or should we say "preempts"?) any natural and proper, proportioned existential act which would constitute this finite human nature as a finite person. This conception of the hypostatic union is but a special case of De la Taille's general conception of supernatural being as created actuation by Uncreated Act.[19] In such a view, the person and supposit is not constituted as such simply by substantial existence but by proper and proportioned substantial existence, the very existence that is naturally called for and befitting this particular substantial nature. But while this view of the person is a step forward in the understanding of the hypostatic union in its metaphysical principles and an opening to a fruitful path of further inquiry in this domain, which will be pursued in a later essay, still it falls short of the adequate account of the metaphysics of the person which would be in some manner applicable to the understanding of the constitution and distinction of the Persons in the Trinity. For again, there is only one proper and proportioned infinite existence in God, which is at once the existence of all three of the Persons. How then could the three be distinguished as Persons on this hypothesis of the constitution of personality? Moreover, even in regard to the hypostatic union and the constitution of the finite person, the theory appears as an *ad hoc* construction which would never have been made but for the fact of the Incarnation. If the person is truly constituted by proper and proportioned existence which raises a mere individual nature to an altogether different level, we should hope to be able to understand this

[18] M. De La Taille, *The Hypostatic Union and Created Actuation by Uncreated Act*, West Baden Springs, Indiana, 1952.
[19] *Op. cit.*

through a more developed metaphysical analysis of the principles concerned – for existence and nature are after all principles knowable and known to reason and to metaphysical inquiry. There are then lacunae both philosophical and theological in the conception of the person implicit in De la Taille's view of the hypostatic union as created actuation by Uncreated Act. Lonergan [20] has modified De la Taille's conception somewhat in order the better to explain the hypostatic union, as will be seen in a later essay; but he does not seem to have made a further advance in the notion of the person beyond explicitation of the view implicit in De la Taille.

The tradition of Capreolus–Billot–De la Taille – and now Lonergan perhaps – seems to be the most successful of the five classic positions in explaining the metaphysical structure of the person and the supposit. And yet it has the deficiencies already pointed out, deficiencies which necessitate further investigation. It would be especially desirable to pass beyond the field of *ad hoc* hypotheses for the hypostatic union to an attempt at a fully metaphysical analysis of the principles of being and of the supposit and person. The results of such an analysis could then be applied to the mysteries of the Incarnation and the Trinity to shed light upon these mysteries and at the same time to be confirmed, shaken, or qualified in the light of these mysteries.

Such an approach to the problem of nature, supposit, and person at the level of philosophical analysis itself is now not only possible but has been begun by Jacques Maritain,[21] and does in fact prove quite fruitful in the understanding of the revealed truths of the Incarnation and of the Trinity – the partial understanding for which we can hope. As was mentioned above, Maritain formerly held the view of Cajetan; but he has refined his teaching to the point that it represents a genuinely new approach to the problem of subsistence. In his "On the Notion of Subsistence — Further Elucidations (1954)" [22] we find the development of this new viewpoint. It includes a philosophical analysis and an application to the hypostatic union; indeed, though the philosophical analysis is independent of the theological application in itself, one is intermingled with the other. But our consideration of the metaphysical structure of the hypostatic union is reserved for another essay; here we restrict ourselves to the analysis of subsistence and the supposit, which

---

[20] Bernard Lonergan, *De constitutione Christi ontologica et psychologica*, Rome, 1961, 58–82.
[21] *Existence and the Existent*, ch. III; *The Degrees of Knowledge*, 434–444.
[22] *The Degrees of Knowledge*, loc. cit.

will then be applied to the consideration of the mystery of the three Persons in the one divine nature.

Maritain begins by noting three fundamental metaphysical points. First, the essence or nature is not the existent but a principle immanent in the existent by which this existent exists, acts, and is manifested as such and such an existent. This is to say that from the very first the essence or nature is to be distinguished from the existent subject or supposit. Second, the essence or nature is simply in potency to existence, which it therefore in no way confers on itself. Third, existence itself is not a static act but a dynamic exercised act, exercised by the existent, an "activity" of the existent, an exerted energy of the existent, Such an act as existence therefore needs a supposit to exercise it, since *actiones sunt suppositorum*. Existence then must be received by the essence and exercised by the supposit; and if being is divided into essence and existence then in some manner the essence must become a supposit even as it receives existence, for this existence must also be exercised. This comes about insofar as existence, in giving being to the essence in order that it can be a potential principle to receive existence, puts the essence in an existential state in which it can exercise existence. This state of active exercise of existence is subsistence, and is thought by Maritain to be a positive actuation really distinct from nature itself, an actuation of the existential order. Such subsistence constitutes the individual nature as a supposit, and if this individual nature be intellectual then such subsistence constitutes it as a person. An ontological depth of subjectivity is in this manner imparted to the individual nature, a depth which carries with it conscious interiority, self-possession, freedom, autonomy, and rights when the nature in question is an intellectual and therefore spiritual one.[23] Subsistence, then, is the state of actively exercising substantial existence as one's own proper existence, therefore in an incommunicable manner. A supposit is an individual essence or nature which has subsistence. A person is an individual intellectual nature which exercises its substantial existence incommunicably and thereby acquires conscious interiority, self-possession, freedom, autonomy, and rights. Such a person is itself a *center* of consciousness and of values, a point of reference and not simply to be referred to others.

Some refinements in this treatment of subjectivity and of subsistence are possible, and it would be desirable to set it into a broader meta-

---

[23] *Ibid.*, 435–439.

physical context;[24] but on the whole it is sufficient for the purposes of this essay. Clearly, here one finds a genuinely philosophical analysis in which the distinction between nature and supposit or person appears reasonably enough, without being an *ad hoc* hypothesis in the face of revealed mysteries. Here the distinction rests upon deeper insight into the relations of essence and existence, rather than upon a mere fact, however certain. One might hope that such a doctrine would be fruitful for the more profound understanding of the hypostatic union (and Maritain immediately proceeds to show that it is), but also of the relation between person and nature in the Trinity itself. And so it seems to be.

Yet before we apply the doctrine to the Trinity, it seems good to make two small refinements. First, a close study of Maritain's text reveals that in fact there are two existential states entering into the picture of subsistence. The first is the existential state of the essence insofar as it is elevated outside of nothingness by and in its reception of existence. This first existential state makes possible the active exercise of existence by the essence, which active exercise is subjectivity formally so-called, while the state of active exercise is subsistence formally so-called. These two existential states are of course simultaneous temporally, while the state of active exercise can be regarded from one point of view as a property consequent upon the state of mere reception of existence (since what is received is an act that at once also needs to be exercised) and from another point of view as an ultimate disposition for the reception of existence (since such existence could be received only in being exercised). While Maritain adverts fully, and indeed this is fundamental to his thought, to the distinction between mere reception and actual exercise of existence, he does not explicitly acknowledge the distinction between two existential states here. Had he done so, he might have felt obliged to reconsider his view that the state of active exercise, subsistence, is really distinct — not only from the nature, but also from existence itself as a kind of intermediate positive actuation of the existential order "like existence itself."[25] For if this state requires, and is, a special positive actuation, then it would seem that the other state (of reception of existence) also possesses a special reality distinct from that of essence and existence. Yet this is not so. Thomists maintain that the essence is immediately actuated by existence in such a manner that this composite exists as a composite of

[24] See my *Inquiry Into Being*, ch. 8.
[25] *The Degrees of Knowledge*, 438, n. 2.

these two without a third. This prompts a few remarks on the meaning of an existential state.

An existential state is a certain manner of facing and receiving the act of existence. We find that it is ordinarily not enough to consider the intrinsic meaning of a determinate form in order to fully understand its relation to actual existence, since the being of such a form is conditioned by the total context of forms in which it finds itself. For example, in the order of intellectual perfection, one may be a scientist; yet this cannot alone adequately describe the being of the concrete knower who is a scientist. His knowing, even in the domain of his science itself, is conditioned by the copresence of other modes of knowledge and other tendencies and achievements. So also in the world of nature, the being of a form is conditioned by the context of forms, substantial and accidential, which surround this particular form. This is why the being of a given substantal form can eventually be rendered untenable by a series of accidental changes which alter the existential state of this substantial form. Yet the reality of such an existential state is hard to locate; it is not a new actuation other than that of form and existence, but the reality of an interrelated context of forms in relation to existence. So here, the reality of the existential states of reception and exercise of existence is not a reality distinct from that of essence and existence, but rather an aspect of the reality of essence precisely as elevated by existence outside nothingness. The distinction of the double existential state enables us to grasp something of the intelligible relation of essence and existence that has hitherto been insufficiently considered; but it does not imply the presence of additional distinct positive actuations in reality itself. The constructed concepts of these states are necessary enough in order to attain more of the intelligibility of the essence-existence relation, but it would be Whitehead's "fallacy of misplaced concreteness" to take every such construct as designating a distinct reality by itself.

One may now object that these remarks seem to have destroyed the effect of the preceding metaphysical analysis. After all, if we are finally left only with essence and existence, we seem to have eliminated the special metaphysical principles of the supposit and person that we were looking for in the first place. But this is not so. In fact, what we have shown is that an individual substantial nature which receives existence also exercises this existence, in virtue of the very meaning of the essence-existence relation, and that therefore existent individual substantial natures are also supposits, and if intellectual, then persons.

And this fact is evident enough in our knowledge of the world. The "ordinary law" is seen to be bound up with the metaphysical principles themselves, and not something resulting from an extra-added positive actuation which the being could just as well do without. If there are exceptions to the ordinary law, in the case of the hypostatic union and the Trinity, then this must have a very special reason; but we at least expect that this reason will have something to do with the special manner of exercising existence that is found in each of these cases. The unique mystery of the person lies in this ontological reality of actual and incommunicable exercise of the act of existence of a spiritual being. If the human nature of Christ is not a human person, it must somehow be that the actual exercise of his human existence is not referred to the nature of the man but to the divine Person – we shall see more of this in a latter essay. And if this is so, it must ultimately be intelligible in virtue of the special character of the human existence of Christ, an existential act not quite the same as that which actuates other human natures. But more of this later; it is the Trinity that concerns us now.

About the Trinity, after all this discussion, we may be rather brief – although our statements here will open the way to much further reflection on various aspects of this dogma. The one divine nature is itself pure, simple existence, and by this very fact also pure consciousness and interiority, self-possession and freedom. This pure existence which is all the rest as well is, of course, exercised existence without being received in anything other than itself. God stands as incommunicable to anything other than Himself, and must be named with an incommunicable name. All this means that God stands as personal, as a Person, utterly autonomous and utterly independent.

But revelation tells us that this God who had been accessible to the philosophers has a mystery of inner life to which the philosophers could in no way gain access, that the philosophers were speaking of the Father but could not know that the Father has with Himself two other coequal Persons. Now we must understand that the one infinite existence of God, incommunicable in itself immediately to any creature, is in fact communicated among three Persons in God. But this existence is exercised existence; and the exercise of existence is itself unique, incommunicable, proper to the Person who exercises it. One infinite existence exercised in three distinct and incommunicable manners by three distinct Subjects – such must be the Trinity of Persons.

But how is one to conceive, in human terms, the ground of such a triadic unique incommunicable exercise of the one same existence? This is to ask what it is that makes the three distinct Subjects in God to be truly and radically and incommunicably distinct from each other, and this will call for a whole new line of theological inquiry in the light of the metaphysics of the absolute and the relative.

II. ARE THE PERSONS RELATIONS OR ABSOLUTES?

The divine Persons cannot be distinguished as three absolute beings, three Gods. In revelation itself, as we have seen, they appear as three Persons in one nature, at least equivalently; and this has been confirmed by the teaching of the Church. Their distinction is one of relative opposition, which arises in virtue of the procession of the Son from the Father and of the Spirit from the Father and the Son, or from the Father through the Son. It is true that Sacred Scripture does not speak of relations as such in the Trinity; but it does speak of the processions, which imply relations of opposition. If the Son proceeds from the Father, they are distinct as principle and principiated, which are correlative in God; here then can be distinguished two real relations, paternity and filiation, which require a real distinction in the Subjects of these relations, that is to say, between the Father and the Son. If the spirit is sent by the Father and the Son, then it proceeds from them in some manner, with a resultant distinction of principle and principiated again; here two more real relations can be noted, spiration and being spirated, which require a real distinction between the spirated Subject and the spirating Subjects. Even the name of the Son is a relative name, as is that of the Spirit or "breath."

Thus there are relations in God, four in number, which are really identical with the three Persons. Three of these relations actually mark out the three Persons, so that they are at least properties of these Persons, namely, paternity, filiation, and being spirated. From these three relations the three Persons each derive their proper names of Father, Son, and Holy Spirit. The fourth relation cannot be such a property since it is common to two Persons taken together. Since this fourth relation of active spiration appears from the outset as something of the Father and the Son, there could never be any question of its marking out a fourth person in God.

But it is one thing to say that there are relations in God which mark the Persons and which are identical with the Persons, and quite another thing to say that the Persons are constituted by these relations – so that the best description of a divine Person would be that He is a subsistent relation. This latter statement is a theological conclusion a little further removed from revelation itself, at least from the explicit revelation of the Scripture and of the teaching Church. The assertion that the Persons are constituted by the relations, and are subsistent relations, bears examination, all the more so since it provokes such an outcry from some of our separated brethren.[26] Does such an assertion mean that the Persons are conceived as secondary to the divine nature, as "tacked on" to the God of natural theology? Catholic theologians emphatically answer that it is not so, but what meaning of subsistent relation can be presented which will remove the problem? Do they really mean that there is no absolute diversity among the Persons, so that there is only absolute unity in which some relative opposition may be discerned in a manner analogous to that in which accidents are found in a substantial substratum? But if this be so, then how could the full notion of the person, as an ontological *center*, with its own unique interior depth, be applied to the divine Persons? The only center in this view would be in the absolute nature; the Persons would be each entirely relative to another, absorbed in exteriority. To one not adequately trained so as to see beyond the theological formulations to the simple revealed truth of the Trinity of Persons, these formulations might make the Three to appear as so many faces of the One Real Person, faces produced by the mysterious processions in the inner life of God. And yet the alternative of positing an absolute diversity among the Persons has problems enough. If God is one simple, pure act of infinite existence, what possible ground of absolute diversity of three Persons could be found in Him? Indeed, it was in the face of this understanding of God that the theological formulation of the doctrine of subsisting relations as constituting the Persons took place. If this formulation should now appear to be inadequate, it will be necessary to produce a better one. Here we shall make a few remarks about the doctrine of St. Thomas concerning the definition of the divine Persons as subsistent relations and the metaphysical context of this doctrine, then consider the meaning of a Conciliar statement which supports this theology, and finally embark upon a reconsideration of the proper place of relation in the conceptualization of the Persons, especially in the light of some reflections upon the metaphysics of absolute and relative.

[26] Vladimir Lossky, "The Procession of the Holy Spirit in the Orthodox Triadology," *Eastern Churches Quarterly*, 1948 Suppl. Is. v. VII, 31–53.

St. Thomas, in keeping with Tradition, distinguishes the Persons of the Trinity in accordance with the relations which we have seen. To understand his doctrine better, as well as some difficulties which arise concerning it, it is helpful to consider the meaning of relation for St. Thomas. Relation for him is, first of all, one of the nine accidental predicaments,[27] which says a certain "looking toward another,"[28] an accident in one being which itself is a looking toward another being opposed to the first. Such a relation could arise simply from the consideration of the intellect and would then be a relation of reason; but other relations do exist in reality itself.[29] A real predicamental relation (and for St. Thomas "relations" are always either predicamental or conceived by analogy with predicamental relations) is a very special kind of being the whole being of which is to be "toward another"; its being is pure exteriority.[30] Thus relation is the very weakest being,[31] an exteriority that is really distinct from the absolute being of the thing in its interiority.[32] Scholastics express this by saying that the relation is distinct from its subject, from its term, and from its foundation.[33] Note that St. Thomas does not himself speak of "transcendental relations," as do later scholastics. A transcendental relation is an essential relation, identical really with the *relatum*, and is found in act-potency pairs, in the dependence of effect on cause, in the dependence of the creature on the creator. While St. Thomas does not speak of such a relation, it is equivalently present; and yet in order to understand his doctrine of the three divine Persons as subsistent relations, we must bear in mind that relation for him is predicamental relation or something conceived by analogy with predicamental relation.

These relations in God of necessity are identical with the divine essence,[34] and yet they are logically distinct from this essence,[35] and, in opposed pairs, really distinct from each other.[36] But of course, if

[27] ST, I, 28, 1, ad 1; 2, c.
[28] ST, I, 28, 3, c.: "De ratione autem relationis est respectus unius ad alterum, secundum quem aliquid alteri opponitur relative." 28, 1, ad 1: "...propria ratio eius quod ad aliquid dicitur, non accipitur per comparationem ad illud cui inest relatio, sed per respectum ad alterum."
[29] ST, I, 28, 1, c.
[30] ST, I, 28, 2, c.: "Sed ratio propria relationis non accipitur secundum comparationem ad illud in quo est, sed secundum comparationem ad aliquid extra."
[31] *De Pot.*, q. 8, a. 1. ad 4.
[32] ST, I, 28, 2, ad 2: "Nam id quod invenitur in creatura praeter id quod continetur sub significatione nominis relativi, est alia res."
[33] A. Krempel, *La doctrine de la relation chez Saint Thomas*, Paris, 1952, 170–179, 245–271, 272–289.
[34] ST, I, 28, 2.
[35] ST, I, 28, 2, ad 2.
[36] ST, I, 28, 3.

they are really identical with the divine nature, then they must exist with the existence of the divine nature, that is to say, they must be fully subsisting relations.[37]

Despite the radical difference between subsisting relations in God and accidental predicamental relations in creatures, the former are conceived by St. Thomas by analogy with the latter. As a consequence, the manner of conceptualizing these subsistent relations includes something of the mode in which relations of the predicamental order among creatures are conceptualized. Though these subsistent relations are not accidental, they are conceived as if accidental. The distinction between the content of a conception and its mode is a stock one for scholastic philosophers and theologians, and must always be made when one uses terms drawn from a knowledge of creatures to speak about God; but to one untrained to disregard the mode even while regarding the content of a conception, it might well, and indeed does often enough, appear that these relations in God spoken of by the theologians are quasi-accidental in comparison to the divine nature – a caricature, of course, but perhaps not a surprising one after all. In any event, St. Thomas clearly must prescind from this mode proper to the conception of finite and accidental relations when he says that *these* relations (however they may be conceived) are really subsistent, because they are really identical with the pure act of existence which is the divine nature.

But if St. Thomas says that the Persons in the Trinity are subsistent relations,[38] still it is beyond the intent of St. Thomas to say that therefore all else in God pertains only to the divine unity. If the relations of opposition give radical distinction and incommunicability to the Persons, still these Persons must *subsist* as distinct and incommunicable.[39] In some manner then, subsistence itself pertains to the constitution of the three Persons as three distincts. This means that there is some kind of "trinification" of the divine subsistence, of the very divine existence of which we have been emphasizing the unity. In the order of *conception*, this trinification of "prior" unity flows from the relations; but in the very being of God there is no such priority or posteriority – God is as much Three as He is One. Thus, in the order of *being*, the relative opposition trinifies the whole, absolute being of God; one could not separate or even really distinguish the relative and absolute being of God.

[37] ST, I, 29, 4, c.
[38] ST, I, 29, 4; 40, 1.
[39] ST, I, 28, 2, ad 2, ad 3; 29, 4, c., ad 1.

In the light of the foregoing, a few comments may be made about the formulation of the Council of Florence, which to a certain extent canonized the conception of the Persons as distinguished from each other through relative opposition, and in this ratified the long tradition of Catholic theological thought in this line, already formally expressed at the (local) Eleventh Council of Toledo,[40] and at the (ecumenical) Fourth Lateran Council.[41] The particular formula of Florence of interest to us is the celebrated *"omniaque sunt unum, ubi non obviat relationis oppositio."* [42] The formula is certainly applicable to the order of conception; for in view of the absolute oneness and simplicity of the divine being, there could be no other way of distinguishing in our thought between the three Persons except in terms of some kind of relative opposition. But even apart from our thought, in the order of being, relative opposition is the ultimate ontological ground of – indeed it *is* — the distinction of the three Persons. But the formula does not deny, could not deny, that the relations in God are identical with the divine nature and existence, and must consequently carry this nature and existence somehow into the distinction of Persons – this is to "trinify" the divine nature and existence. Therefore we may speak of one nature in itself, but trinified in the relative opposition of the Persons.

It is the *"ubi"* in the formula that presents some problem. It must be interpreted a little more broadly than some have done – there are some theologians so literal as to disregard the spirit breathing through such a pronouncement and consequently miss even the real meaning of the letter. Such theologians interpret the *ubi* in a very formal sense and make so sharp a split between the absolute and relative terms applied to God as to deny all meaning to any trinification of the divine being and to end in fact, even though not at all in intention, in a split between the nature and the Persons. This means regarding the Persons as relations *alone*, and importing something of the (necessary) *mode* of conceiving finite predicamental relations into the analogically conceived content of relations in God. But all this opens the door to that caricature of Trinitarian relation-theology that was seen above, in which the relations – and therefore the Persons – appear as quasi-accidental entities, "tacked on" to the God of natural theology. Here all predicates except relative ones pertain wholly and entirely to the divine absolute unity, which is really conceived as *prior* to the Trinity, in accordance with the princi-

[40] DB 278.
[41] DB 428.
[42] DB 703.

ple that the absolute is prior to the relative. (I do not wish to suggest by this last remark that absolute predicates taken precisely as absolute pertain to anything other than the divine unity, but rather that there is also a certain relativization and trinification of such absolute terms in virtue of the identity between the pure existence and the relations.)

Such theologians are ordinarily not unaware of the difficulties of their view. Sometimes they will tend to minimize the whole theology of relations in the Trinity, as conveying a somewhat misleading view of the Persons; they may even go so far as to deprecate the whole role of philosophical ideas in the understanding of dogmas. More commonly and reasonably, the inadequacies are explained as flowing from the faltering of human conceptualization before the mystery of the Trinity. Yet perhaps something else is possible. Could not the concept of trinification of being be employed to overcome the apparent split between the one nature and the three Persons? This concept fits in well enough with the formula of Florence, for such trinification of being could not be found in God except insofar as there are in God really distinct relations of opposition which are nevertheless really identified with the divine being. In place of trinification of being, there is only pure unity in God, *ubi non obviat relationis oppositio.*

But now it is necessary to explain what is meant by trinification of the divine being, lest it appear as a pure verbalism. In order to do this we must employ, with regard to the inner life of the divine being, some terms the connotations of which in natural theology must be disregarded here. Natural theology presents us with the traditional dichotomy between "being of itself" (*esse a se*) and "being from another" (*esse ab alio*), the former referring to the being of God and the latter to the being of creatures, the former designating uncaused being and the latter caused being. Now when we come to speak of being within God Himself, where the idea of cause has no application whatsoever, still such terms could be used at a higher, transcendent level of meaning (attainable by analogy under the light of divine faith and theology), by reason of the procession of the Persons in the Trinity. Here the Father could be said to have "being of Himself" or "being from no one" (*esse a nullo*); the Son would have "being from another" (*esse ab alio*); and the Holy Spirit would have "being from others" (*esse ab aliis*). The usefulness of this terminology will be evident in a moment.

In the previous essay, a "person" was seen to be an intellectual substance incommunicably exercising its own proper existence, and this definition was applied even to the Persons of the Trinity. Within the pure existence of the divine being, there are three incommunicable exercises of this existence. Their distinction is in the relative opposition, in the opposed relations with which this pure existence is identified. But nevertheless they are not just opposed relations but opposed incommunicable exercises of existence. The exercise of *esse* as *a nullo* is proper to the Father, of *esse* as *ab alio* is proper to the Son, and of *esse* as *ab aliis* is proper to the Holy Spirit. Such a focus upon existence as exercised (yet never *apart from* relative opposition but precisely as identified with this relative opposition) gives an absolute dimension to the Persons (yet never *apart from* their relative aspect). This focus consequently allows us to see the Persons as interiorized *centers* and not merely as absorbed in relativity and exteriority in the face of each other. The perfect communion of the Persons of the Trinity can here be seen, not as pure ecstatic exteriorization of utter extroversion but rather as the mutual transparency and oneness of hearts of infinite depths.

No doubt, one will now ask what then in the Persons is truly prior, the absolute or the relative. Both are in fact contained in the data of revelation – the relative is always there, even in the very names of the three Persons; but through revelation we encounter genuine interiorized *centers* of being, consciousness, love, and action. It is indeed this *being a center* that really justifies our giving the name of Persons to each of the members of the divine Trinity. But of course, there could not be three such centers in God, and they could not be manifested to us as three distinct centers in God, except on the condition that they be and be manifested as essentially relative.

Yet, granting that revelation gives us both aspects of the divine Persons, we may still ask whether it is the absolute or relative aspect that is prior ontologically. In the older metaphysical context there is a certain difficulty here; for in it the absolute should always precede the relative, and yet here this would mean that the nature must be prior to the Persons ontologically. But this is clearly not the case, since the Persons are in no way additions to the nature but really identical with it, simultaneous with it, without any priority or posteriority in relation to it. In this question, one can only abandon the principle of the priority of the absolute to the relative as a principle that is relevant only to created reality. And a similar response must be given to the problem of the priority of the absolute or the relative in the very constitution of the Persons themselves. There could be no real priority or posteriority within the divine Persons; they are neither primarily absolute nor primarily relative, but they could not exist as three distinct Persons in one God without being at the same time both absolute and relative being. Again then, the principle of the priority of the absolute to the relative must be set aside as irrelevant outside the domain of created reality.

Such a simple recognition of a *special case* in regard to the divine nature and Persons and in regard to the being of the divine Persons themselves is in a certain sense a solution to the problem of priority and posteriority in the ontological reality of God. But such an abandonment of so firm a metaphysical principle as seemed to be that of the priority of absolute to relative is unsatisfying; we would expect that this principle either applies throughout the entire domain of absolute and relative being or itself is only a principle of *conceptualization* of the absolute and the relative. This latter possibility suggests that the metaphysics of the absolute and relative is susceptible of further development, even of a certain degree of revision as regards the position of St. Thomas and his ordinary followers. The principle in question ultimately depends on the conceptualization of relations, all relations, as either predicamental relations in the sense described earlier or at least relations *like* predicamental relations. Predicamental relations are always posterior to the absolute being in which they are found, for these relations are conceived and judged by St. Thomas as metaphysical accidents inhering in the related being. Any development of relation-theory which considers all relations on the model of such predicamental relations must end by stating the priority of the absolute to the relative and face the fact of the same exception in God.

One can of course answer that we should not expect to find a perfect intelligible scheme in which to conceptualize a mystery, and should not be surprised that there are exceptions to our metaphysical principles in the mystery of the divine being. Such an answer should be firmly rejected. Granted that mysteries cannot be perfectly conceptualized, granted that the application of metaphysical principles may be obscure when we come to consider the mystery of the inner being of God, still this inner being of God is *being*, and therefore cannot mean a simple pure exception to genuine metaphysical principles. In fact, it is quite possible that a present metaphysical formulation is inadequate, that the principle of the priority of the absolute to the relative is really only a principle of conceptualization, that the being of the absolute and relative is not quite as it has been conceived by many in the Thomist school, that the metaphysical analysis of the absolute and the relative admits of more refinement. Indeed, there are contemporary Thomists who insist that the complete real distinction between predicamental relation and the being which is related was a mistake.[43] But if that is so, then the analogical conception of other relations after the model of predicamental relation must also be modified, and the metaphysical principle of the priority of absolute to relative reconsidered. This in turn may enable us to conceive the relativity of the Persons in the Trinity not as an exception to the general metaphysical principle but rather as the highest instance to which a more refined statement could be applied. May we then be permitted to embark upon a new analysis of relations, which holds out hope of fuller success?

First let it be noted that scholastic philosophers have not been immune to a common tendency of philosophers to project various aspects of the life of the intellect onto reality itself – the Whiteheadian fallacy of misplaced concreteness. If Plato made the mistake of projecting the attributes of ideas into reality, and an earlier scholastic like William of Champeaux dabbled with the idea of a common nature subsisting as such in the real world of individuals, even the "good school" of Aristotelian-Thomist scholasticism has tended to give being, distinct real being, to what are more properly categories of conceptualization. There is no question about the distinct reality of the first three predicaments: substance, quantity, and quality; but the last six are rather commonly acknowledged to be much more categories of conceptualization than distinct formal categories of being itself precisely in the manner in which they are conceived. Father George Klubertanz has used the happy distinction between formal and formalized accidents to express this difference between the first three categories and the last seven, including relation.[44]

Certainly, among the things of the physical universe and among persons there are real accidental relations; the problem is whether these relations have any reality distinct from that of the absolute being of the related things. Every such relation presupposes relata (related things), in which can be distinguished the subject – that which has the relation; the term – that to which the subject has the relation; and the foundation – the reason why the subject has such a relation to the term. Now if the relation does have a distinct reality of its own, then this

---

[43] Bernard Lonergan, *Insight*, rev. ed., New York, 1958, 490–497; George Klubertanz, *Introduction to the Philosophy of Being*, New York, 1955, 243, n. 6; Joseph Sikora, *Inquiry into Being*, 72f. But see also John of St. Thomas, *Ars Logica*, II, 17, 4, 593a–594b (ed. Reiser), and Krempel's discussion (*op. cit.*), 245–254.

[44] *Introduction to the Philosophy of Being*, 239–247.

reality must be other than that of the subject, term, and foundation. While one can prove the non-identity of the relation with any one of these three, it is quite another thing to show that the relation is more than all three of these taken together. Moreover, consider the notion of such a really distinct relation. Since any intrinsic intelligible content would make it a category of absolute being, it can have none of this. But if its total intelligibility is extrinsic, then its being is likewise extrinsic and reduced to that of the subject, term, and foundation. Thus, the really distinct predicamental relation appears to be inherently unintelligible.

But if such a relation is identified with the subject, term, and foundation, it can nonetheless be real (with whatever reality the subject, term, and foundation have). The mere fact of real interaction, for example, means real interrelation, without the need of any extra added reality beyond the interaction itself; the mere fact of dependence in being means real relation, *is* real relation, without need of any distinct, added relation. The reality of all accidental relations can thus be reduced to the reality of absolute accidental modes of being; they are but the relative aspects of absolutes. Only because of the weakness of human conceptualization is it necessary to know these relative aspects in separate concepts, and therefore to assign relations to a distinct category of conceptualization. Relations are known through constructed "relation-fictions" and are not objective forms but rather formalizations of the intellect.

Let it be emphasized that this view of relations of the predicamental order does not minimize the reality of the relative as such; rather, it simply locates this reality elsewhere than before – not in the content of the objective formalization of the intellect but rather in the very reality of absolute being. At this point, the dichotomy between predicamental and transcendental relation disappears – in each case some principle of absolute being – accidental, substantial, existential – not only *has* a relation but *is* a relation. Such a view of the reality of relation has far-reaching implications wherever the concept of relation, however analogical, is employed, be this in the universe of knowing which is the concern of logic [45] or in the inner, Trinitarian life of God. In this view, the metaphysical principle of the priority of the absolute to the relative becomes a principle governing not real being but rather our conceptualization of real being. Since the meaning of a relation includes the subject

---

[45] On this point, see my "Thomist Reflections on the Foundations of Formal Logic," *Notre Dame Journal of Formal Logic*, VI, 1965, 1–38.

and term, it of necessity includes a reference to absolute being; but, while it is true that every absolute being in the world is also relative at least to God but also to other finite beings, this relativity need not be explicitly conceptualized in the conceptualization of absolute content. So it is that the priority of the absolute is a law of our conceptualization. But it is not a law of being, for the absolute and the relative in real being are identified and neither is prior to the other.

When we come then to the inadequate conceptualization of the mystery of the Trinity, according to this metaphysical conception of relation, we can better understand that the Persons are in no way ontologically posterior to the nature, and that the very existence of God is trinified – not by the addition of relations but rather by its identification with the relations of opposition. There is a peculiarity in our mode of conceptualization such that the nature might *appear* prior to the Persons, which would then appear as quasi-accidental and purely relative, and even "split off" from the nature so to speak; but this peculiarity can be compensated for by our awareness of its origin and necessity. But there is no need to declare any exception to any previously affirmed metaphysical law of the priority of the absolute to the relative.

From a theological perspective, one can now see the relative as truly transcendental, found in all being whatsoever. Philosophy by itself could affirm the transitive relativity of all creatures to God and then to each other, and the immanent relativity in each creature in virtue of its act-potency composition; but the philosopher alone could discover no trace of real relativity, either immanent or transitive, in God, who appears to him as one, simple, absolute, and utterly independent being. But in the light of the revelation of the Trinity we know of immanent relativity in God, identical with His absolute being. This enables us to make the rather sweeping affirmation that being *is* relation as well as absolute, an affirmation verified in a supereminent manner in the mystery of the Trinity.

We have come rather far from the mere description of the Persons in the Trinity as subsistent relations and from a rather simple, overly literal, interpretation of the formula of Florence that *"omniaque sunt unum, ubi non obviat relationis oppositio."* But there is no question of altering this formula in any way; rather, it is a matter of setting it into a more adequate metaphysical and theological context, in which something of its profound richness previously hidden may be permitted to shine forth.

III. THE SELF-CONSCIOUSNESS OF THE THREE PERSONS

When we speak of God in human language, we must make use of ideas drawn from our understanding of created being. That which such ideas analogically designate – without ever being able to express in its full reality – in God must somehow correspond to what they signify when they are referred to creatures.[46] Anything else would mean a simple equivocity between speech about creatures and speech about God, and therefore complete agnosticism about the divine being. But Christian revelation, and its clear explanation by the magisterium of the Church, excludes such agnosticism; Christian theologians must always attempt to say something about the mystery of the divine being, even though this must be through the faltering manner of human language and thought.

Assuming then the correspondence between what is designated in God by an analogical idea and what this idea signifies when it is applied to creatures, and assuming also the meaningful distinction between person and nature both in the world of created persons and in God, and therefore the distinction between the unity and the trinity of God, one may legitimately inquire about how definite terms are to be applied to God. Should a given term be applied to the divine nature or to the divine Persons, to the divine unity or to the Trinity? And the answer to such questions must necessarily depend upon the use of the term in relation to creatures, upon the place of the designated perfection in the metaphysical structure of finite being and particularly of the finite person.

From the preceding essay it should be evident enough that formally relative terms are not necessarily the only personal terms to be applied to the Trinity. We have seen that even the divine existence is in some manner trinified by these relations, which are not just tacked on to this existence but rather identified with it and therefore draw it along in some manner into the real distinction of the Persons. Such trinification of the divine existence must also mean trinification of other divine perfections often enough heretofore associated solely with the divine unity and the divine nature as opposed to the Trinity of Persons. For example, the divine intellect and the divine intellection – while of course one with the one divine nature and existence, and one, again, in

---

[46] I have treated the problems of human thought about divine perfections from a metaphysical viewpoint in *Inquiry into Being*, ch. 20.

virtue of the fact that intellect and intellection, as faculty and act, follow upon nature so that for one nature there must be only one intellect and one intellection – still, this divine intellect and divine intellection is trinified with the trinification of the divine existence. There is then a common fund of (infinite) knowledge of the divine being itself and of the being of creatures possessed by all three divine Persons, and in a unique manner by each.

Now the primary mode of divine knowledge, which really contains all others, is that of self-consciousness or self-awareness, the auto-transparency of the subject to itself. If the divine intellect and the divine intellection are trinified through the trinification of the divine existence, the divine self-consciousness is all the more so trinified. And, of course, this must be still more true because in fact there is not just one conscious subject in God but three; for the conscious subject is the Person. If one does speak of an "absolute consciousness" in God, he must at the same time understand that it is identified with three distinct relative consciousnesses.

Such a statement as the last cannot but scandalize theologians of an older school, for whom consciousness was a secondary and rather neglected adjunct of knowledge in created persons and therefore also in God. For them, knowledge pertained to the divine unity of nature, and with knowledge also consciousness. (This supposed, of course, that only formally relative terms could be applied personally, in a "trinitarian" manner; but this supposition has already been dealt with in the preceding essay.) This attitude toward consciousness rested on a conception of consciousness as either a secondary reflective act of knowing one's direct acts or, alternatively, a concomitant reflexive awareness of one's acts of intellect and will in virtue of the very spirituality of these acts. In either case, the acts would be known not only as acts but as acts *of a subject* and would therefore yield an awareness of the subject – in the former view, of the subject as objectified; in the latter view, of the subject as subject. Such concepts of act-consciousness are with difficulty applied to the divine being, and in any event scarcely suggest any trinitarian character in the divine consciousness; for the divine acts are identical with the divine existence.

But if act-consciousness arises in virtue of the spirituality of conscious acts, as a consequence of the fundamental reflexivity of spirit (I pass completely over the now thoroughly obsolete position that consciousness is a secondary reflective objectification of primary direct knowing – one must after all have regard for the phenomenological data in this domain), may we not also speak of being-consciousness where existence is itself spiritual and consequently endowed with reflexivity?[47] But this is in fact so in every person – persons are such only because of their spiritual being, and even human existence is first of all the spiritual existence of a spiritual soul communicated to matter. This being-consciousness, deeper than all act-consciousness, deeper even than intellect itself in the finite existent, is the ground of the unity of the finite consciousness and the fundamental initial horizon of being to be transcended by the finite intellect. Such being-consciousness is in fact identical with the substratum of the intellect in the subjectivity of the existent; it is nothing other than the obscurely (at least in the human person) reflexive, and therefore conscious, exercise of substantial existence in the subject. Such finite, conscious exercise of finite existence, of existence separated from the fullness of existence and consequently striving to unite itself with this fullness in whatever way may be possible, is the finite ground for the emanation of the intellective faculty as a tendency toward transcendence of the finite existent in which it is and even toward transcendence to the infinite being of God. We find then that consciousness in the most radical sense as being-consciousness is identical with the actual exercise of existence in the spiritual person; this is consciousness of the incommunicable exercise of existence by a spiritual subject, and therefore *is* conscious subjectivity. Such being-consciousness is, then, an attribute not of nature but of person.

It is important at this point to emphasize that the consciousness of God, which is His fundamental act of knowledge containing all the rest, should be conceived not as act-consciousness but as being-consciousness – not an obscure being-consciousness such as that possessed by the human existent but an utterly luminous being-consciousness in which is clearly seen the totality of the divine perfection as well as all the possibilities and actualities in the domain of creatures. But this being-consciousness, we have just said, is an attribute of person rather than of nature, at least in the world of finite persons. A difficulty arises when we come to God, for the being-consciousness of God is identical with His existence and therefore also with His nature. One might therefore hesitate about placing it in the line of person rather than of nature in God, in the line of Trinity rather than of unity. But it was seen in the preceding essays that in God not only is existence itself trinified through its identity with the relations of opposition but also there is a threefold incommunicable exercise of this one existence,

[47] See *Inquiry into Being*, ch. 8.

therefore a trinity of Persons, marked out by these relations of opposition. Now, the being-consciousness of which we have been speaking has not been identified simply with spiritual existence but with *exercised* spiritual existence. There is therefore more than a trinification of being-consciousness in God; there is in fact an actual Trinity of such being-consciousness, identical with the Trinity of Persons.

This Trinity is a Trinity of relative consciousnesses, for everything distinctly attributed to the Persons is somehow marked by relativity in accordance with the principle of Florence. At the same time, the three relative consciousnesses are identical with one absolute consciousness, itself identified with the pure act of exercised spiritual existence which is God. But one could not speak of any priority of this absolute consciousness to the relative consciousnesses, no more than one could speak of any other priority of the absolute to the relative, of the nature to the Persons, in the being of God. There are then three radically distinct centers of knowledge and love in the Trinity, but the consciousness (and everything else too) of each is entirely relative to the other two and in the closest immediacy with them. We can see here at least the outline of the very perfection of social being among distinct personal centers, a most intimate community, to which we ourselves are destined to be admitted in a mysterious manner, so far as is possible for a finite person.

So far, revelation making use of theological reason has led us to distinguish sharply between person and nature in God, to consider the respective places of the relative and the absolute in God, to speak even of a Trinity of relative consciousnesses in the Trinity of Persons. But underneath all this meditation, perhaps reasonable enough, about the Trinity, a still deeper question lurks, one to which perhaps no definitive answer can be given, and yet one which calls for at least an attempt at an answer – so far as this be possible for a mere human intellect, but one endowed with at least some degree of light through divine revelation. Why should there be a distinction of three Persons, three Consciousnesses, relations of opposition? Revelation tells us that the Son proceeds from the Father, that the Holy Spirit proceeds from the Father and the Son or from the Father through the Son, and these processions bring about all the rest. But then we must ask about these processions and their nature. Why I have asked this question in the chapter entitled "The Self-Consciousness of the Three Persons" will become clearer as we go along.

The inquiry may begin at a point apparently somewhat removed from the actual questions we have asked, with the consideration of the nature of finite consciousness, of finite knowledge and love. We shall speak primarily of consciousness in knowledge, understanding that our remarks are also applicable in an analogous way to consciousness in love; for love in fact follows right along with knowledge, and its structure is conditioned by that of knowledge. Note that our concern is not with knowledge of anything distinct from the knower himself, however much it be that such knowledge of the other is always found with self-consciousness, but rather with self-consciousness itself. Moreover, we consider not any merely reflective, secondary consciousness through some second act of knowing, not even primary reflexive act-consciousness, but rather the being-consciousness of the finite person. We shall see also that even at this level, deep in the heart of being and prior to the emanation of the faculties of intellect and will, there is a mode of being-consciousness not only in knowledge but also in spontaneous love.

Earlier scholastic analyses of knowledge emphasized the duality between knower and known that was always present in knowledge, even while this duality was somehow transcended in union. Recent attention to the reality of reflexive consciousness and its role in all our intellectual knowledge has tended to focus attention on the unity between knower and known, on the fact that the knower in some way must *be* the known in order to know it; this of course is especially true as regards self-consciousness in knowledge. But this focus upon the immanence of the act of knowing and upon the unity of the known with the knower in the act of knowing must not be allowed to obscure the necessary affirmation, now possible from a deeper perspective than that of the old scholastics, of a duality even within the structure of self-consciousness itself. Always in knowledge, even here, there is found a formal structure of relations of opposition; the known as known is somehow opposed to the knower as knower, and the structure even of self-consciousness is radically bipolar. There is a kind of circle in consciousness, in which the subject as subject goes out of itself to discover itself as subject. Whether this subject goes out of itself through an act in act-consciousness or through existence in being-consciousness, always it is in the spiritual reflexivity of an exercised act that the subject comes upon itself as subject; this is indeed why consciousness is always *con*sciousness as opposed to simply direct knowing.

In order to complete the picture of being-consciousness as including duality within its formal structure and ontological base we must also point out that this duality is in fact a double duality. For such being-consciousness is not only being-consciousness in knowledge but also being-consciousness in love. For the spiritually reflexive exercised act of existence is not only (materially) possessed, which would suffice to constitute being-consciousness in knowledge, but also (formally) exercised, which consitutes being-consciousness in love. This second mode of being-consciousness flows from the first; for the formal exercise and affirmation of existence by which it is made one's own and embraced as one's proper good presupposes that this exercised act has been received first so as to constitute the being of the subject which exercises this act. A double set of relations of opposition then appears in the deepest heart of the finite subject and its being-consciousness, those between possessor and possessed and those between exerciser and exercised, the former giving rise to radical being-consciousness in knowledge, and the latter – posterior to and dependent upon the first in the constitution of being, though not in any temporal order – giving rise to radical being-consciousness in love.

One can of course note that the dualities noted in the formal structure of being-consciousness have their parallels in the structure of act-consciousness, whether this be primary reflexive act-consciousness or secondary, reflective consciousness through some second act of knowing the direct act or an act of love following upon a direct act of knowledge. This very last case, in which a distinct act of love follows upon some direct act of knowing, is the ordinary one with which philosophers and theologians have been familiar for a very long time; here the duality-structure is apparent enough in both the knowledge of the other as other (or of the self as other), and the consequent love of the other known as other (or of the self known as other). But such parallels in the order of act-consciousness to our analysis of being-consciousness are not of special interest here. For our whole aim is eventually to gain some insight into the nature of the divine consciousness; and the divine consciousness must not be conceived according to some analogy with act-consciousness but rather according to an analogy with fundamental being-consciousness – all being and action in God are identical with the pure being of the infinite act of existence.

The problem as regards God is obvious enough. God, so far as He is knowable to our reason, manifests Himself as pure and simple infinite existence, seemingly excluding any kind of duality from His being. But, on the other hand, if He is truly infinite existence, then He lacks nothing of the perfection of existence; and it seems obvious that self-consciousness is not only a perfection but among the highest of perfections. Moreover, as a spiritual being, He *must* be self-conscious in virtue of His spiritual reflexivity. Indeed, it was already pointed out above that self-consciousness must be the primary mode of divine knowledge; for God's knowledge could not be determined by anything outside Himself. And all who have considered the evidence of natural theology will understand that in God this is not only self-consciousness in knowledge but also self-consciousness in love.

Could it be then that consciousness in God lacks the formal structure of consciousness as we have come to see it in finite persons? But if this be so, are we really justified in using the same term of both God and creatures? Have we not ended with an equivocal usage, so that it would be just as true to say that there is not consciousness in God? We may recall that similar considerations induced Plotinus to locate the supreme reality, the One, beyond consciousness altogether. One could, of course, reply to these considerations that just as the duality of essence and existence is surmounted in God, so also the dualities of consciousness in knowledge and love must be surmounted. But while the name being is drawn from the act of existing and has a meaningful significance when it is applied even to the pure act of existing, the names of knowledge, love, and consciousness seem to carry with them necessarily the idea of opposition and duality, and therefore perhaps to lose their formal significance when they are applied to God. And yet not only Christian theology but even philosophy declares that such names are truly and analogously applicable to God. Certainly we will not say that God does not know, that He does not love, that He is not self-conscious. Have we perhaps hit upon a genuine antinomy of natural reason? This would say too much. But we have at least come up against a mystery in God (where indeed we might well have expected to encounter mystery!), a mystery which might even dispose us to listen for any possible word from God about His inner life and being. Certainly, if there *were* to be found any kind of duality in God, any relations of opposition immanent to the divine being, we should attempt to correlate them with the self-consciousness of God in knowledge and love.

In fact, revelation has told us of the distinction of Persons in the Trinity, of their relative names of Father, Son and Holy Spirit; of the processions of the Son from the Father (with consequent relations of opposition), and of the Holy Spirit from the Father and the Son (with other consequent relations of opposition). Theological reflection has led us to affirm three distinct relative Consciousnesses, all identical with the one absolute consciousness of the divine being. It has also led us to pose the general question of the nature of the processions and why they and the relative opposition should be present at all, why there should after all be such a distinction of three Persons in the one divine nature. Now there appears to us the possibility of shedding light upon a philosophical mystery through the revealed doctrine of the Trinity and its theological interpretation, and at the same time making use of the already-given philosophical analysis of self-consciousness in order to achieve this very theological interpretation of the revealed truth. There would thus come to pass a kind of symbiotic relationship between the philosophical effort and the theological effort. While it will be difficult to affirm with certainty the truth of the hypothesis to be presented, we will be able to point to various confirmatory evidences which seems to increase its probability.

Within pure existence as also pure consciousness in knowledge, within this absolute consciousness, we would look for relations of opposition and some kind of duality, from the viewpoint of philosophical reason. That there should be no such relations of opposition in God leaves us with a certain mystery in the understanding of the meaning of consciousness in God. But revelation tells us that the duality and relations of opposition that seemed out of the question in the pure and simple infinite act of existence are actually found there; that there is a procession of the Son from the Father by a kind of spiritual generation. Both the usage of Scripture, which calls the Son the Word, and the common tradition of Western theology, which has even made its influence felt in statements of the Church's magisterium, strongly suggest – if not more than suggest – that this spiritual generation is intellectual generation. Such a view of the procession of the Son from the Father yields a duality and relations of opposition precisely in the line of consciousness in intellectual knowledge, just what is suggested by the philosophical consideration of the meaning of absolute consciousness in the infinite act of existence – even though this suggestion has to be set aside by the mere philosopher. Theology then would conceive of a relation-structure within the absolute divine consciousness, a relation-structure whereby two relative consciousnesses are constituted, one as a kind of going out or ecstasy of the other, and therefore the former as second in relation to a first. It is not that there is first an absolute divine consciousness and then a relation-structure constituting relative consciousnesses. Rather, the very being of the absolute consciousness is necessarily at once also this relation-structure and the two relative consciousnesses. Thus the Father and the Son are not results of, but indeed constitutive of, the absolute consciousness and absolute being of God.

Within pure existence as also pure consciousness in *love*, within this absolute consciousness already structured by the relations of opposition between Father and Son and by the duality there, we must look for still further relations of opposition and another duality. For consciousness in love again seems to the philosopher to call for such relations and duality, above and beyond those of knowledge alone since love follows upon and is in accordance with knowledge, and consequently to leave the mere philosopher with a rather mysterious notion of the divine consciousness in love. But revelation does speak of a second procession, of the Holy Spirit from the Father and the Son, and consequently of further relations of opposition and further duality in God. This second procession is contrasted in revelation with the first, as non-generative, since the Son is called the *only-begotten* Son. While Scripture is rather unclear about the nature of this procession, it does in some manner present the Spirit as of both the Father and the Son; and the common tradition of Western theology, again making its influence felt in statements of the magisterium, suggests that the procession of the Spirit from the Father and the Son is in the line of love. But this yields new duality and new relations of opposition precisely in the line of consciousness in love, just what is suggested by the philosophical consideration of the meaning of absolute consciousness in love in the infinite act of existence (but of course set aside by the mere philosopher). Theology here conceives of a second relation-structure within the absolute divine consciousness, a relation-structure whereby a third relative consciousness is constituted in relation to the first two, as a kind of going out or ecstasy of the first two taken together, or perhaps of the first through the second. Once again, this second relation-structure and duality is not in any sense an ontological consequence of absolute consciousness but rather is constitutive of this absolute consciousness as consciousness not only in knowledge but also in love. Here then, the Holy Spirit as proceeding and constitutive of the duality and relation-structure of consciousness in love is not in any sense a result of, but rather constitutive of, the absolute consciousness and absolute being of God.

In the order of revelation and of theological understanding of revelation, first is seen the distinction between the three Persons in one God and the two processions, of the Son from the Father and of the Spirit from the Father and the Son. Consideration of the meaning of the processions reveals the presence of relative opposition between the Persons and therefore of relations of opposition which are identical with the Persons and mark them out as mutually distinct. The processions and relative opposition are then interpreted as constitutive of the formal structure of divine consciousness in knowledge and love. This interpretation is welcomed by the philosopher, who prior to this could only be mystified by the fact of divine consciousness, a fact surely enough, but one seemingly calling for dualities and relations of opposition which the philosopher could hardly admit as possible in the simple infinite act of existence, which indeed he could only set aside as seemingly impossible.

But although the theory elaborated sheds light both on the revealed doctrine of the processions and the Trinity and on the philosophical problem of the nature of consciousness in knowledge and love in God, still, is it anything more than a plausible hypothesis with very satisfying confirmations? Some have in fact suggested that the entire attempt to make some analogy between the psychology of finite consciousness, knowledge, and love and the processions and distinction of Persons in the Trinity is a mistake, an intrusion of merely philosophical reason into domains which utterly transcend it. Even without taking so extreme a view, one might wonder whether the testimony of revelation and of the Christian theological tradition is really sufficiently clear to justify firm confidence in the use of the psychological analogy for conceptualization of the Trinity. And of course the theory presented is only one form of the psychological analogy, although I believe that it is by far to be preferred to those which consider self-consciousness as merely act-consciousness of some kind or other.

It should be unnecessary by now to make any further response to objections against the use of philosophical reason by the theologian in order to shed some light upon the revealed mysteries. But it may be well to add a few words in support of the psychological analogy in general, without actually coming to a firm decision as to whether it passes from the realm of highly plausible hypothesis to that of unshakeable theological certitude. As was noted earlier, the evidence in Scripture, small though it be, does suggest that the first procession is in the line of knowledge; and even while Scripture is unclear about the second procession, the mere fact that it is second and from the Father and the Son tempts us to place it in the line of love. But the hints of Scripture do not stand alone; a whole line of Fathers and the common teaching of theologians have settled upon the use of the psychological analogy from intellectual knowledge and love to "explain" the Trinity, and this teaching has gradually penetrated into the belief of the faithful, the liturgy of the Church, and even into the pronouncements of the magisterium (although so far not in a clearly infallible pronouncement). But of course one could object that non-infallible pronouncements, the liturgy, the belief of the faithful, can make use of the theology of the time in the expression of the faith without necessarily committing us to the whole of such theology. Certainly the evidence is not so clear as to place Catholic authors who remain unconvinced of it in bad standing in the Church.

Perhaps the best evidence for the use of the psychological analogy is its power to illuminate both revelation and the philosophical problem of consciousness in God. A more negative argument might run as follows. Since the divine existence is utterly simple, no conceptualization of the Trinity could arise out of a consideration of this existence alone; no foundation of the relations of opposition in the Trinity could be conceived by us solely on the basis of the one and simple infinite existence. Therefore the processions and the relations of opposition should be conceived as grounded in, not the divine existence, but the divine activity. How this could be done might well appear very problematic since the divine activity is identified with the divine existence; but these can be distinguished in our conceptualization, and our problem is precisely how to *conceptualize* the ground for the distinction of Persons. Now the divine activity does seem more open to the notion of relations of opposition than does the divine existence, and indeed, since every created activity involves some kind of procession, we might well hope to find here some more or less suitable analogue in terms of which to understand the divine processions. But there can be no question of any transitive activity of God here; for any such activity would be specified by a created term and terminate in a creature, while here we are seeking to understand processions in which both terms – beginning and end – are divine. For a similar reason, the formally immanent and virtually transitive activity of God in creation and conservation of creatures is likewise excluded; while the immediate specifying term of such activity is indeed God (since it is formally immanent), this term is not God according to His total reality (since the activity is virtually transitive). The procession in such a case is not that of God from God (as in the Trinitarian processions) but rather of a created being from God. Therefore we must turn to consider the immanent activity of God. But since God does not have parts, the only immanent activity to be found in Him is that proper to a pure spirit, namely that of knowledge and love, which for Him means self-consciousness in knowledge and love (for the primary object of His knowledge and love, which contains all other secondary objects, can only be Himself). One might, of course, suggest that perhaps there are still other immanent activites of which we know nothing at all, which would be more relevant to the conceptualization of the divine processions. But such an hypothesis would be not only gratuitous but utterly destructive of any attempt on our part to conceptualize these processions. Moreover, such an hypothesis is extremely unlikely, both because of the testimony of revelation that man is the image of God and because there is a certain well-founded totality and enclosedness in the notion of infinite spirit self-conscious in knowledge and love. Such a spirit is infinitely happy and sufficient in Himself, without need of any other; and this happiness needs nothing more than joyful self-acceptance by One who totally comprehends the inexhaustible riches of His own being. And of course, be it pointed out that this happiness is also a social reality, since this one infinite spirit is in fact three Persons in the closest interpersonal communion in knowledge and love. In this light the hypothesis of other unknown aspects of the immanent life of God, which would account for the Trinitarian processions, seems even worse than gratuitous; and this in turn suggests that the account of these processions in terms of self-consciousness in knowledge and love is a good deal more than a fruitful hypothesis strongly confirmed by the data of revelation, philosophical inquiry, and theological understanding.

Finally, theologians have long noted that the psychological analogy leads to a certain dissymmetry in the understanding of the two processions, a dissymmetry which very neatly corresponds with a dissymmetry in the revealed data concerning these processions. For if the first procession is truly in the line of knowledge and in virtue of the necessity of a mediating term for perfect self-consciousness, this procession must by its essential nature be generative of a term perfectly similar to the Generator; for only such perfect similarity would permit this mediating term to mediate a perfect self-consciousness in the line of knowledge. Such a procession essentially productive of a perfectly similar living term from another living term can be called generation in the true and proper sense, and the end-term of the procession (that is, the mediating term of self-consciousnesss in knowledge) can be called a Son in the true and proper sense. But all this corresponds very well with the manner of speaking in the data of revelation and the teaching of the magisterium about the second Person and His relation to the First. On the other hand, if the second procession is truly in the line of love, which is not formally assimilative but rather outgoing (although, of course, there is a perfect – material – similarity here too between the mediating term and the beloved, Who in this case is also the lover), this procession cannot be called generation in the true and proper sense, and the end-term (that is, the mediating term of self-consciousness in love) cannot be called a Son in the true and proper sense. It would be better to call the procession a kind of "out-breathing," or *spiration*, and the end-term a kind of "breath," or *Spirit*. But this of course is the very word employed in revelation and by the magisterium in speaking of the Third Person, who proceeds from the Father through the Son as a "Breath," and therefore as the *Spirit* of the Father and the Son. So it is, in the light of the psychological analogy, that the Father is the ultimate source, *fons et origo totius Trinitatis*, of both processions, even while He has just one, the only-begotten, Son. This consideration could only serve to strengthen our confidence, already very firm, in the value of the psychological analogy from the structure of finite self-consciousness in knowledge and love as an instrument to understand more fully the divine self-consciousness, both as absolute consciousness and as the relative consciousness of three distinct Persons.

In the approach we have taken, a consideration of the formal structure of the absolute divine self-consciousness in knowledge and love led to the distinction of the three Persons and their three relative consciousnesses. This leads us to make a further inquiry into the three distinct relative consciousnesses themselves, to discover if possible what diverse nuances of meaning are contained in the "self-consciousness of the Father," the "self-consciousness of the Son," and the "self-consciousness of the Holy Spirit." For each of these is in fact a distinct center with His own unique relativity to the other two Persons, and therefore with His own unique self-consciousness. While the three Persons and their three relative consciousnesses are constitutive of the formal structure of the divine absolute consciousness, and identical with this absolute consciousness, still each of the three Persons is a distinct central reference-point for a reflexive circle of consciousness in knowledge and love, with the appropriate duality-structure and relations of opposition. We may wonder then where such duality and relations of opposition are to be found in each of the three Persons as distinct relative consciousness. Clearly, we should not look for a substructure of duality and opposition within each Person; this would set us off on an infinite series of such substructures. Rather, we must reemphasize the point that the distinct consciousnesses of each Person are *relative* consciousnesses and not absolute; the self-consciousness of each Person is a consciousness of Himself as with the other two Persons and even through the other two Persons. Each Person is conscious of an exercised existence which is itself trinified and triply relativized; immanent therefore to His self-consciousness, even constitutive of it, is the very interiority of the other two Persons present in "perichoretic" [48] immediacy. Thus, the dualities and relation-structures of the divine absolute consciousness can also serve to structure the three relative consciousnesses in knowledge and love. This is not, after all, so paradoxical as it may sound: the three relative consciousnesses are completely identical with the absolute consciousness, and can be distinguished as three central (relative) points of reference within the one absolute consciousness, even while they are regarded not as consequences of but as constitutive of the formal structure of this absolute consciousness. Each relative consciousness is itself a unique perspective on the trinification of the absolute consciousness, and is therefore a most intimate communion with the other two such unique perspectives of the other two Persons. This intimacy may be described as the utter spiritual compenetration of the very interiority of consciousness among three Persons.

But even with this utter spiritual compenetration of the interiority of consciousness, there is distinction between the perspectives and self-consciousnesses of the Father, Son, and Holy Spirit. The Father sees Himself as the source of the others and Himself without a source; the Son sees Himself as generated and spirating; the Spirit sees Himself as spirated from the other two Persons. The Father's self-consciousness in knowledge is through the Son, and His self-consciousness in love is through the Spirit – thus the duality structures of the absolute consciousness serve also to constitute the self-consciousness of the Father. The Son's self-consciousness in knowledge is of Himself as the mediating term for the self-consciousness in knowledge of the Father; His self-consciousness in love is through the Spirit spirated by the Father and the Son. The Spirit's self-consciousness in knowledge is again through the

---

[48] I refer here to the traditional understanding of the mutual immediate presence of the three Persons, which means that no one could ever be found in any manner separated from the others. This mutual immediate presence is called *perichoresis* by the Greeks and *circumincessio* by the Latins.

Son; His self-consciousness in love is of Himself as the mediating term for the self-consciousness in love of both the Father and the Son taken together. Thus the reflexive circle of consciousness in the relative consciousnesses of the distinct Persons is not enclosed *within* each distinct Person (that would be to embark upon the infinite series spoken of earlier) but rather between the Persons; such a reflexive circle would be impossible between really distinct absolute consciousnesses such as those we find in really distinct finite persons, and is possible here only because of the perichoretic immediacy of the three Persons, which is the complete compenetration of the most profound interiority of each of the three relative consciousnesses.

Finally, a few words seem desirable concerning the analogy that is so often made between the Second Person as Word and the human concept as an expression of the content of one's insight; these remarks are also applicable in a way to the other analogy between the Third Person and the interior expression of human love in the will. If our analogy resting on the formal structure of self-consciousness in knowledge and love is correct, there is clearly some foundation for the analogies mentioned; and yet these analogies appear to limp, for they present the Son and Spirit as consequences of a prior divine consciousness, as derivatives from the divine nature as possessed by the Father. But if we are right, Son and Spirit are themselves constitutive of this very divine consciousness rather than posterior to it; this would seem to be necessarily so if the Son and Spirit, together with the Father, are to be regarded as in no sense posterior to and derivative from the divine nature. We have already taken considerable trouble to get rid of this mistaken conception of the Persons as somehow superadded and "tacked on" to the divine nature. One might also wonder why the divine self-consciousness finds need of expression and formulation through the Word and the Spirit. If there is already given a divine self-consciousness prior to the expression of the Word, why should it be expressed at all? Is not the divine self-consciousness already clear and exhaustive enough? The necessity for such expression of the concept in human knowledge has reasons in the mode of human insight, but these reasons seem lacking in the divine self-consciousness. And if there could be such a divine self-consciousness in knowledge antecedent to the expression of the Word, could there not also be such a divine self-consciousness in love antecedent to the emission of the Spirit? Such difficulties confirm us in the determination to seek for analogical understanding of the processions, not in this common form of the psychological analogy, in which the Word is expression and formulation of consciousness, but rather in the analogy drawn from analysis of the formal structure of consciousness in knowledge and love as constituted by dualities and relations of oppositon. Here the Word is still proceeding Word, but not so much like an impressed or expressed species of the scholastic philosophers, as the necessary opposed term in the constitution of self-consciousness in knowledge. And the Spirit is still proceeding Spirit, but not so much like the *pondus amoris* of John of St. Thomas, as the necessary opposed term in the constitution of self-consciousness in love. The earlier analogues are not therefore to be dismissed as invalid and useless; far from it! But I suggest that even better understanding, halting though it be, of the mystery of the divine processions can be gained by consideration of the most profound structures of being-consciousness in knowledge and love in the spiritual self.

5

THE HYPOSTATIC UNION AND THE
CONSCIOUSNESS OF CHRIST

Before beginning any attempt to understand something of the mystery of the hypostatic union and of the consciousness of Christ, it is necessary to insist most firmly upon the absolute transcendence of God in regard to the world. The Uncreated Life of the three divine Persons stands eternally immutable and untouched by the decision to create, by the existence of creatures, and even by the hypostatic union of the human nature of Christ with the Second Person of the Trinity. No creature could ever rise to God, touch Him, cling to Him so as to comprise His utter transcendence of every creature. The total being of every creature is entirely dependent on God, and this dependence includes even the union of the creature with God. Therefore, if there is some union of creature to God, it is God who with complete gratuity and preserving His complete transcendence unifies and is the bond of unity between the creature and Himself. There is nothing between the creature thus unified to God and God, no created claim, which would in some sense pull God down to union with the creature. If God should choose to enter into a fuller union with some creature, this will be accomplished by the divine knowledge, love, and decree of all three Persons acting in concert and wholly prior to the actual drawing of the creature into such a union. Indeed, this decree of the three Persons, with its infallibility in producing its created effects, *is* already the union itself (in the active sense). The created effect primarily produced by the decree, a created term or reality referring the creature to God in a new way, can be called union (in a passive sense); but this is only secondary and consequent union depending entirely for its being on the primary active union which is the uncreated divine decree.[1]

In the preceding paragraph we have suggested the possibility,

---

[1] This aspect of union has been explained by Lonergan in *De constitutione Christi ontologica et psychologica*, 51ff., 57–82.

specifically, of the hypostatic union, and more generically, of "fuller union." Under the second would be included any of the diverse modes of supernatural union with God through some mode of divine grace. Three such modes come inmediately to mind: the beatific vision, supernatural union through sanctifying grace, and the hypostatic union. Only the third concerns us here; the former two will be considered later. But all three are modes of union transcending any natural union of persons with God. Such a natural union would be a union of knowledge and love mediated through the knowledge and love of creatures. In such a union the acts of the created person would remain properly his own acts, although of course in total dependence for their being upon God. But even the fullest and most stable such union, such as might be the final end of a human being existing in a state of pure nature, would still be only mediated through union with other creatures. In supernatural union of a created person to God, a more immediate union is given (though there is always a created term through which the whole created person is passively drawn up into union); and the acts of the created person performed in consequence of this union transcend the natural powers of this person and so cannot simply be called his acts alone. But the hypostatic union which is manifested to us in the Incarnation, as the Church has come to understand it through the development of dogma and the formulations of Councils, especially Chalcedon—this hypostatic union is much more than a supernatural union of a created person to God. Rather, here a human nature so belongs to God that its human acts must be attributed wholly and properly to a divine Person, to the Second Person of the Trinity. This is not a union of persons, but a personal union of a human nature to a divine Person.

A priori we should be inclined to wonder whether such a personal union would even be possible, but it is a factual datum in the mystery of the Incarnation. Given to us even in Scripture that Christ is true man and also God, this doctrine was clarified through the struggles with the early Christological heresies and through the later progress of theology; but this work of clarification and deeper understanding continues even today, and the present essay seeks only to push the investigation a little farther. Two points are of particular interest to us: What is the metaphysical structure of the hypostatic union? What is the consequent structure of the consciousness of Christ, at once divine and human? The former is a long-discussed question among scholastic theologians; the latter question has only recently been posed in a sharp manner, although it could hardly ever have been purely and simply overlooked.

The generic structure of the union of a creature to God, given earlier, can be applied to the understanding of the hypostatic union. Always it is God in utter transcendence who is the cause of the union, who *is* the union in the active sense by His uncreated knowledge, love, and formal decree to unify. Always a created term corresponds to the divine decree, which infallibly produces this term. Here one should distinguish the material term, which is the creature itself which is unified to God in some manner, and the formal term, which is the precise creaturely correlate and product of the decree to unify. This formal term of union could perhaps be called the created conjunction of the creature to God; but it must be emphasized that this term does not enable the creature to touch God, but on the contrary entirely flows from God in order to relate the creature to God in a new way. This term is thus not a means of holding God on the part of the creature, but rather a mode by which God holds the creature to Himself.

This formal term of union is of primary concern in understanding the metaphysical structure of the hypostatic union. By the very nature of the hypostatic union, this term must somehow replace and exclude whatever it is that renders the ordinary created human nature a created supposit or person; only thus could the acts of this human nature truly be also the acts of a divine Person. But this sharply poses the question as to what distinguishes a mere created nature from a supposit or person, the same question that we have already seen to be posed by the mystery of the Trinity. Historically, the problem of understanding the hypostatic union seems to have been the predominant concern in the treatment of the intrinsically philosophical question of the relation of nature and person. Indeed, so much has this been so that some have wondered whether the latter question is really by right a philosophical question at all. But we have already considered this question as a properly philosophical one and then applied our results to the effort to understand something of the mystery of the Trinity even before coming to consider the Incarnation. In doing this, we relied to a great extent upon the work of Maritain, which itself is centered on the problem of the hypostatic union. It would in fact be very profitable at this point simply to read his treatment in order to gain much light on the metaphysical structure of the hypostatic union. While I propose to set down my own development of this theme, I must acknowledge the greatest debt to Maritain's work here. But before we actually apply our already achieved understanding of the relation of nature and person to

[2] Maritain, *The Degrees of Knowledge*, 434–444.

the clarification of the mystery of the hypostatic union, it seems useful to make some brief remarks about the five classic views here.

In fact, the inadequacies of these five views, of Scotus, Tiphanus, Suarez, Cajetan, and Capreolus (with the modifications of the latter by De La Taille and Lonergan) have already been noted in the first chapter on the Trinity; but we may here briefly recall their difficulties as regards the hypostatic union. Scotus thought that the finite person or finite supposit added to the notes of the individual nature a double negation of dependence on any other being; it was simply an individual nature which neither is nor can be communicated to any other being as some kind of part of that being. Such a notion of the person can be applied successfully to the hypostatic union, but only because this notion is purely descriptive and not explanatory; it does not really come to grips with the problem of nature and person but merely points out their factual difference. The same can be said about the opinion of Tiphanus, that person and supposit add to the individual nature the note of wholeness. This is basically a more positive formulation of the description of Scotus, and in that respect a better description; but it still falls short of a really metaphysical statement about the ontological root of personality. Neither view can actually illuminate our partial understanding of the mystery of the hypostatic union. The hypothesis of Suarez, that personality in the finite person is a special *mode* beyond the individual nature, and that the hypostatic union can take place because the individual human nature of Christ is in fact deprived of this substantial mode, is unsatisfactory from the outset by reason of the philosophical context in which this mode is to be understood, namely in the context of the denial of the real distinction between essence and existence. But beyond this, the Suarezian mode appears to be an *ad hoc* hypothesis without any real metaphysical reason other than the simple fact that in one case there is found an individual human nature which is not a person, namely in the hypostatic union. The view of Cajetan attempts to go a little deeper, pointing out that the individual nature needs a termination analogous to the point which terminates the line, in order that it be able to be a subject, that which is and not merely that by which something is. This substantial termination of the nature is a mode in the line of essence itself, completing the essence and enabling this essence to subsist. While this does appear as an attempt at some metaphysical explanation of the constitution of the person, and of why the individual human nature of Christ is still not itself a person (since it lacks this substantial mode in the line of essence), still this mode itself and the possibility of its absence seem rather incomprehensible and therefore radically as *ad hoc* hypotheses. The most common view among Thomists at present is that of Capreolus and Billot, that the person and the supposit are constituted not by anything in the line of essence at all but by substantial existence. In the earlier, simpler form of this opinion, Christ was thought not even to have any finite human existence but to exist in virtue of the infinite existence of the Word. But in response to the obvious difficulty of understanding an immediate actuation of Christ's finite human nature by the infinite act of existence of God, and of understanding how this actuation would be an actuation by the Word and not by all three Persons in common, De La Taille proposed the notion of a created actuation by uncreated act. This created, supernatural, existential act, which is simply a medium through which God Himself actuates the obediential potency of the human nature of Christ, replaces, preempts the place of, the natural and proper and proportioned existential act which would ordinarily actuate the substantial human nature. But while this conception does give some account of the metaphysical structure of the hypostatic union without the special problems of Capreolus and Billot, inasmuch as it avoids immediate actuation by the infinite existence of God and also accounts for this actuation as an actuation by the Word and not by the other two Persons (for this created actuation in the supernatural order refers essentially to the Word), still the metaphysics implicit in this view of the hypostatic union seems *ad hoc*, made in view of the problem of the Incarnation. We would prefer to be shown how a proper and proportioned existence actually raises a mere individual nature to a new level, through an analysis of the metaphysical principles involved, namely existence and nature. But this seems to be simply postulated in order that the supernatural created actuation by uncreated act may then be introduced to preempt the place of such a proper and proportioned existence (thus preventing the human nature of Christ from being also a human person) and to join the human nature to the Word (thus effecting the hypostatic union). Lonergan's attempt to improve the theory of De La Taille by emphasizing the transcendence of God and of the Word even while the union is actively effected, and by describing the created actuation itself as the secondary appropriate created term produced by and corresponding to the divine decree – a created passive union entirely posterior to and totally dependent upon the uncreated active union in the divine knowledge, love, and decree – is indeed an improvement; but one does not find in Lonergan any more than in De La Taille the kind of metaphysical understanding of the constitution of the finite person that we seek in order the better to understand something about the nature of the hypostatic union.

In our earlier discussion of the problem of person and nature in the Trinity, Maritain's metaphysical treatment has already been noted and has provided the basic guideline according to which was evolved a more satisfactory metaphysics of the constitution of a person. His discussion of the metaphysics of person and nature, and the application of it to the understanding of the hypostatic union can be considered as another development in the line of De La Taille and Lonergan, and therefore of Capreolus and Billot, although he in fact began by adopting the perspective of Cajetan in his earlier treatment of the problem.[3] It is not necessary here to repeat the basic metaphysical analysis, which can be found in our earlier essay on the nature and Persons in the Trinity. Here we shall proceed immediately to the problem of the hypostatic union, taking up the matter in our own way rather than following the treatment of Maritain step-by-step.

We saw in the earlier essay that the person or supposit is constituted as such precisely through the incommunicable exercise of the act of substantial existence. Accordingly, the individual nature of Christ as man lacks this exercise or affirmation of its own substantial existence; moreover, this exercise must even be positively excluded by the formal term of union to the divine Person of the Word. But this is not to say that the finite existential and substantial act of the created human nature is itself lacking or excluded. If this finite human existence were in fact absent, then the human nature would have to exist in virtue of the uncreated and infinite divine existence, which would bring us back to the position of Capreolus and Billot. But in fact, if there is no finite existence of the human nature, it is difficult to see how there could really be any genuine human action at all in Christ; for action follows upon and is a function of being. There is a growing conviction, as we have seen with Maritain, De La Taille, and Lonergan, that the finite secondary human existence of Christ is actually found, and a growing tendency to emphasize those texts of St. Thomas in which he speaks of just such a finite and secondary existence in Christ.[4]

Yet, if this finite, secondary, substantial existence of Christ is indeed present – though it is not actually exercised by the finite individual human nature of Christ – an obvious difficulty must be met. Existence,

[3] *Ibid.*, 430-434.
[4] *De unione Verbi incarnati*, a. 4.

by its very "nature," is an exercised, dynamic act; it could never be merely possessed. But here a finite existence is found which is not actually exercised by the individual nature to which it gives being. How could this be so? It must be said that if this existence is not actually exercised by the creature, by the finite nature, this can only be because this exercise of the act has been in some manner preempted by the Second Person of the Trinity. In this way, instead of the human nature affirming and making fully its own the act of substantial existence that it receives and merely possesses "on loan," instead of the human nature having a quasi-efficient and emanative causality in regard to this existence, on the contrary this existence is affirmed by, emanates in some manner from, and pertains as to a subject of exercise to the Word. But note some important differences in the mode of emanation in this case and in the ordinary case in which actual exercise is not thus preempted by a divine Person. In the latter case, an existent essence affirms the very act which has made this essence to exist, in a kind of mutual causality; but now the Word who is Existence affirms a secondary act of existence which He does not at all need in any manner, which in fact is totally dependent for its being on the three divine Persons acting in concert to produce it. In the ordinary case, the emanative causality of the finite nature derives ultimately from the very act of existence itself, which gives being to the finite nature; now the emanative causality of the divine nature is in no way dependent upon the finite existence but rather is the total transcendent cause of this finite existence, and not by an emanation in the strict sense but rather by a formally immanent and virtually transitive act which perfectly safeguards the transcendence and untouchability of the divine nature in itself even while it gives being in a quasi-emanative manner to the finite existence as essentially referred, in the line of exercise, to the Person of the Word although it is the actuation (as merely possessed) of the finite human nature. While the human nature would ordinarily possess its act of existence even more fully in virtue of its affirmation and exercise of this act, in this case the individual nature is more possessed by the act of existence than possessing this act; but since this existence already pertains to the Person of the Word, through it the nature also so pertains to the same Person of the Word and is thus the human nature of a divine Person.

In view of the aforementioned differences between the ordinary emanation of substantial existence from the self-affirming finite existent and this quasi-emanation of substantial existence (of a finite nature) from a divine Person, it must be said that the substantial existence in the ordinary case is quite distinct from the substantial existence in this special case. If the former is the natural, proper, and proportioned existence of the finite nature, the latter is a supernatural, special existential act which can still give existence to the finite nature but which has pronounced differences in the relational order from the ordinary natural and proper existence. This supernatural existence, therefore, does not actuate the natural potency of the finite nature, but rather its obediential potency in relation to the supernatural order and the interior life of God. It can still be said to preempt the exercise of natural, proper, and proportioned existence in so far as it actually renders this latter existence unnecessary at all. Since this created supernatural actuation in effect joins the created nature to the Uncreated Act of Existence (as exercised by the Word), one could speak of the human nature as being actuated by Uncreated Act through the medium of a created actuation. Such was the manner of speaking of De La Taille, who used this idea to reach a unified conception of supernatural union with God not only in the hypostatic union, but also in the life of grace and in the beatific vision. We shall return to this in a later essay. But from this viewpoint it is possible to see the divine causality here not only as quasi-emanative but also as quasi-formal; for the created actuation not only "emanates" in some manner from God but also joins the human nature of Christ to the Uncreated Act as if to a formal term. But such a quasi-formal causality here seems similar to that suggested by Rahner.[5]

The supernatural, created, existential actuation of which we have been speaking thus cannot be understood without pointing to several functions of it at once and to diverse modes of causality which produce it. It preempts the place of a natural, proper, and proportioned existence in the finite nature by being itself an existential actuation, but already referred as to exercise to the Person of the Word. Since it cannot be affirmed by the created nature in such a manner that it be fully *of* this nature, it rather holds the nature than is held by the nature, and therefore draws the nature with itself in its reference to the Person of the Word; from this viewpoint, this actuation is the formal term of union (in the passive sense) and the medium of assumption of the created nature to the Word. Since through this actuation the human nature is joined to Uncreated Act, the actuation can be called a created

[5] Karl Rahner, *Theological Investigations*, I, transl. by Cornelius Ernst, Baltimore, 1961, 319–346.

actuation by Uncreated Act and thus a quasi-formal cause mediating another quasi-formal causality, this time of the very Uncreated Act of the Word Himself. But of course it is necessary to guarantee the complete transcendence of the Uncreated Act by recognizing that the mediating term itself is entirely dependent upon and flowing from the determination of the three Persons of the Trinity in concert that the word actually *be* a quasi-formal cause of a created nature. The mediating actuation is only the appropriate created term resulting from this determination in God, just as it is the appropriate created term, as we saw, resulting from the determination of the three Persons together, that the Word be the quasi-emanative cause of the substantial existence of the human nature. These two divine determinations are, of course, really one determination with two aspects; and the appropriate created term has two corresponding aspects. It is the aspect of quasi-emanative causality that comes to the fore when we think of the Word as pre-empting, by the created actuation, the place of the natural, proper and proportioned existence of the human nature; and the aspect of quasi-formal causality comes to the fore when we think of the Word as assuming this human nature to Himself by the same created actuation. Both of these aspects of the causality of the Word and of the corresponding created term can be embraced in the happy phrase of De La Taille: created actuation by Uncreated Act, where actuation is understood both formally and emanatively in reference to the Word. Lest it seem that the matter of efficient causality has been overlooked, it should be pointed out that it is already contained in the idea of a determination of the three Persons together, to which corresponds an appropriate created term. The created term flows from the determination of the Trinity, by their common efficient causality; but what they efficiently cause is a term that is referred in the lines of formal and emanative causality to the Person of the Word. So it is then that the Infinite Person of the Word exists not only in His divine nature but also in a human nature.

Such a hypostatic union would be impossible between two creatures, for the exercise of substantial existence could be referred only to a substance which itself has this existence or which is the plenitude of infinite existence containing in a supereminent manner the existence of all things. Only in such a case could the quasi-emanative causality or properly emanative causality be found, for such causality is really a kind of flowing from the depths of subjectivity of what is already in some manner there. This is true even in the cases of the emanation of accidents from finite substance and in the emanation of operation from the same finite substance through the medium of the operative powers; for the substance in the first case, and the substance together with the operative powers in the second case, are not simply in passive potency to the accidents and to the operations. Rather, there is a quasi-active exigency in the first case and a properly active exigency in the second case. But no finite existent has such an active or quasi-active exigency for the substantial existence of another distinct finite existent, and therefore no finite existent could be the emanative or quasi-emanative cause of the substantial existence of another finite existent.

What has been said regarding the substantial existence of Christ's human nature as an actuation "exercised" by a divine Person is also analogically applicable to the various modes of accidental existence in this same human nature. Ordinarily, such accidental existence is possessed by the accidental forms and exercised by the subject in which the accidents inhere. Here it is, of course, possessed by the accidental forms; but it is referred as to exercise to the same subject to whom the substantial existence is so referred. But such accidental existence is quite distinct from the primary formal term of union, and is only a set of secondary, consequent terms of union, referred to the Word through the mediation of His secondary, substantial human existence. There is in the existing human nature of Christ a quasi-active exigency for His accidents, but this exigency is modified by the unique mode of His substantial existence – it is an exigency for accidental existence to be possessed by the human nature but not to be exercised by this nature. It is similar in regard to the human operations of Christ; the active exigency for them in the human nature and active powers of Christ is not an exigency that these operations emanate from this human nature and active powers, but rather that such operations be genuine operations of the Word acting through the human nature and its powers. And the actual operations of Christ as man are so referred to the Word in accordance with this exigency of the existent human nature and powers. Here again the principle is verified that the mode of operation follows upon the mode of being.

Is the human nature of Christ then in any sense the subject of His accidental perfections and operations? If by subjectivity we mean the actual exercise of existence and activity, then Christ's human nature is not a subject in the proper sense. However, it is possible to speak of a purely receptive subject, as prime matter is said to be the subject of substantial form; and in this sense Christ's human nature can be said to be a subject both of existence—substantial and accidental—and of operation. But such a purely receptive subject is not what is ordinarily meant nowadays by the term "subject," and is not what we have meant by this term in this and earlier essays. Accordingly, the purely receptive subject is here regarded as a subject only in a secondary and qualified sense, with the subject of actual exercise being regarded as the subject in the full and proper sense. This distinction will prove to be of some value in understanding something about the consciousness of Christ.

We come now to the knotty problem of the consciousness of Christ, a question of much recent interest to theologians in view of our greater awareness of this dimension of human and of intellectual existence in general. Although it would be possible to discuss the matter in the context of recent speculations, it seems better here to proceed to a rather straightforward analysis in the light of the principles elaborated in earlier essays concerning consciousness and in this essay concerning the metaphysical structure of the hypostatic union.

That there are in fact diverse modes of divine and human intellection and volition in Christ, flowing from His diverse natures, is evident enough in the tradition and teaching of the Church. The theologians have ordinarily distinguished three fundamental modes of human knowing in Christ: the beatific vision, infused knowledge, and knowledge acquired through the ordinary human mode resting on experience. The special problem concerning the presence of the beatific vision in the human being of Christ will be considered later, and we will not dwell on the other two modes of human knowledge which He has. Rather, we are primarily interested in that mode of self-awareness which is concomitant with all human knowledge and volition, and indeed with all intellectual being, with all spiritual being, which has already been described in the treatment of the Trinity. And here we shall focus principally upon the human self-consciousness of Christ rather than upon the divine self-consciousness of the Second Person in His uncreated eternal being. The latter has already been sufficiently considerd in the essays on the Trinity, and will be referred to only when we come to a synoptic view of the total structure of the consciousness of the Word-made-man.

Earlier, we distinguished three modes of consciousness: reflective and secondary act-consciousness, reflexive act-consciousness, and reflexive being-consciousness. The first of these presents no special problem here; it is not really consciousness in the proper sense, which is a reflexive awareness without any need for a special act of its own, but only another act of knowing among other ordinary objective acts of knowing – special only in that it has as its object other acts of knowing rather than the real being to which these other acts refer. That some scholastic philosophers and theologians should have regarded, and perhaps even continue to regard this as the deepest reality of consciousness, betrays the inadequate phenomenological base of their thought.

We come to consciousness in the proper sense with reflexive act-consciousness. Its nature has already been described in the chapter on "The Self-consciousness of the Three Persons." Briefly, it is a reflexive awareness of an intellectual act of intellection or volition as exercised, and therefore as the act of a subject; but this is also to say that it is a reflexive awareness of the subject in its very exercise of such activity. This kind of reflexive awareness arises in virtue of the spirituality of the subject of the act and consequently of the act itself. The very presence of such a spiritual act in such a spiritual subject makes the act (and the subject) actually intelligible and understood (by the obscure understanding which is consciousness – obscure at least in man). But note that it is the mere presence of the act, and not its exercise, that makes it thus knowable by consciousness. This means that such consciousness will be found even in a purely receptive spiritual subject, such as is the human soul of Christ in relation to the human intellectual powers, habits, and acts of Christ. But this consciousness is not simply consciousness of the purely receptive human subject of these acts, but also of the subject of actual exercise of these acts, who is the Uncreated Word. For these intellectual acts are not merely received in the human nature of Christ but also actually exercised by the divine Person; and their reflexive consciousness includes not only awareness of the acts as possessed but also as exercised. Yet this actual exercise of such acts takes place through the medium of the existent human nature. Therefore, in speaking of the subject-term of consciousness, we may here distinguish the intermediate, proximate term of the act-consciousness of Christ, which is the purely receptive human subject – subject in only a qualified sense – and the ultimate remote term of this same act-consciousness, which is the infinite subject of actual exercise who is the Word. This ultimate term is attained only obscurely in this act-consciousness considered precisely as such, for the intermediate term itself is known only obscurely and indirectly in virtue of such act-consciousness alone.

Reflexive being-consciousness is analogically similar to reflexive act-consciousness, as was seen in the earlier treatment; such being-consciousness is a reflexive awareness of an act, not of activity but of existence, as exercised by a subject. Fundamental being-consciousness, which is of special interest here, is such a reflexive awareness of the exercise of substantial existence by any spiritual subject. It is in fact found in any spiritual and intellectual being, and in man in so far as his existence is primarily the existence of his spiritual soul, though here such being-consciousness is very obscure because of the union of the spiritual soul with prime matter. Once again, however, it is the mere presence of such an act of existence in a spiritual subject, even apart from its exercise, that renders this act reflexive and therefore conscious and leading to a reflexive grasp of the subject which has this act, whether this subject be only a purely receptive subject or also the subject of actual exercise of the act. Therefore, in Christ there is such a consciousness given of the purely receptive human subject of His human existence through this very existence itself as spiritual and reflexive. But this human existence is, of course, also of necessity an exercised dynamic act and essentially referred to whatever be the subject of actual exercise, namely, the Person of the Word. This means that in the conscious living of His human existence, Christ is conscious at once of the finite, human subject which only receives this existence and also of the infinite, divine Person who actually exercises this act of human existence. There is no reason to think that the human consciousness of the finite, human, purely receptive subject is any clearer than that which other men have; for the metaphysical structure of form in matter, and of existense in a matter-form composite is here the same as in other men, and therefore yields only a very obscure grasp of His human existence in the human consciousness of Christ. But in view of this obscurity, and in view of the fact that this obscure consciousness of His human existence as in the receptive human subject is also the very medium through which is given the consciousness of the divine Person and Subject of actual exercise, Christ's human consciousness of assumption to the Word is itself very obscure, so obscure that it could not be formulated in the conceptual and propositional level of Christ's knowledge without the aid of infused knowledge, whenever such knowledge is actually conferred. There is of course no doubt that the beatific vision would illumine the obscure awareness of assumption, but we must defer consideration of this kind of illumination until we come to consider the problem of the beatific vision in Christ at least to some extent.

But it *does* seem possible to say something about the mode of Christ's human consciousness of the actual Subject of exercise of His human existence and therefore of His assumptiom to the Word. Ordinary men are in some manner aware of their own self-affirmation and relative autonomy in the line of existence; they are aware of being at their own disposal to some extent through their free action. All this points to their radical being-consciousness of themselves as subjects of actual exercise of existence and not merely as purely receptive of existence. But in the human being-consciousness of Christ, this ordinary human awareness of radical independence and autonomy must be lacking, since the human subject here is purely receptive and not a subject of actual exercise of existence. Rather, in place of such an awareness, is given another awareness, of His human existence as affirmed by another, by a certain obscure plenitude of being darkly present even in this human consciousness. This awareness is much like the mystical awareness of supernatural graces precisely as given by God, and indeed is the primary mystical union of Christ's human nature as purely receptive subject with the Word. Would it be possible for Christ as man, even without the aid of infused knowledge and apart from the beatific vision, to bring His acquired knowledge to bear upon this substantial mystical union and thence to conclude that He indeed is God? It seems that it would be difficult for Him to come to such a conclusion, since this mystical mode of awareness is so obscure and hard to distinguish from other mystical modes of awareness which mean much less than such a mode of union. We are sufficiently acquainted with the stumblings of mere human reason when it seeks to interpret mystical modes of union with God apart from the infused light of faith and the insights of theologians.

It is now possible to present a synoptic view of the consciousness of Christ, both from the perspective of the Second Person of the Trinity and from the perspective of the human nature of Christ as purely receptive subject. From the former perspective, the ultimate ground of unity of the total consciousness of Christ must be sought in the divine, uncreated consciousness of the Second Person. In this consciousness the Word knows both Himself and the other two Persons and all other actual or possible reality; in it is also known the special created reality of His secondary human consciousness precisely as His, and this knowledge in no way depends upon the secondary consciousness but rather is the transcendent cause of such consciousness. The created secondary consciousness, both being-consciousness and act-consciousness, is entirely distinct from the infinite and transcendent reality of the

Second Person and His uncreated self-consciousness, but is essentially referred to this properly divine consciousness by quasi-emanative and quasi-formal causality, and held to the Word by Himself as His.

From the perspective of the human nature of Christ as purely receptive subject, the reality of the uncreated, divine self-consciousness recedes from view. There is given a consciousness of the finite action and being of the human receptive subject, and therefore of this subject itself. In this consciousness of the finite subject is found a radical awareness of dependence, of createdness, such as would be found in any other created spirit or created intellectual being; but beyond this there is also found reference not to the finite subject but to an Other as the true owner and affirmer of the finite action and being of the receptive human subject. This Other, a plenitude of being, remains obscure at the plane of this human consciousness itself, but is illumined by the infused knowledge of Christ and by His beatific vision, and to some extent at least, even by His acquired knowledge. Of particular interest here, because of its seeming relevance in interpreting the created consciousness of Christ, is the beatific vision. We would like to know about how this beatific vision is actually present in Christ, and how it affects the created consciousness of Christ, either as an ultimate form of unity or in some other manner.

Some theologians have felt rather uneasy at the idea of the beatific vision in the human Christ even while He lived, suffered, and died here on earth. The "temptations," the seeming ignorance of certain matters, the intense suffering, the utter humanness of Christ, His likeness to us in all things save sin, all these aspects of Christ's life on earth make it more difficult for us to conceive of Him as at the same time enjoying the face-to-face vision of the Trinity which is our final beatitude and eternal rest for all our desires. And yet, if Christ's human nature is hypostatically united to the Word through the supernatural grace of union (which is the formal term of union of which we have spoken at length), the beatific vision is due to this nature right from the first moment of its being. For it is truly God who exists in this human nature and who through it first of all enters in communion with the Trinity even before going out to the created world. There could be no question of meriting the beatific vision here, for the natural Son does not have to merit what is His due. Is it possible that God would deprive His natural Son of what is His due? Such an hypothesis of deprivation for a time of the beatific vision that was Christ's by right might still be a tempting one to some, despite the intrinsic repugnance in the idea, unless it could be shown that the presence of the beatific vision is somehow compatible with the obvious utter humanness of Christ as man in His life on earth.

Although the problem of the nature of the beatific vision will be considered in a later essay, some brief remarks must be made here, perhaps more adequately intelligible only in the light of the later discussion. Since no creature can rise to God, "touch" God in any manner, God Himself must draw the finite intellect to Himself in order that it enjoy the beatific vision. This drawing is not accomplished through the infusion of any intelligible species, since no creature, no finite species, stands as a medium in the immediate face-to-face seeing that is the beatific vision. The "light of glory" conferred upon the finite intellect in order that it be able to see God is not such an intelligible species, but only places the creature in a state in which it can immediately see God. This state is only the immediate union of the finite intellect with God manifesting Himself as the supreme intelligible object (and Subjects). This union, again, had God alone as its unique transcendent cause; and the created term corresponding to the divine determination is the light of glory. Again, the union in the active sense is the divine decree itself, while the union in the passive sense is the light of glory. In virtue of this passive union the finite intellect is open to the immediate presence of God and to the radiance of His uncreated light, which is His very being. But there is no further active response on the part of the finite intellect appropriate to such a union, for this is union with the very infinite being of God Himself. There can only be adherence, a simple entranced gaze, and the profoundest joy of the intellect in this simple adherence and gaze. The only created response to the uncreated decree and union (in the active sense) is the created term corresponding to this decree; thus the created term, the light of glory, is both the condition under which the finite intellect can see God immediately and the appropriate created response to the divine determination of God to manifest Himself to the finite intellect. In this way, this created term is both the primary formal effect of the beatific vision in the finite intellect and the ultimate material disposition of this finite intellect for the beatific vision, which is only a new case of the scholastic principle that the act itself brings with itself the ultimate formal disposition for the act. Any further active response of the created person requires the mediation of infused knowledge in addition to the beatific vision, with the single exception of the act of charity in the will (a complacent love immediately specified by the beatific vision itself). Such infused knowledge and charity are genuine properties of the beatific vision, since they are contained in the requirements of complete subjective beatitude of the finite person; but they are not essentially constitutive of this beatitude. This does not mean that charity is unnecessary to beatitude; it is at once the immediate material condition for the reception of the light of glory and a property, a formal effect, consequent upon the possession of the beatific vision. Nor does the fact that charity does not actually enter into the essential constitution of beatitude mean that there is a lesser degree of communion (lacking the affective component of our ordinary communion with being) with God, in virtue of the vision alone. For the supplement to merely cognitive communion that affective communion ordinarily brings is already present in the beatific vision, which is a presence of God not only as objectified but also in His very subjectivity in most intimate communion with the created spirit, and a presence which is not only seen but also tasted as fully gratifying the infinite desire of the intellect. A further act and joy of the will is actually found, but it is in the manner of a superabundance. If in our ordinary life it is otherwise, so that the will gives us a fuller entry into communion with being than does the intellect alone, this is because the intellect cannot in any other case enter into the fullness of presence either of self or of other that is given to it in the beatific vision.

But if the above remarks about the beatific vision be true, then this vision in itself is a principle of rest and not of activity in the finite person. Only when something of its content is mediated through lower, infused knowledge can the vision become a (remote) principle of activity. But then the presence of the beatific vision at the summit of Christ's spirit does not necessarily imply that any of his human acts on earth, or indeed in heaven either, are elicited in the immediate light of the vision, so as to destroy their human mode. When infused knowledge does in fact mediate the light of the beatific vision, so that Christ acts humanly according to a light that is far beyond the human, His acts indeed range far beyond those of ordinary men, but they still retain their human mode to some extent in that they are still finite acts at such and such a point of space and time. So it was that the historical acts of Christ's life all remain historical acts, despite their transcendent significance; and Christ's human being is a truly historical being. Moreover, mediation through infused knowledge of the content of the beatific vision in Christ during His actual life on earth might not have been the ordinary rule at all; this could have been the exceptional event, perhaps only at moments such as the baptism by John or during those mysterious periods of prayer alone with the Father. In this light, one might entertain the idea of a gradual growth, at the lower, ordinary level of human consciousness below the beatific vision, of Christ's awareness of Himself as Messiah and of some of the details of His mission. To some this might seem to introduce a certain element of imperfection into Christ in His human being. But one may wonder whether the true manhood of Christ is not far better safeguarded and conceived so as to accord with the data of the Scriptural accounts of His life on earth when we admit such a level of ordinary human consciousness below the beatific vision and not utterly transfigured by this vision at every moment. To posit a non-mediated influence of the beatific vision on the human acts of Christ, or to posit a continual mediation through infused knowledge at every moment in every matter and detail of Christ's life both make it difficult to recognize Christ as truly one of us, like us in all things save sin, and to regard many of the events narrated by the Evangelists as anything but a kind of play-acting instead of the real drama of a flesh-and-blood human being.

In the light of the preceding remarks about the beatific vision in Christ, it is possible to make some suggestions concerning the relationship of this beatific vision to the created consciousness of Christ. This vision in Christ stands in a certain relative transcendence as compared with all lower knowledge in Christ, analogous to the absolute transcendence of the uncreated knowledge and consciousness of the Second Person of the Trinity even in relation to the human consciousness and beatific vision He has through the hypostatic union. And just as there is an ultimate unity of the consciousness of Christ in the uncreated self-consciousness of the Word, so also there is an ultimate (relatively ultimate) unity of the *human* consciousness of Christ in the beatific vision – in this vision Christ discovers His human being more fully and completely and adequately than He could through any lower level of His knowledge and consciousness, and He sees here not only His human being but also all the diverse levels of His human knowledge and consciousness all unified in this light, together with the very emanation from and union with the divine being of the Word.

But because of the transcendence of the beatific vision in relation to the lower levels of human knowing in Christ, this vision provides only an extrinsic unity of consciousness so far as the lower levels of the consciousness of Christ are concerned. The intrinsic unity of the human consciousness of Christ must be sought outside the beatific vision itself. And yet it cannot lack all reference to this beatific vision, since a true intrinsic unity of human consciousness must somehow embrace in itself a reference to all the diverse modes of human knowledge, at least in the sense that all these modes refer back to and evoke this unity. In Christ, then, this true unity must be found in the created self-consciousness of the human receptive subject outside the beatific vision but precisely as concomitant with the beatific vision. Even as Christ discovers Himself in His depths of human (purely receptive) subjectivity in the beatific vision (this is the medieval *cognitio matutina*), He simultaneously discovers Himself in this same human subjectivity in His being-consciousness outside the beatific vision (this is a form of *cognitio vespertina*). Despite the transcendence of the beatific vision, it remains present in the very same finite subject which has this being-consciousness; and the reflexivity and auto-transparency of spirit prevent the *cognitio vespertina* from being utterly unaffected in any manner by the *cognitio matutina*. The former, of course, cannot itself be transmuted into clear vision but it is obscurely illuminated by the latter in a warm and pleasant night; this warm and pleasant night is the only immediate "manifestation" of the presence of the beatific vision, to the lower levels of human consciousness. Now, this same "illuminated" *cognitio vespertina*, which is the being-consciousness of Christ as human and having the beatific vision, is at the same time the focal point of all other aspects of the human consciousness of Christ, the center and reference-point for all act-consciousness and really identical with all fundamental being-consciousness in Christ as man. Here then is the ultimate intrinsic ground and form of unity of the human consciousness of Christ. Let us also note that this analysis reveals, in the obscure illumination proceeding from the compresence of the beatific vision, a new dimension to the substantial mystical union of Christ's human nature to the Word; for it is this same radical being-consciousness, which is thus "illuminated," that is also the substantial mystical experience of the grace of hypostatic union to the Word.

Thus there is a real unity of human consciousness in Christ, dominated by the pure light of the beatific vision but intrinsically constituted in the darkness of the concomitant (and obscurely mediating) human being-consciousness. From the perspective of the lower modes of knowing and consciousness the beatific vision itself here is a warm, comforting, and consoling night, but without any determinate influence in the details of life, action, and lower knowledge apart from the mediation of infused knowledge. In this manner it is quite possible to hold the presence of the beatific vision even during His life on earth, without any prejudice to His humanity and to the utterly human mode of His life and action. At certain moments and during certain periods, the light of the beatific vision might be mediated by infused knowledge with a radiance and a clarity that would utterly surpass the illuminations of the highest of merely human mystics; but at other times, this light could remain only at the summit of the human soul of Christ in the pure form of the vision itself, with only a memory of previous illuminations at the lower levels of human awareness. While always resting in the pure light of the Trinity at all times at the highest peak of His being, the human Christ might go about much of His human life in the dimmer light of acquired knowledge and recollections of previous illuminations and expectancy of new illuminations to come.

6

THE FINITE SUPERNATURAL AND ITS MODES

The notion of the finite supernatural is not at all univocal and must apply to such diverse realities as the infused virtues of faith, hope, and charity, sanctifying grace, actual grace, the grace of the hypostatic union in Christ, the beatific vision of creatures, and anything else that can be grouped together under the general heading of created grace. But perhaps it is possible to achieve an understanding of the finite supernatural in general through a notion analogically applicable to all the diverse instances. Such a unified notion of supernatural created being was the goal of De La Taille,[1] in his conception of the finite supernatural as created actuation by uncreated act. Lonergan,[2] and Rahner too,[3] have also sought for such a unified grasp of the various modes of this being, Rahner through the idea of quasi-formal causality and Lonergan by a refinement of De La Taille's conception. In fact, we have already encountered something of their views in the discussion of the nature of the hypostatic union. Without dwelling further upon them here, we will proceed to our own examination and elaboration, beginning with some general observations on the mode of procedure, recalling something from our discussion of the hypostatic union in order the better to compare the mission of the Holy Spirit as sanctifier with that of the Son as incarnate, reflecting upon the actual created term of the mission of the Holy Spirit in our life of grace here below and noting the analogical similarity between this created term and that found in the hypostatic union, moving to a consideration of the structure of the beatific vision in the light of the foregoing considerations, and finally summing up our investigation in a statement of the unified conception of the finite supernatural and the diverse mode of its

---

[1] *The Hypostatic Union and Created Actuation by Uncreated Act*, p. 29-41.
[2] Private mimeographed notes, *De ente Supernaturali*.
[3] *Theological Investigations*, I, 319-346.

application in each of the three cases discussed, namely the Incarnation, the life of grace here below, and the beatific vision.

Finite supernatural being, the created favors by which God raises us to a participation in His own divine life, comes from God as a radically unmerited and utterly gratuitous gift. Presupposed to the gift, of course, is the loving regard, the favor of God Himself, which indeed is already a kind of uncreated grace. But this uncreated grace in fact is not something simply reducible to the divine oneness and simplicity of being; rather, it is already structured by the Trinitarian mode of divine being. This grace and favor within God Himself is the very determination of the Trinity that the Son be sent by the Father, and the Holy Spirit by the Father and the Son together, to bring to the world the created grace of God. This is to say that the uncreated grace and favor of God is identical with the divine missions, the mission of the Son and the mission of the Holy Spirit. The entire finite supernatural order for men in some manner or other flows from these two missions, the hypostatic union and the entire life of grace here below being direct results of these missions and the beatific vision being a kind of fructification of the benefits of the missions for us. We speak of course of the present economy of grace and salvation for men, and not of other possible orders or of the divine plan for the angels. In such other economies of grace and salvation, the structure of uncreated grace would be somewhat diverse; and yet always it would retain some kind of Trinitarian mode, if it is truly to introduce created persons into the very life of God Himself, which is irreducibly Trinitarian. Although we may hope to reach an analogical conception of the finite supernatural which will be applicable even to other economies than our own, it seems proper to begin with our own, by a consideration of the missions of the Son and of the Holy Spirit, and of the created terms – finite supernatural being – which arise in consequence of these missions. We have already said much concerning the structure of the hypostatic union, and our treatment of the created term of the mission of the Son will only be summary. The primary focus of this part of the paper is on the mission of the Holy Spirit. Only later will we turn to the beatific vision and its relation to the other modes, in order then to arrive at a unified notion of supernatural being.

The missions of the Son and of the Holy Spirit begin in eternity and terminate in time. But each of these missions is already constituted as a mission in the eternal procession of the Son from the Father and of the Spirit from the Father and the Son. The missions of the Son and of the Spirit are identical with the processions of the Son and the Spirit. Thus the Son and the Holy Spirit may be said to be sent from all eternity in so far as the Father, the Son, and the Holy Spirit together determine in the one intellect and will of God that the Son be sent and that the Holy Spirit be sent. But if this determination has truly been made from all eternity, then it is necessary that at some point in time a created term arise corresponding to the eternal mission, a term through which the Son or the Holy Spirit comes to be present in a new way in the world of creatures. For example, if it has been determined from all eternity that Christ be sent into the world of creatures, that He become incarnate as man, then at some point in time it is necessary that the Incarnation actually take place, and that a created term by its very nature referring to the Son and to the presence of the Son arise in the world. This created term in the hypostatic union of the Word made flesh is nothing else but the assumed existence, the *esse assumptum*, of the human nature of Christ. This *esse assumptum* has been called by Father De La Taille a created actuation by uncreated act. Similarly, in the mission of the Holy Spirit, an invisible mission into the souls of the just, the created term is sanctifying grace and the life of grace which flows from the possession of sanctifying grace. As was the case with the *esse assumptum* of the hypostatic union, this grace and life of grace can be described as a created actuation by uncreated act and must refer by its very nature to the Person of the Holy Spirit. It must be in some sense of the Holy Spirit; it must involve the personal presence of the Holy Spirit.

Now the created term of the uncreated mission must in both cases be the common effect of the whole Trinity. But just as the *esse assumptum* of the human nature of Christ can be said to be signed by the uncreated Word, so also there must be something in sanctifying grace and in the life of grace which is signed by its reference to the Holy Spirit.

What is the manner in which this signing by the Holy Spirit takes place in the created term of the mission of the Holy Spirit? In order to penetrate into its nature, first a preliminary metaphysical account, in part repetitive, of some relations of essence to existence, of substance to accident, and of natural being to the supernatural, accidental being that has been engrafted in grace onto the natural being of man is necessary. This metaphysical account will in turn lead to a deeper understanding of the internal structure of sanctifying grace as well as of actual grace in the souls of the just, and consequently to a fuller understanding of the invisible mission of the Holy Spirit in its created term. Finally, some remarks will be made concerning the freedom of man in living the life of grace.

Lest the preliminary metaphysical discussions on which we are about to embark appear completely unrelated to the question at hand, let it be noted that for us sanctifying grace, and indeed the entire life of grace in us, is regarded as it was by St. Thomas as pertaining to the accidental order. Created sanctifying grace is an accident within the soul, pertaining to the genus of quality. The same is true of whatever supernatural habits accompany or are added on to sanctifying grace in the soul. And the works of grace, just as the other operations of man, are activities pertaining to the accidental and not to the substantial order. (Of course, activity pertains to the accidental order in a way entirely other than that in which quality does; for activity pertains first of all to the existential order, while quality is a formal accident conferring a determinate grade of accidental existence.)

And yet, surely, neither entitative nor operational grace pertains to the accidental order in exactly the same manner as do the accidents known to natural reason. For ordinary accidents are not only in the subject in which they happen to be found but also can be said to be of this subject. But no natural subject can make grace, however accidental in its essence, to be of this natural subject in such a way as to be fully called its own (*tamquam suum*). It is this difference between the accidental being-in of supernatural grace and the accidental being-in of ordinary natural accidents that prompts us to investigate more fully the manner in which accident is related to substance. This in turn demands, as a presupposition, a deeper understanding of the relation of existence to essence in created being.

It is a commonplace of Thomist metaphysics that essences do not exist; subjects alone exist. An essence is only an intelligible content in being capable of being known, of showing itself to a knower. But the substantial existent must be more than a substantial essence; it is more than a face to be shown to a knower – it affirms itself, through its substantial existence, in an incommunicable manner. It is indeed this self-affirmation of the substance which is its subjectivity. Self-affirmation of substantial being is in its way analogous to activity. It is possible to understand better the self-affirmation of substantial being in the light of a few observations concerning the presuppositions of activity.

To conceive an agent as a mere passive potency to which further act is simply added from outside, as is form to matter, would be a serious mistake. While the agent is in potency for the activity, this agent is also in some manner the "spring" or depth from which the activity flows. This "flowing from" is what is meant by "exercise," when it is said that activity is an exercised act. Such exercise is of necessity unique and incommunicable; it can only be the exercise of this act by this thing. This exercise of act is subjectivity, as opposed to objectivity, which is mere possession of act. That which exercises the act is the subject, and the subject is unique and incommunicable in its exercise of act.

Now activity presupposes that the substantial agent is not a mere object but a subject. This is to say that the substantial agent cannot be a mere essence existing; the mere existence of an essence-intelligibility is not a sufficient ground for activity. For the further actuation which activity implies could only come to such an existing essence-intelligibility as added from outside, as is form to matter. This means that, before there can be an active subject, there must first be an existent subject – a subject the subjectivity of which is somehow constituted by existence itself. Therefore it cannot be correct to say that existence only gives being to essence, to objectivity; this existence is also the existence of a substantial subject.

But existence cannot be the existence of a subject rather than of a mere object unless existence itself is an exercised, dynamic act. In fact, it is this very affirmation and exercise of existence which constitutes the subjectivity of the existent and renders each existent unique and incommunicable, in some manner apart from every other existent and on its own in the world. Therefore, when existence is given to the objective essence to be possessed, it is also exercised, in virtue of the new existential state of this objective essence, a state which of course is itself correlative with and in some manner due to existence. This existential state is precisely the state of having existence, the possession of existence as a dynamic act demanding not merely to be possessed but also to be exercised. Resulting from this state of having existence, therefore, is the further state of exercising existence – and this state of exercise of existence is the very subjectivity of the existent. The fact that the objective essence is no longer merely held in existence by the existence which it possesses, but now makes this existence its own, means that the existent now has the fullness and interiority of the subject and not the mere exteriority of objectivity. Of course, in all this it must be remembered that the succession of states or moments is the result of our conception; in fact the possession and exercise of existence must be simultaneous. What has been said here could perhaps be summarized in more conventional terms as follows: the intelligible essence is as a material cause in relation to existence, at least a quasi-material cause (since it is constituted in being by the very existence which determines it); but the possession of existence, the state of possessing existence, also constitutes the intelligible essence as a subject, as a quasi-efficient cause of existence (but only quasi). We have already called this causality *quasi-emanative*.

Subjectivity, then, is constituted by objectivity in this existential state, or rather this double existential state. But the objectivity here must be the objectivity of substance. Accidents can never exercise their own existence, for they are only beings of substance. If an accident were to exercise its own existence, it would be thereby constituted as both a subject and substance.

In virtue of the foregoing analysis, it appears that every created substance should also be a subject, and that every created intellectula substance should also be an intellectual subject, or person. And yet we know of one created intellectual substance which is not a person, namely the human nature of Christ which was assumed into the hypostatic union. This substance surely exists in a finite way, possesses a finite existence; this is to say that it is actuated by a finite substantial act of existence. And yet this substance could in no way make this substantial existence *its own* and thereby constitute itself as a person. How could this be so? After all, is not existence of its very nature an exercised, a dynamic act, and therefore demanding to *be* exercised by a subject? It must be, then, that the finite existence of the human nature of Christ finds itself referred back to the uncreated Word as the subject who "exercises" this act – in an immanent, yet virtually transitive manner, by supplying itself all that would ordinarily be supplied by the subject of this act. Thus one might say that the divine subject who is the Word has pre-empted the exercise of the existence of the human nature of Christ. It is this very pre-emption that constitutes this *esse* as an *esse assumptum*, as a created actuation by uncreated act.

It is evident that the distinction between mere possession and actual exercise of existence can be, and indeed has been for us, very fruitful in the understanding of this particular actuation by uncreated act which is found in the hypostatic union. It therefore seems quite possible, indeed rather likely, that this same distinction may be of considerable value in understanding the created actuation by uncreated act that is involved in the created term of the mission of the Holy Spirit, that is to say, in the entitative and operational supernatural grace given to us by the Holy Spirit.

The parallel between substantial and accidental existence as regards possession and exercise is obvious enough. In the ordinary case, the same subject which possesses accidental existence (conferred through its various accidental forms) also exercises this existence as its own. At least those accidents proper to the thing and not superimposed on it from outside emanate from the substance in a manner analogous to that in which activity emanates from the subject. This emanation consists precisely in the exercise of the accidental existence by the substantial subject. Of course, every natural accident has an existence exercised by the substantial subject in which it is; but only in the case of proper accidents can this exercise properly be called an emanation.

But grace and the life of grace, far from being emanations of the natural subject in any sense, cannot really be said even to be actually exercised by the subject in which they are found. The work of grace is a work of God in us; as a participation of God, but even a share in the very life of God Himself, grace must of its very nature be referred to the divine being in a manner far beyond that in which any merely natural creature is so referred. The life of grace is an existence of God in us much more than it is a higher existence of ourselves. Action performed under grace is much more the action of God than our own action, although it is also our action. How this can be so will be seen later in the analysis of the structure of operational grace. But at present it can at least be said that the expression "created actuation by uncreated act" is as applicable to created grace and the life of grace in us as it is to the created term of the mission of the Word in the world. And if this is so, it means that the existential act (*esse* and *operari*) in the domain of grace is referred to a divine Person or Persons in a manner analogous to that in which the *esse* (and indeed also the *operari*) of Christ's human nature is referred to the Person of the Word.

But in noting the analogical resemblance of these two created actuations by uncreated act, in so far as an existential act is in a creature but referred to a divine subject as regards its exercise, we must also take care to point out the profound differences. In the union of a human nature to the Word, it is first of all a substantial existence that is the *esse assumptum;* other secondary *esse* and *operari* are assumed only in consequence of this primary assumption. But in the union of a soul to God through grace, the *esse assumptum* is entirely in the accidental order. Also, in the former union the nature assumed in virtue of the *esse assumptum* is itself a "natural" nature, like any other human nature; but in the latter union, the "nature" corresponding to the (accidental) *esse assumptum* is a "nature" itself belonging to the supernatural order, none other than the very "nature" of grace itself. In the former union, two substances are united in one hypostatis; in the latter union, two hypostases are united in one life (through a participation of one in the unparticipated life of the other). In the former, the entire natural life of the finite substance is "exercised" by the divine Person; in the latter, the natural life of the finite substance and person is exercised by this same finite person, while its supernatural life is engrafted into it as a work of God in it, and therefore "exercised" by God. Yet, if in the former, no room is left at all for any exercise even of activity by the finite substance, in the latter even supernatural activity can truly be said to be exercised – in a subordinate manner – by the finite subject under grace, so that it is truly *his* activity as well as God's (although much more God's than his). Finally, while the former actuation is effected by all three Persons but referred personally to the Word (so that the union is brought about by all three but between only the Word and the human nature), the latter actuation is also brought about by all three Persons but may be referred personally to the Spirit (so that the union brought about by all three Persons is the union of created grace to the Spirit – and through this union a union of a finite subject with the Spirit).

But it is one thing to say that supernatural grace is referred, as regards exercise of existence, to God, and quite another thing to say that this reference is uniquely personal to the Holy Spirit, as the exercise of the substantial existence of the human nature of Christ is referred uniquely and personally to the Word. The first point seems firm enough; the second is presented more as an hypothesis.

And yet this hypothesis has good grounds. It does give a better understanding of those texts of Scripture which designate the Holy Spirit in a special way as the sanctifier and giver of grace. It also seems to explain how even Christ Himself could be in some sense under the regime of the Spirit. And especially, it enables us to designate more clearly a created term for the invisible mission of the Holy Spirit, a term according to which the Spirit is truly present in a new way in the world of creatures.

In order to understand this created term of the invisible mission of the Holy Spirit more fully, let us begin by distinguishing between entitative grace and operational grace. Entitative grace is grace which consists in an infused habit of some kind, while operational grace is grace which consists in some supernatural operation. In entitative grace, the most fundamental reality is that of sanctifying grace – whether this be identified with or distinguished from supernatural charity. In the present discussion of the nature and structure of entitative grace, we focus out attention entirely upon sanctifying grace, understanding that the remarks made about it can be applied in an analogous way to the other modes of entitative grace.

Since sanctifying grace is an accidental quality (or habit) inhering in the soul, it is necessary to distinguish in it between its form and its "being-in" the subject who has this grace. If what has been said above be true, then the form of sanctifying grace calls for, demands, a peculiar type or mode of being-in completely unlike that of ordinary, natural accidents. For the exercise of this existence or being-in must not pertain to the subject who has this grace but rather to God who gives this grace. Sanctifying grace is not a created actuation by uncreated act by way of exception to some common rule; rather, the nature of sanctifying grace requires that it be such a created actuation by uncreated act by virtue of this "exercise" of its being-in by the divine being. But since the exercise of act pertains to a subject, then the exercise of existential act of sanctifying grace must pertain to a divine subject or to more than one divine subject. This is to say that this created actuation by uncreated act is not an actuation by the divine nature, but rather an actuation by one or more of the divine Persons. According to the hypothesis here presented, it is to the Holy Spirit that the created actuation which is sanctifying grace is uniquely and properly referred (even while this actuation is produced, by efficient causality in the strict sense, by the three Persons acting in common).

Now if the being of sanctifying grace is of its nature referred, as regards its exercise, to the person of the Holy Spirit, then where sanctifying grace is found in the soul, there is also found a new personal presence of the Holy Spirit. From this point of view, such created grace can indeed be regarded as a kind of seal imprinted on the soul as a sign of the presence of the Holy Spirit. But if the Holy Spirit is truly present in a new way through such created grace, then the entire Trinity is also present at the same time by the principle of circumincession. This "material" presence of the Trinity in virtue of the proper personal presence of the Holy Spirit could itself give deep meaning to the idea of the indwelling Trinity in the souls of the just. And yet there is more to be said concerning this presence of the entire Trinity through sanctifying grace. If grace has an existential and personal proper reference to the Holy Spirit, it also has an objective and intentional reference to the whole Trinity; for such grace is a participation in the very life of God Himself, which is irreducibly Trinitarian. The formal structure of sanctifying grace, its intelligibility, is essentially Trinitarian. Sanctifying grace is life in the Spirit, which makes us brothers of Christ, through which we come to the Father. If this grace refers properly to the Holy Spirit, it also refers to Him as proceeding from the Father and the Son, and thus refers through Him to the Father and to the Son. And if, on the one hand, sanctifying grace be regarded as identical with habitual charity, while, on the other hand, the Holy Spirit be considered in the light of the psychological analogy as proceeding Love, the proper reference of sanctifying grace to the person of the Holy Spirit becomes especially fitting, but at the same time such grace ought to have an intrinsic reference, as does the proceeding Spirit Himself, to the Father and the Son. And yet, even all this falls short of the full reality of the divine indwelling, as we shall see later.

If we suppose the supernatural organism of entitative grace – sanctifying grace, the infused virtues, and the gifts – as already constituted and with such a unique personal reference to the Holy Spirit, there still remains the problem of operational grace – the grace found in operation. For the mission of the sanctifying Spirit does not stop with the infusion of the supernatural organism; it must extend also to the promotion of supernatural activity through the already constituted entitative structure. But here is found a special difficulty. Such supernatural activity is in some sense the activity of the created subject, and therefore exercised by this created subject. And yet, if it be truly supernatural, our earlier analysis should compel us to refer its exercise in some manner to a divine Person or Persons (on our hypothesis, to the Holy Spirit). The problem is not just one of understanding the activity of a secondary agent under a First Cause; rather it is one of understanding how the same activity can be truly said to be exercised by a creature under grace even while it is also referred as to its exercise to a divine Person. This problem does not arise in the mission of the Word, for there is no finite subject to exercise the acts of the human nature – they are all referred to the Word as to the one subject of both the divine and the human nature. Nor does this problem arise in the mission of the Holy Spirit as regards the domain of entitative grace, for here it is not necessary to attribute exercise but merely possession of the accidental being-in of grace to the creature who has it. What then can be said about the metaphysical structure of operational grace in order to shed light upon the problem?

It should first be noted that while there is a fundamental difference between the operational grace that precedes sanctifying grace and that which follows and in some manner flows from sanctifying grace, operational grace in the strict sense – intrinsically supernatural operation – does exist in the created subject before the advent of sanctifying grace. Even before the coming of sanctifying grace, "operational grace" is more than a set of intrinsically natural inspirations and illuminations that would be supernatural only in so far as these illuminations and inspirations are ordered under the principal causality of God so as to dispose the soul more and more proximately for the free reception of justifying grace. Intrinsically supernatural operational grace is necessary if acts preceding justifying grace can be genuinely dispositive for justification, for no merely natural acts can positively dispose in any manner for supernatural grace. Yet these acts are not simply infused *in actu secundo* by God as operating grace. They presuppose in the will an already grace-inspired tendency (operating grace) that will fructify in the acts themselves (supernatural cooperating grace) if the free will of the agent remains freely open to this fructification. In this respect, both before and after justification operational grace presupposes prior supernatural grace – either the organism of entitative grace or at least the transient tendential actuation just spoken of.

In order to understand how supernatural operation can be truly said to be at once God's, and even personally the work of the Spirit, and at the same time that of the justified person (as it must be if the created person truly merits by this operation), it is well to consider the proximate principle (*principium quo*) of such operation, namely the organism of entitative grace in the created subject. This organism is truly possessed by the created subject; hence, acts performed through it are acts of the created subject. This point should become clearer when we come to the consideration of the genuine freedom of the created subject in regard to supernatural acts. But this same accidental and supernatural organism of entitative grace in the created subject is referred, as regards the exercise of its being-in, to God, or even to the Holy Spirit. Hence, acts performed through it must also be referred to God, or to the Holy Spirit, as to a Subject who exercises them in a mysterious manner, immanently but also in a virtually transitive way. So it is that God, or the Holy Spirit, performs in us the operations of our life of grace.

Something similar must be said also about grace-inspired operation in the non-justified person. Even here this operation is a fructification of an intrinsic tendential actuation of the created person, as has already been noted. Despite the absence of the organism of entitative grace, the structure of divine-human supernatural operation is fundamentally the same.

One other special case of operational grace, which was left out of consideration in the division between operation preceding and operation following justification, deserves mention. This is the case of supernatural operation in one who is without sanctifying grace but nevertheless has faith, or faith and hope. Can one speak of strictly supernatural operational grace in this instance, and of a proper reference of this grace to the person of the Holy Spirit? Since strictly supernatural habits of faith and hope or at least of faith truly remain as proximate principles of operation, and since these proximate principles can be themselves referred, as regards the exercise of their being-in, to the person of the Holy Spirit, the resulting operation can belong to the order of operational grace properly and personally referred to the Holy Spirit. Such operation is a form of supernatural life, but a truncated and qualified life deprived of its due fructification in charity, not life *simpliciter* but only *secundum quid*. And yet this is not the fault of God operating; it is the result of a free resistance on the part of the created subject.

At this point, a few remarks concerning the freedom of the created subject under grace can be made. In general, activity is a fructification of being, flowing from the inner dynamism of being itself. Freedom of choice is a capacity for the moderation of the dynamism of being through the possibility of nihilation, of saying no (this is the negative aspect of such freedom) and of non-nihilation, of letting this dynamism fructify (this is the positive aspect of such freedom). Now this possibility is truly left to us by grace. Grace enters in and remains by our sufferance; we can reject it and we can say no to its fructification, and God will respect our choice. While God is and acts in us through grace, still even the acts of operational grace are a fructification of supernatural ontological principles in us, a fructification in which we must acquiesce in order that it take place just as we must acquiesce in the fructification even of such natural principles as depend for their exercise upon our freedom. In both cases, since the acts are the fructification of ontological principles within us, and a fructification which is freely permitted and acquiesced in, the acts are truly our acts, just as the corresponding refusal to act would be our refusal. But since supernatural grace is a share in the life of God which involves also a special presence of the Holy Spirit and the Trinity, free acquiescence or refusal is not only acceptance or rejection of a created gift of God but even acceptance or rejection of the personal advances of the Holy Spirit Himself and of the Trinity. There is not only true freedom in the life of grace, but a freedom even in the very presence of God knocking at the door, before the Spirit sent from God to sanctify us and to enter in ever more fully as the Guest of the soul.

We have already seen that the supernatural organism of entitative grace in man is only the primary created term of the mission of the Holy Spirit, and of the determination of the Holy Spirit, and with Him of the Trinity, to indwell in the souls of the just. It is evident that it is not finite grace which "draws down" the Holy Spirit and the Trinity to the soul of the just man; rather, it is their loving and condescending regard which causes the being of the finite supernatural in the soul. If the supernatural organism of entitative grace is in some sense a material condition for the indwelling, this grace is itself much more the "primary formal effect" of the indwelling Spirit and Trinity, a formal effect proceeding in a quasi-emanative manner from God while conditioning our union with Him as with a quasi-formal cause.

But this is very much reminiscent of the discussion of the hypostatic union and of the relation between the grace of union, which is a created term corresponding to the uncreated mission of the Son, and the Word Himself as a quasi-emanative cause of this created term, and the human nature of Christ, to which the Word joins Himself as quasi-formal cause. Here there emerges a certain analogical unity in the concept of the finite supernatural as applied to these two cases. The notion of created actuation by uncreated act through quasi-emanative causality so as to produce a quasi-formal union of a divine Person to a finite being in fact sheds much light on the nature of each of these two modes of finite supernatural being. Could it perhaps also be applicable to the third mode of the finite supernatural, that is, the beatific vision of the saints and of the human Christ? To answer this question it will be necessary to make some observations about the ontological structure of the beatific vision (as well as we can conceive it).

This beatific vision is an immediate, face-to-face presence of God known clearly in His inner being and life to the finite person. God is here present to the finite person not just as objectified or as a vicariously present subject; His infinite subjectivity is physically present in the finite intellect and renders all mediation in knowledge of him unnecessary. He has, of course, always been omnipresent and present by His causality of the creature, present even in the very intellect itself of the creature – but this presence did not suffice for the finite intellect to possess the beatific vision. Though God was there, this finite intellect could not *see* Him in an unmediated manner but had to know Him only through the medium of His created effects, and therefore only to the extent that these created effects could reveal some fragmentary aspect of the infinite being that He is. Moreover, the unmediated seeing of God must forever remain beyond the finite natural capacity of any created person. This natural capacity is necessarily of finite scope, simply lacking any proportion to the infinite divine being, unable to find any suitable (necessarily finite) medium through which to know the absolutely infinite in itself, infinitely distant from the utter transcendence of this being.

But if the finite intellect is radically unable to rise to direct intuitive knowledge of the divine being, God does nevertheless raise this intellect to such vision in a strictly supernatural manner as the climax and final goal of the supernatural vocation that He has given to men and to angels. This divine gift is surely as mysterious as are the other modes of the finite supernatural that we have already seen; and yet, just as in the latter cases, it is possible to understand something about the ontological presuppositions and structure of this crowning mode of supernatural elevation of the created person.

Since the beatific vision is itself unmediated by any creature, the act of vision here requires only the divine being and a created intellect open to the immediately present divine being. Yet this created intellect is not thus "open" in virtue of itself. This openness is brought about through a special supernatural gift, given to the finite intellect, joining this intellect to God – a gift not itself a mediating principle of knowing, but rather a principle of union in openness between the being of the finite intellect and the being of God. One may call this gift a created supernatural union with God, a union which is not itself a formal means of vision but which nevertheless is a necessary condition for the vision of God. Theologians have called this gift the "light of glory."

But as in the cases of the grace of the hypostatic union and of the wayfarer on earth, we must observe that this created union (union in the passive sense) is not the primary supernatural reality (by which we could "cling" to God) but rather presupposes the loving regard, favor, uncreated grace of God Himself and is only the created term corresponding to the divine determination, the decision of the Trinity, to communicate the very life of the Trinity. God's determination so to manifest Himself in vision to the created person is uncreated grace and is already uncreated union (union in the active sence). God remains utterly transcendent, His independence of being in no way compromised by admitting created persons into His intimate society and the community of the Trinity. If the created person is actually unified, in an irrevocable manner, to God by the light of glory, this can only be because God has raised the creature, not because the creature has ascended to God; because God holds the creature to Himself, not because the creature holds fast to God and will not let go.

Moreover, the light of glory is no more the property of the created person than was the grace of the wayfarer. Here too, the light of glory cannot be in any way an emanation from the natural subject, nor can the existential act of this supernatural light be said to be actually exercised by this natural subject; for such emanation and exercise would make this light of glory to belong truly to the creature as something of its own. What was said of the grace of the wayfarer is all the more true of this light of glory. It is a work of God in us. As a participation of God, but even a share in the very life of the Trinity, this light must of its nature be referred to the divine being in a manner far beyond that in which any merely natural creature is so referred. The existence of this light in us will be an existence of God in us much more than a higher existence of ourselves. Here again, then, one may speak of a created actuation by uncreated act through quasi-emanative causality so as to produce a quasi-formal union of (not just one but all three) divine Persons with the finite person.

Already the outlines of a unified conception of finite supernatural being begin to appear. But before pursuing this idea further, it is necessary to enter much more fully into the ontological structure of the beatific vision. In fact this vision is the goal toward which all the modes of finite supernatural being tend, and further understanding of this vision will shed considerable light even on the other modes of the finite supernatural.

In view of what has already been said, no elicited finite act is either required or possible in the beatific vision as such. Such a finite elicited act would in fact be an intervening finite medium between the finite person and the infinite being of God which is seen, a totally disproportionate and inadequate medium. Moreover, no such medium – which would "open" the finite intellect to God – is at all necessary; for God Himself is physically present as quasi-emanative cause of the light of glory, which unifies the finite intellect to God in such a manner as to open this intellect to the immediacy of the uncreated light of the

Trinity now present as a quasi-formal cause in union with the finite intellect. The light of glory is a medium of union in the ontological order, but not in the order of the vision itself; the union effected by the light of glory is not the vision but only the condition for the vision. How this is so will be better seen in the more technical analysis to follow.

In order to understand more deeply the nature of the beatific vision it is helpful to compare the immediate illuminating presence of God in it to the traditional role of the impressed and expressed species in ordinary human knowing. Although there is no exact correspondence at any point, nevertheless this ordinary process does provide some basis for an analogical consideration of the beatific vision itself.

Ordinary human intellection terminating in the objectifying and formulated knowledge of the concept and judgment requires, according to the scholastics, the presence of intentional forms in the intellect: first, the impressed species – the form of the thing known, now present not in its physical reality but with a spiritual, representative, relative reality as the formal principle of the act of insight; second, the expressed species – a formulation by the intellect to itself of the content of the act of insight, again a spiritual, representative, relative reality of the form of the thing known. The impressed species is not itself known in the knowledge of the thing but is only the necessary principle of this knowledge, therefore a *medium quo* in the terminology of scholastic philosophy; but the expressed species is itself known and through it the thing is known immediately (without discourse of reason) — it is thus a *medium in quo*. The act of knowing is itself identical with the existence of the impressed and expressed species in the intellect. The terminology of impressed and expressed species is properly applied in the analysis of conceptualization, with the impressed species as the formal principle of the moment of insight which precedes conceptualization, and the expressed species as the formal principle of the formulation which is the concept. But a similar structure must be noted in the analysis of judgment, since there too is found a moment of insight and a moment of formulation in the act of judgment. The intellect does not rest in the moment of insight in either case but proceeds to formulation out of a desire to stabilize its possession of new intelligibility and to delineate and articulate to itself the precise and total content of the act of insight. The insight is a momentary act occurring in a complex and transitory context; the formulation is a stable and well-defined, more or less permanent possession, and a necessary requirement for any hope of accumulating a *store* of knowledge.

We have said that the beatific vision is itself a non-mediated presence of God to a finite intellect in a condition of total openness to God in virtue of the light of glory. There can be no question of envisaging the vision itself as a result of some finite impressed or expressed species or as itself a finite medium between the finite intellect and God in the manner of an impressed or expressed species. Nor can the light of glory be conceived as an impressed or an expressed species, for it is not a formal principle of but only a condition for the vision. Can God Himself be conceived here after the manner of an impressed or expressed species in the intellect? Before this question can be properly answered it is necessary to examine more closely the manner of God's presence in the beatified finite intellect and His relation to the light of glory.

The presence of God in the finite intellect trancends and precedes anything in the finite person. As so present and intent upon communicating Himself more fully in the beatific vision, God produces efficiently the light of glory, which is also referred back to God as to a quasi-emanative cause and is therefore a quasi-property flowing from the actual active communication by the divine being of itself. The light of glory puts the finite intellect into an existential state of immediate and apprehending openness to God's intelligible and illuminating immediate presence in this intellect, and is therefore from the point of view of the finite intellect a dispositive cause for the vision. Thus, this light is at once the ultimate disposition in the finite intellect for the communication of the divine being in vision and a property of the divine being (a *quasi*-property) as actively communicating itself in vision and as a quasi-formal cause in the finite intellect, in a manner analogous to that in which in the communication of natural forms the ultimate disposition induced by the agent cause is at once also a formal effect of the form which is induced.

The finite intellect was always open to being and even to the divine being (as mediated through creatures); but however immediate the divine presence in the finite intellect, this intellect of itself was previously unable to apprehend in an immediate manner the divine being. The being of God was too intelligible, too simple, too transcendent, and therefore was darkness for the finite intellect except for the mediation of some creatures; for the finite intellect could elicit only finite acts of knowing which would be radically inadequate for any immediate understanding of God. And this finite intellect had to rely upon such finite acts, whether elicited or imposed or natural, as mediating principles for all of its knowing; these acts are the light of this intellect, and this intellect must follow its light. From another viewpoint, natural understanding is first of all *self*-understanding, in auto-presence and in the reflexive possession of mediating intentionalities; therefore the understanding, and the object of understanding, of the finite person is necessarily conditioned by the finite mode of being of this person. If the finite intellect is in any manner ever to escape this predicament, this can only be by some radical transformation of its mode of knowing.

The light of glory draws the finite intellect outside its natural state and mode of knowing. This light is the "property" of the divine entry into the finite intellect to be known in an immediate manner, a "property" which is at the same time a disposition elevating the finite intellect, drawing this intellect into the immediacy of the divine light in a union so close as to eliminate the necessity and preclude the possibility of any finite elicited act of knowing. Thus the finite intellect does not here see by its own light but rather by the divine light itself; this finite intellect is "comforted" (in the old scholastic sense) by the immediacy of this divine light, and rendered able to see, and actually seeing as well, by God's self-communicating presence. In this comforting light God is already present as an *intelligible understood*, strengthening our faculty by this mode of presence – so that without any new act the faculty simply *is still* and *sees* what is in it already as known, pure self-conscious Light. But this can only take place if the light of glory act as a mediating disposition in the finite intellect (while quasi-emanating from God) for the quasi-formal union of God Himself to the finite intellect.

But if the intrinsically constitutive principle of the beatific vision is the quasi-formal union of the divine being to the finite intellect, then some analogical similarity between the role of God here and the role of an intentional form in ordinary human intellection can be noted. But if God here has a role similar to that of the expressed species, in so far as He gives Himself in a stable, clear manner so that no further formulation of this knowing is either necessary or possible, still there is a great dissimilarity in so far as the expressed species is by its nature a product and a formulation of prior understanding, which is certainly not the case in the beatific vision and the being of God. In so far as the impressed species in some manner comes from without and, being present, is a principle of insight, the role of God in the beatific vision is similar to that of the impressed species. But the impressed species as such is a relative, representative, mediating principle, which is only a first step in the process of human intellection, while God in the beatific vision is the absolute, original, unmediated, ultimate term of knowing. The presence of God in the beatific vision is of such a nature as to render any kind of impressed or expressed species, or any of the rest of the ordinary intellectual process, totally unnecessary. The analogical comparison of the presence of God in the beatific vision to the presence of finite intentional form in ordinary human intellection is of some help to understanding the beatific vision, but at the same time reveals only a very limited likeness. One might wonder whether a better analogy might not be found than that to the impressed or expressed species.

The doctrine of the impressed and expressed species was developed in order to explain the process of objectifying (conceptualizing) and quasi-objectifying (judging) intellection. It envisaged only the kind of intellectual insight that could be directly formulated in such a process. In fact there are other modes of intellectual insight than this, modes of non-objectifying intellection through affective connaturality or through conscious living of existence or activity. Such insight and intellection can lead indirectly to some kind of formulation, but the ordinary account of the impressed and expressed species must be modified here. Moreover, even in the ordinary case of objectifying intellection it is possible to give a somewhat different explanation of inquiry and insight than that ordinarily given by scholastics, as I have done in my *Inquiry Into Being*.

But even with all this, the basic distinction between the moment of insight (mediated) and the moment of formulation (produced) is still found in every case of our knowledge of the *other;* and consequently there is always a structure analogous to that of the impressed and expressed species. Only one other possibility remains, that of the concomitant consciousness which we have of the lived exercise of existence and of the activity of intellect and will. Such concomitant consciousness itself lacks the structure of mediation or production; it is immediate awareness of the act itself in virtue of the act itself. It is true that even here this immediate awareness is itself involved in, immersed in, a context of intentional reference and mediation – through the act one also becomes aware of the subjectivity of the self and even of the being of another. But such concomitant consciousness does reveal the possibility for the finite spirit of non-mediated intellection in virtue of immediate presence. Here this non-mediated intellection (intellection only in a reductive sense, since there is no distinct *act* required) is always intrinsically finitely conditioned by the finitude of finite acts of existence or activity that are truly possessed by the finite subject in some manner. This would not be so in the non-mediated intellection of the beatific vision; for (1), in the union between the finite intellect and the divine being through the light of glory it is God who holds the finite intellect to Himself and thus is more possessing than possessed, and (2), the intellection itself, precisely as non-mediated, is not finitely conditioned by the finitude of the light of glory except as regards the degree of openness of the finite intellect to the immediately present infinite being of God. Still, despite these qualifications, non-mediated concomitant consciousness does provide, along with the impressed and expressed species, some analogical basis for a limited understanding of the beatific vision.

At this point it might seem appropriate to embark upon some investigation of various "properties" of the beatific vision as the final state of man. For the beatific vision is essentially only in the intellect, and yet man is more than intellect. Indeed, even as regards the intellect itself, the beatific vision in some manner transcends all other human or finite intellectual knowing. It seems evident enough that if the beatific vision is in fact concretely the ultimate good of man, the infinite good already possessed, still there is need for something further to constitute, no longer the essence, but at least the integrity of beatitude. We have already said something about the role of infused knowledge in mediating between the beatific vision and the lower levels of human consciousness, and about the connection between the acts of charity and joy and the beatific vision, in our discussion of the consciousness of Christ in an earlier essay. But to go further into the detailed aspects of this problem of the integrity of beatitude and the properties of the beatific vision would take us away from the central problem of this paper, which is to understand the various modes of the finite supernatural in the light of a unified concept of finite supernatural being.

It is time now to begin weaving together some of the strands of thought that we have followed up in this essay and in some earlier essays concerning the various modes of finite supernatural being. In this essay we have considered sanctifying grace, actual (operating) grace, the hypostatic union and the grace of union, and the beatific vision. A more extensive account of the grace of hypostatic union was seen in the essay on the hypostatic union, and the grace of faith was treated at length in a series of chapters. In each of these cases, there was noted the divine presence in the human being. In all but the case of one not justified by God, there was noted the quasi-formal union of

God to the human being and His quasi-emanative causality of a created actuation unifying the creature to Himself in a supernatural manner. This structure is required for the act and habit of living supernatural faith, and it should be unnecessary to carry out the detailed analysis here. That supernatural charity demands a similar structure is evident enough if charity is to be identified with sanctifying grace. But it would be equally certain even if the two be distinguished in the manner of conventional Thomism. The habit of supernatural charity would require this structure for the same reason as does sanctifying grace, as a part of the living supernatural organism of entitative grace; the act of supernatural charity would require this structure, since it presupposes the habit of charity in the order of efficient causality. And of course if entitative and operational charity, as modes of supernatural being in the will, demand such a structure, so also must living hope.

But in order to round out this inventory of the finite modes of supernatural being and to prepare better the way to the unified concept of finite supernatural being, it is well to consider briefly the actual relation of sanctifying grace and charity, and the ontological reality of dead faith (and hope) as opposed to faith (and hope) living by charity. In the light of this consideration we hope to be able to formulate still more precisely the formal note of divine indwelling in the souls of the just, more precisely than in the earlier part of this paper.

The heart of the organism of entitative supernatural grace is sanctifying grace, which is the root principle of participation in the life of God in us. But this heart could be conceived as a quasi-substantial principle for the rest of the supernatural organism in us, an underlying habit in the soul, which is the ontological principle for the operation of habits of faith, hope, and charity and for the acts of these supernatural virtues. Such a concept of sanctifying grace has some difficulty when we consider that faith and hope could remain in a man even though he is deprived of sanctifying grace. Moreover, the concept in question seems to rest on a vision of our supernatural life and action as more ours than God's. While these are certainly in some manner ours and in some manner God's as working in us, it seems sufficiently certain from all that has been said in this essay that they are more God's than ours. In this light there seems to be no need for such a created quasi-substantial principle of our supernatural life. Rather, both sanctifying grace and charity (and in a qualified sense the rest of the entitative supernatural organism in us) are quasi-emanative formal effects of the divine indwelling through a quasi-formal union and causality. But then there is no need any longer to distinguish charity from sanctifying grace at all. In this way, sanctifying grace as the heart of the entitative supernatural organism in us is viewed as a fundamental orientation of the created person in his will, giving a new direction to everything he does, turning him toward the saving God not in some automatic manner but in a radically voluntary manner (at least habitually so, but also actually in adults). The concept of sanctifying grace as a quasi-substantial principle was an attempt to conceive of the life of grace by analogy with the structure of finite, natural beings. But if grace is not just ours but God's working in us, we should not be surprised to find that such an analogy finally proves to be mistaken, and that the heart of the supernatural life of participation in God's own knowledge and love is to be found at the level of our own intellectual life of knowledge and love rather than at the level of some quality modifying, inhering in, the substantial being of the soul. The attempt of St. Thomas to put sanctifying grace in this latter position was perhaps a necessary trial in view of the rediscovery of Aristotle and the application of his philosophy with such fruitful results in theology. But we should not be afraid to abandon such a theory in the face of a better understanding of the being of the finite supernatural and of its relation to the indwelling of God.

The question has already been raised concerning the ontological reality of dead faith, faith (and ordinarily also hope) in one who lacks sanctifying grace and the indwelling presence of the Trinity. This faith is still supernatural faith, and therefore entitative and operational supernatural grace referred to God not only as to an efficient cause but also as to a quasi-emanative cause. But here this quasi-emanative causality of the habit and act of faith by God is not conjoined with a quasi-formal union of God to the finite person. Here the habit and act of faith are not the ultimate dispositions on the part of the finite person for the union with God as with a quasi-formal cause, dispositions which at the same time would be the primary formal effect of such a quasi-formal union. Rather, here the habit and act of faith (and so too with hope in such a case) are in themselves only more remote dispositions for this union, which look toward the ultimate disposition, and primary formal effect, which is charity itself. It is entirely necessary that the ultimate disposition and primary formal effect be charity; for God will not join to Himself in a quasi-formal union a creature that is not freely and totally centered on God Himself as the supreme good loved above all things, and He will not enter into such a union without bestowing this gift of charity on the creature.

The nature of God's presence to the creature as *locutio increata* has been described in the series of chapters on faith and intersubjectivity. That presence is mediated to the intellect through the affective connaturality of the will inspired by grace, and even the presence of God to the will there is a mediated presence, through this same grace-inspired connaturality. In virtue of charity as a disposition, and producing charity as a quasi-formal effect, God enters into a more immediate, quasi-formal union with the will of the finite person; but this immediacy of presence is between God and the *will*, not the intellect. In relation to the intellect, God's indwelling presence is still mediated, through the will; therefore this quasi-formal union of God to the finite person does not mean a beatific vision for the finite person. That could only take place through a quasi-formal union of God to the finite intellect as itself conditioned and disposed by the light of glory. And yet the will is in the intellect, and what is in the will is in some manner present to the intellect as well. The quasi-formal union of God with the finite will disposed through charity will enable us better to understand something of Christian mysticism, as we shall see in a later chapter, and of its roots in the fundamental structure of any Christian life. This obscure presence of God to the finite person is never vision, but it is a prefiguration of such a vision; and the testimonies of the mystics prefigure the joy of the blessed.

Another mode of immediate, quasi-formal union of creature to God was seen in the hypostatic union. But again it must be emphasized that this union is not precisely between the finite intellect and God but rather between the finite substantial nature and God. Once again this union is mediated, through the substantial nature, in relation to the finite intellect; therefore once again it does not mean a beatific vision as an immediate result. Of course, the grace of hypostatic union does imply a beatific vision as well; but this vision has as its immediate dispositive principle the light of glory and not the hypostatic union itself.

An overall view of the finite modes of supernatural being must center upon the beatific vision as the central reality toward which they all tend. This is the highest mode of being to which any created nature or person could rise, and every supernatural grace is finally directed to this end, to the attainment of this beatific vision and participation in the inner life of the Trinity either for oneself of for oneself and others as well. Faith, even dead faith, is already an anticipation of this vision. With charity, quasi-formal union with God is already given, a union which will endure even with the beatific vision, but union of the will and not yet immediately of the intellect. Yet such a "dark" prefiguration is required if we are to be truly able to respond to the divine advances not only with freedom of autonomy and independence (freedom which will remain even in the light of vision) but also with the freedom of choice proper to wayfarers whom God wishes to give a genuine option with all the consequences allowed in a spirit of fair play. In Christ himself, the created supernatural life and, above all, the light of glory and the immediate presence of the Trinity in beatific vision, are the most precious gifts, compared to which every other creature in the universe of creatures and even all of them taken together are inferior. Christ also comes to give supernatural life to others, but again a life which culminates in the beatific vision.

At last we can speak of the general structure of the being of the finite supernatural. This means, of course, the being of the finite supernatural that is substantially so, of which we have been speaking almost always in this essay. The modally supernatural, which is nothing but the ordering of the substantially natural toward some supernatural purpose, has been generally set aside, precisely because it is not intrinsically supernatural. This does not deny its intrinsic interest, but one must set limits somewhere to this lengthy essay.

The modes of finite supernatural being arise in so far as God determines to raise the finite intellectual being to a higher life of participation in the uncreated life of the Trinity, in fact by a communication of the divine being itself in the beatific vision with all its consequences. If such finite intellectual beings were created as already elevated to such participation in the Trinitarian life, there would be no need of any other modes of the finite supernatural than the light of glory and whatever is a consequence of the vision itself. But when such finite intellectual beings are not created as already in their final state, then the varieties of entitative and operational grace already described have a place. All these varieties, as well as the light of glory itself, are only the appropriate external, created terms corresponding to the divine determination to communicate the Trinitarian life, a determination made in utter freedom and motivated by nothing but the divine love itself, completely gratuitous, and therefore well called uncreated grace. The created terms are, of course, distinct from God and therefore require the divine creative efficacy in the line of efficient causality to give them being.

But we have already seen that such created supernatural reality, though *in* the creature, must still be conceived as more *of* God than of the creature. Grace never becomes the property of the creature but is always "something of God" in the creature. This has led us to conceive this grace as everywhere referred to God as to a quasi-emanative cause. This quasi-emanative causality of God must be described in a manner analogous to that in which we speak of the transitive activity of God in creating the world. Neither form of activity is *formally* such as we name it but only virtually so, since all the activity of God can be formally specified only by the divine being itself. The manner of this quasi-emanative causality has been understood from the viewpoint of the created term by the introduction of the metaphysical distinction between the mere possession and the actual exercise of existential act. Although the distinction itself rests upon a simply metaphysical analysis of the relation of essence and existence, and has a certain applicability in the metaphysical discussions of the relation of nature and person and of substance and accident and other problems, it has been employed here in an analogical manner going beyond anything that reason alone might suggest as possible and in view of data concerning supernatural being that have come to us only through divine revelation. There is no adequate natural analogue for the reference of the possession and exercise of entitative grace to two distinct substantial beings – God and the creature, or for the reference of the exercise of operational grace to two distinct beings – again God and the creature. But if such created supernatural being is always referred virtually to God as to a quasi-emanative cause, it must also be considered as a formal cause (in the cases of faith, hope, and charity – sanctifying grace) or as a quasi-formal cause (in the case of the grace of substantial hypostatic union in Christ) or as an operational act (in the case of operational grace) in the creature itself. This two-fold reference of the finite supernatural to God and to the created nature in which it is enables us to speak of it as always a created actuation by uncreated act.

But such a created actuation by uncreated act always looks toward a non-mediated primary union with the uncreated act itself as with a quasi-formal cause. The created actuation of its nature disposes for such a union, calls for such a union, and would if possible be a quasi-formal effect of such a union; or in the case of operational grace, it tends toward or is a consequence of such union, not in the order of being but in the order of operation. From this point on, we will set aside the latter, operational grace, altogether and focus our attention entirely upon the various modes of entitative grace, in order to examine their relation to non-mediated primary union with the uncreated act as with a quasi-formal cause.

Such created actuations by uncreated act are either adequate or inadequate dispositions for the diverse modes of non-mediated union. The graces of faith and hope in themselves are inadequate dispositions for the non-mediated union and indwelling by quasi-formal causality in the will that would exist with the grace of charity. Faith and hope in themselves are only preparations, or remainders that are preparations, for a future return of such indwelling of God along with the return of charity. If charity is the adequate disposition (necessarily presupposing faith and hope, of course) for the non-mediated union in the will, the light of glory is the adequate disposition for such non-mediated union in the intellect, and the grace of hypostatic union – the *esse assumptum* – is the adequate disposition for such non-mediate union in the substantial being of the creature.

When such an adequate created actuation by uncreated act is actually present, the quasi-formal causality of the divine being has two aspects. First, the divine being here becomes the non-mediated formal term of union, unifying itself to the adequately disposed creature. Second, the divine being principiates the ultimate disposition itself – the created actuation – as the mediating term of a derived created union and the primary "formal effect" of the non-mediated union. This principiation, as we have already seen, consists in both an efficient and a quasi-emanative virtual causality constituting the created term as a mode of finite supernatural being.

Finally, a few remarks should be made concerning the value of the conception of the finite supernatural to which we have come. As a theory concerning the nature of such supernatural being it does integrate elements from recent theologians, especially the created actuation of De La Taille and the quasi-formal causality of Rahner, in the light of the key distinction between possession and exercise of existence that has been developed by Maritain.[4] From this point of view it appears more adequate as a theory of supernatural being. But more than this, it seems required by the application of metaphysical understanding to the reality of the supernatural and to the adequate conception of this supernatural in Scripture and Tradition. Grace must never be regarded as our property, for in itself it completely transcends our nature. Grace must never be given such a reality as would enable it to be separated from the inner life of the Trinity itself, dissociated from uncreated grace

---

[4] *The Degrees of Knowledge,* Appendix IV.

and standing on its own. Grace must always be God working in us, as St. Paul says: "For it is God who of his good pleasure works in you both the will and the performance." [5] "God ... works in you who have believed." [6] "The charity of God is poured forth in our hearts by the Holy Spirit who has been given to us." [7] "It is now no longer I that live, but Christ lives in me." [8] "And because you are sons, God has sent the Spirit of his Son into our hearts, crying 'Abba, Father.'" [9] "For by grace you have been saved through faith; and that not from yourselves, for it is the gift of God; not as the outcome of works, lest anyone may boast. For his workmanship we are, created in Christ Jesus in good works, which God has made ready beforehand that we may walk in them." [10] "Now, to him who is able to accomplish all things in a measure far beyond what we ask or conceive, in keeping with the power that is at work in us..." [11]

Grace is not a creature like any other creature; created grace, even though distinct from God, has essential reference to the inner life of the Trinity. Grace exists as a relation to this Trinitarian life and to the Persons of the Trinity. But this mode of existence proper to supernatural grace becomes intelligible through the distinction between possession and exercise of existence and the referring of exercise of this existence of grace to one or more of the Persons of the Trinity. Nor could this mode of existence of grace be intelligible to us without the application of this distinction; for grace conceived in some other manner would have to be regarded as more of the creature than of God, metaphysically and abstractly conceivable even as dissociated from uncreated grace, in some manner the property of the creature.

Moreover, this conception of the finite supernatural renders possible a better understanding of the union of God to the finite intellectual being in the hypostatic union, the indwelling in the souls of the just, and the beatific vision by a quasi-formal causality. Its fruitfulness will also be apparent in the account of mystical experience in a later chapter.

For all these reasons, the conception of finite supernatural being elaborated in this essay deserves much reflection. At the same time, it

---

[5] Phil. 2, 14.
[6] I Thes. 2, 13.
[7] Rom. 5, 5.
[8] Gal. 3, 20.
[9] Gal. 4, 6.
[10] Eph. 2, 8ff.
[11] Eph. 3, 20. Cf. also Rom. 8, 14ff; I Cor. 12, 3–6; II Cor. 3, 5, 17.

poses some problems for further investigation. Having spoken of the existential aspect of the finite supernatural, we might begin to ask about its essence-structure, both in general and in each of its particular actual or possible modes. How is the essential Trinitarian reference actually contained in this essence-structure in each case? To which Person or Persons of the Trinity, or in what order, are each of the finite modes referred as regards virtual exercise of existence? Is Scheeben's hypothesis, which we have recalled in the course of this treatment, concerning the Holy Spirit as the subject to which the entire supernatural life of the wayfarer is personally referred, anything more than a very attractive and somewhat plausible theory? What other theories could be proposed as alternatives? What actually is the relevant evidence from Scripture, Tradition, and the magisterium? But such questions, though posed by the reflections of this paper, go beyond its scope.

7

THE WAYS OF GRACE OUTSIDE THE CHURCH

"No salvation outside the Church." In the older interpretation of this theological epigram, some allowance was made for the possibility that God's grace might work even outside the framework of the visible Church and its sacraments in certain instances. But this was conceived of in the manner of an exception to the ordinary law, so that, almost inevitably, little hope was held out for those living in pagan lands or outside the Church in Christian lands. In this view, the ordinary work of saving grace did not begin until the rather proximate call to baptism in the Church. But since grace alone can keep man from sinning mortally for a lengthy period of time, because of human weakness in consequence of original sin, mortal sin was thought to be the ordinary state of persons outside the visible Church; and since one dies as one lives, as a rule, there could be only grave fear as regards the salvation of the vast majority of such persons.

Such a view could hold a firmer grip upon even learned men in the Church in times when Christendom was a rather compact and homogeneous unit without a great deal of awareness of other non-Christian cultures and of world history. It also provided a strong impetus for the great missionary movements in response to contacts with alien cultures. Paradoxically, these very contacts failed to shake the theology in question; for the contacts were ordinarily not so much opportunities for mutual understanding as opportunities for European expansion in the political, military, economic, and cultural domains. When resistance to the missionaries was encountered, it could easily enough be taken as a sign of the strong influence of the devil and all his forces in such lands previously untouched by the Christian doctrine. There were those who protested against such ready interpretation in the worst possible light of all the elements of pagan culture, but the temper of the times was against them. The outcome of the "Chinese Rites" controversy is indicative here. Secular European expansionism and the missionary spirit in fact were symbiotic; and if theology of the kind we describe could stimulate this missionary spirit, it could also take a certain comfort in the way in which it so admirably fitted in even with the great secular movements of the time. There is a certain kind of theologian for whom this coherence of teaching with secular aspirations is most highly valued, and for him there should be some lesson in the rather mixed success of the missionary enterprise of the last four centuries.

The pattern for the radical denunciation of non-Christian culture can already be found in St. Paul's Epistle to the Romans, with its denunciation of the corruption of decadent Roman culture. But St. Paul did not make a universal theological statement about all human culture so much as a practical and particular statement about the culture before his eyes. Certainly, early Fathers of the Church like St. Justin Martyr and Clement of Alexandria saw "friends of the Word" and "evangelical preparation" in pagan cultures. But the first contacts between Christian teaching and the decadence of Rome had to be unfriendly and lead to conflict, for the whole Roman way of life was challenged by Christianity. Only much later could the best elements of Roman culture become assimilated into Christian culture, so much so that now we fear that we have become too Roman and Latin to achieve the full universality required of our mission to the world.

This sense of cultural limitation and fear of its consequences for the missionary Church has penetrated deeply into Christian awareness in recent years, and we are no longer so ready to resist every element of alien cultures in the alleged interest of Christian life. With greater sympathy for the diverse cultural achievements of the human race has come also some awareness of the possibilities that grace might work in secret ways in these cultures, and that the previous theological generalization concerning those outside the visible Church might not be so well-grounded after all.

Perhaps just as important in shaking this theological conviction is the growing realization of the length of man's existence on earth; it is no longer possible to make a neat and compact "Biblical history" of some six or seven thousand years of human existence – we must think in terms of hundreds of thousands and perhaps of millions of years. But in such a perspective we find it hard to think that, apart from the years since Abraham, and indeed even since then, grace has as an ordinary rule been lacking for the salvation of the vast majority of the human race. What would become of the genuine divine universal salvific will, if this were the case? It is not enough to say that God intended to save all men through Adam, and that Adam frustrated this. We have become too aware of the dignity and value of each individual human person and of the unique relation if each such person to God to be content with such an answer. We now believe that God does in some manner or other call each individual person personally to Himself, and that every adult – that is capable of free moral decision – can and must respond in some manner to this call. (This leaves aside the status of the unbaptized infants, who may not have received any proximate call to the supernatural life at all, but who in any event have some kind of call, perhaps only in the natural order, to some manner of life with God.) If good Jews of Old Testament times could be saved in virtue of the foreseen merits of Christ, and therefore really by the grace of Christ, and if Mary could be preserved from all stain even of original sin in virtue of these foreseen merits, then there is no reason why God could not in His own ways save good men of all times, both before and after Christ, who have never even heard of Him but who nevertheless seek Him in their gropings toward the plenitude of truth and of good. The great scene of the Last Judgment depicted by Christ in Matt 25, 31-46 suggests that many who did not know the Christ whom they actually were serving or rejecting will still be saved or damned because of their attitude toward Him. Always it is the grace of Christ, and always it is the Church – in which Christ lives and through which He works – that saves men of all times and all places. "No salvation outside the Church" remains true, but true on a grander scale than before; and Christ appears more clearly as He in whom all things hold together.

    A manner in which the grace of Christ can enter into human freedom, even in the very first human act, has already been seen in the earlier chapter on faith of pure intersubjectivity. And the analysis there presented can be applied not only to the very first moral act but also to any subsequent moral act of the human existent in which the very last end of all his action is put into question so that he must take a position in this matter. But if grace is present whenever there is question of the fundamental moral option, then there is no reason to suppose that it is absent at other moments, either to confirm and to deepen the choice already made or to dispose the man gradually to reverse such an option badly made. Even if God is never conceptually and propositionally apprehended and considered, even if no determinate act of faith expressed in propositions is enunciated, even if commitment here shows itself to formulating reason only as commitment in an unlimited way to certain created values, still God in His hidden reality and His graces of faith, hope, and charity, and other supernatural helps can be at stake in such a manner that the individual person really knows this obscurely in an unformulated manner even while not knowing it in any expressible fashion. He might only be able to say that the commitment he makes, and tries to keep and to follow, whatever it be, is of transcendent importance for himself and even independently of his own good; or he might not even be able to rise to this degree of formulation (we certainly would not expect much formulation as regards the fundamental option made in the first moment of genuine moral choice). Nor is this way of grace confined only to those who have great commitment to great causes, such as scholars, politicians and rulers, and religious leaders; it works also among the most ordinary of men, where the issue is "only" that of mutual regard and practical love showing itself in works. Indeed, love of neighbor is perhaps always the great test, at least in some implicit manner, at least perhaps in the radical unselfishness and readiness to follow the divine ways that could transform mere devotion to some created truth or created good as one's own final good into loving consent to and promotion of the fullness of God's plans not only for oneself but for all creation.

But let us consider this way of grace without apparent reference to the visible Church of Christ, in relation to the way of grace that is more "ordinary" for us Christians. The former way is a way in the darkness as regards conceptual and judging reason, one in which only the barest essentials of faith may be present to give only the most obscure illumination for the course of one's life. Here there is no awareness of various special means of grace given to us by God, no understanding of the favorable conditions for the expansive growth of the grace-life in us, no realization of the opportunities for merit and for the apostolate, perhaps even a conflict between many aspects of one's action and the true end to which he is committed in virtue of his fundamental option. If this conflict does not mean formal mortal sin, because of the excuse of ignorance, still the very weight of material sins and sinful habits of itself militates against the basic option and tends to prepare the way for its abandonment at a later date under the pressures of human passion and pride. Such a state of spiritual and moral being is something less than that really called for by the dignity of man as a rational being, and God does gradually lead men out of this darkness into His wonderful light, through His revelation and His Church.

But it should be noted that even for Christians the ways of grace are ordinarily marked with obscurity. Though the light of the faith and the teaching of the Church allow us to formulate for ourselves the contents of faith and standards of life, to aim at more favorable conditions for the growth of supernatural life, to minimize the possibilities of conflicts between lines of activity embarked upon even in good faith and the actual dynamism of the life of grace, still there is a certain obscurity about the actual workings of grace in us and therefore the possibility of some lack of correspondence between the formulations of conceptual and propositional reason and the actual reality within us. God knows us with a completely exhaustive knowledge, scrutinizing the inmost reality of the human heart; but we are never able fully to articulate ourselves to ourselves. If this is a source of anxiety, it should also be a source of hope; "... in his sight we set our hearts at rest. Because if our heart blames us, God is greater than our heart and knows all things. Beloved, if our heart does not condemn us, we have confidence towards God...." [1]

It is possible to achieve a sufficient conceptual articulation of one's choice of and adherence to various finite goods. But the commitment to God demanded in the life of grace is quasi-infinite. Our formulations are always finite and cannot express such a total commitment; these formulations are always compatible with a merely finite commitment. Thus our deepest moral option remains obscure and eludes our efforts to seize it in its reality – at least if this option really is the quasi-infinite commitment to God. The Christian condition then must remain radically one of faith and hope, barring some special revelation from God in a special case, until the Christian finally does actually enter into the life of vision and possession.

These things being said concerning the obscurity of the ways of grace even among Christians in the Church, it remains true that under the providence of God there has taken place in human history a progressive movement of ever more explicit formulation of the call of God to men, a formulation stimulated and guided by a series of divine in-breakings into human history all the way from the dealings of God with Adam and Eve to the teaching of Christ and of the Church with which He remains until the consummation of the world. And in response to this ever brighter and clearer illumination and more and more explicit formulation, there has been in man an ever more articulate and elaborated belief and action, culminating in the life of the Church, in which the last age of the world has come, but in which progressive development of dogma

[1] I Jn 3, 19ff.

and greater growth of moral consciousness still go on even in an accelerated manner. From the very moment of the fall of man, this new movement of human history under and in response to the continuing call of God to all men to enter into His own life has been stimulated, guided, and dominated by the grace of Christ, given to all men of all times in virtue of Christ's redemptive sacrifice at the center of temporal history. Wherever this grace works in men, it points toward Christ's sacrifice and toward His continuing presence in the Church until the end of time; it is therefore both the grace of Christ and the grace of the Church, and it has always been true that there is "no salvation outside the Church." Moreover, this grace calls for greater formulation and explicitation, and therefore for the clear and ever clearer teaching accessible to all men through the Church. It therefore moves men toward entry into the Church. We have noted above the difficulties under which grace labors when it works in darkness, and the need for a fuller illumination which is inherent in the dignity of man as a rational being. But grace working in the light, and the fuller illumination which man needs, are found precisely in the Church in which Christ continues to teach and to save.

Yet if we insist on the need for the Church to illuminate the workings of divine grace by its preaching of the revealed word of God, one immediately wonders why the Church did not appear earlier in human history, why Christ did not come to teach men much earlier. The Fathers and Doctors of the Church have met such questions by pointing to a divine pedagogy, gradually leading men to an awareness of their radical misery and need, so that the divine grace might be better received by men. Before grace working in the dark might become grace working in the light, men had to be brought from the vague awareness of inadequacy that has troubled all men to a more explicit recognition of the vanity of all things under the sun and the profound need of the human heart for the coming of the Kingdom of God. But the Word was there all along, illuminating every man that has come into this world in an obscure manner at least sufficient for the free acceptance or refusal of God and of His grace.

But the movement of human history under God toward God through the Church has not ceased with the actual coming of the Church. The preaching of the word committed to the Church must take time, and during all this time the work of divine preparation of the nations to receive the light of faith continues even as it did before the coming of Christ. Even now, in the midst of the final stage of temporal history, there are diverse degrees of approach to the fullness of the light in the diverse cultures, philosophies, and religions of mankind. Negatively, one can of course say that all such merely human achievements fall short, *are not* the divinely appointed spiritual and temporal instrument for the salvation of men. But positively, each of them is more or less conducive to the working of grace that actually goes on in and through them, however mysteriously. The moral philosophy of Confucius and Lao Tze, the thought of Plato and of Aristotle and Plotinus, the devotion to the one God of Mohammed, the Roman sense of justice and the Soviet awareness of the values of social man, all such human illumination and moral triumph is only human in itself; and yet through it – as through the obscure presentation of the *bonum morale honestum* at the first moment of human moral choice – grace can work and indeed does, more easily, with fewer obstacles, than in the total absence of any moral ideals or in an atmosphere of utter indifference to the objective truth of things.

Similar comments may be made in regard to even post-Christian culture, which to a great extent still lives on something of the treasury of – now-secularized – Christian truth. But they must be made more strongly about separated Christian communities; here, since something of the institutional forms of the Church remains – and indeed in many cases very much of these forms – and also a great deal at least of the actually formulated belief of the Church, we cannot simply speak of grace working in darkness. Rather, there is a high degree of illumination and the use even of the institutional forms of such communities as a means for the communication of the life of grace. Despite historical wounds both to unity and to faith, such separated Christian communities do in some manner pertain to the Church and represent diverse degrees of approach to the fullness of the light as well as, at least as well as, diverse degrees of separation from it. What is past is past, and the judgment of final responsibility for the breaking of unity in doctrine and in life can be left to God. In our age there is much evidence that the Spirit again is drawing us back toward the unity we long for.

But it is quite possible that human cultural achievements may also hinder the work of grace in men, to the extent that we can rest content in them with a kind of complacent pride that is not really open to the call of God and to the coming of the Kingdom. Still more is this so when there is question of the confrontation of grace working in the light in the Church with the various human cultures and non-Christian religions, and even with the separated Christian communities. It is one thing to accede to the obscure pull of grace at the heart in darkness or in a dimmer light, and another thing to face the apparent opposition between so many of one's formulated ideals and convictions and the formulated teaching of the Church. Some of this cannot be avoided; for in merely human culture there is always a residue, more or less, of human error, human passion, and human pride. But a great deal of conflict can be avoided or diminished if Christian teaching is presented, not in the trappings of an alien, but still very human, culture, but rather as adapted to the new cultural system. We would like to show Indians that the true values of Hinduism are in no way destroyed, but rather more firmly guaranteed, when they are viewed under the light of Christian wisdom. So also with other non-Christian cultures and their values, but also as regards the thought and values of the non-Christians even within our own pluralistic society. We ourselves can become very much attached to the merely human cultural system and its values in which Christian life and thought has become incarnated for ourselves, so that the Christian message is offered by us to the world precisely as incarnated in our particular culture. But in this case it is not so much the alien cultural system which is the obstacle as our own manner of presenting the supra-cultural Christian message on our own terms. And yet all this is not to say that a universal theological and philosophical synthesis is impossible; we must only insist that such a synthesis must transcend a particular cultural context, in a manner analogous to that in which modern natural science has succeeded in doing, by a fuller recognition of the richness of the multi-dimensionality and analogicity of being and knowledge and affective life in man. Such a fully scientific synthetic view would be able to recognize the possibility and value of radically non-scientific, poetically or mystically orientated expressions of religious truth, and of approaches to religion that are more moral and pragmatic than speculative. Indeed, not only is such a scientific philosophical and theological synthesis not impossible, but it is even a condition for the genuine transcendence of the particular Western cultural context in which Christian life and thought have had their principal incarnation. Cultural relativists will insist that such an enterprise is impossible, that there is simply no possible transcendence of cultural context, that cultures are totally disparate and that consequently genuine communication is rendered impossible. But the Church has never thought this, and indeed the divine command to teach all nations the message of Christ would be absurd if it were so. Moreover, Christian philosophers maintain that a "perennial philosophy" does exist and can be used by faith and theology in the elaboration of such a Christian synthesis. But such philosophy and such a synthesis could not be adequately achieved within the Western cultural context alone; for the richness of being transcends such a particular culturally conditioned understanding, and indeed the very existence of other modes of understanding in other cultures is a clear testimony to the limitations of our own view. If we insist that Thomism, as Maritain says, bears with it the progress of philosophy, this does not refer to an already achieved work of the Middle Ages but rather to a living and organically growing metaphysical and theological synthesis ever open to assimilate new manifestations of the rich potentialities of the human spirit in its communion with being. Such a Thomism could assist greatly the missionary enterprise of the Church and perhaps is even a necessary instrument for which we must wait, even while exerting all possible efforts without it. The cultural adaptation which we require for the presentation of the Christian message could hardly be fully achieved in any satisfactory manner without such a new and fuller Christian synthesis which would transcend all particular cultures even while it does justice to the variagated riches of each – but this could hardly come to pass without an utter openness at the level of insight and a tremendous expansion at the level of systematic conceptualization in the perennial Christian philosophy.

In the light of all the foregoing remarks concerning the ways of grace outside the Church, it seems opportune to add a few more regarding two aspects of the missionary problem of the Church. The first is a certain frustration at the slow pace of missionary progress in recent times, further aggravated by the seeming collapse of so much of the work done as a result of recent anti-colonialist and therefore anti-Western and even anti-Christian reactions to Western expansionism. The second is a certain anxious questioning of the value of the whole missionary effort, prompted by the new theological trend to see the working of grace among all men, even where the message of the Church has never been preached. Some wonder whether it would not be better to leave things as they are and not provoke conflicts and tensions, with confidence that God will see that every man capable of moral decision will have his chance to accept or to reject the grace of God. But against this there is the command of the Lord to teach all nations.

Both of these problems arise in great part from some failure to consider deeply enough the divine ways in the operation of grace. The slowness and very partial success of the missionary work of the Church in Asia and Africa, and among large masses in our own pluralistic society, itself suggests that perhaps we are doing something wrongly. The earlier justification and stimulus for missionary activity rested on the conviction that the pagan world was thoroughly alienated from God; too many Christians, even very holy men, failed to recognize the light illumining *all* men present everywhere in varying degrees. Instead of appealing to the most enlightened elements of pagan culture as a natural base on which grace could build, many missionaries seemed to think it necessary to replace the indigenous culture by a foreign transplant, so that in order to become a Christian one had to become less an Indian or African and more a European. It was a very human mistake for ordinary men who could hardly even think of the Christian teaching except in the Western terms in which they had learned it. We know a little better now, and are perhaps a little humbler. But if much of this seems commonplace enough in an age in which Paul VI goes to India and sits down to discuss matters with non-Christian religious leaders, still it will take time for the new consciousness of the true universality not only of the divine call but also of the actual operations of grace in obscurity as well as in the light to penetrate into the ordinary viewpoint of many missionaries – who after all are at heart still Westerners even after they learn Hindi or African folklore.

But some missionaries are actually asking whether the whole missionary effort is really so important after all, if grace is already present before their arrival. An implicit presupposition of such questioning would seem to be that justice is satisfied as long as everybody has his chance for salvation, in one manner or another. But, even setting aside the problem of the unbaptized infants who die in that state, one must point out that as regards the divine call and the dispensation of grace, justice is never the primary consideration; for our salvation is first a gift of love, which desires for us not only a minimal degree of life but that we may have it more abundantly. True, the Word works in the darkness as well as in the light; but in fact God would call all men to clearer light, and so he tells us to preach the Gospel everywhere. If that is not enough for us, we can ask whether we are really at one with God's designs as opposed to our own private opinions and inclinations. It is as though some almost want to believe that God's hands are, or should be, tied without their help.

There is no salvation outside the Church, for the grace of all men is the grace of Christ and of the Church of which He is the Head. But who has ever maintained that all the ways of the Spirit, who breathes where He will, should be evident and open to our view? And if grace works in the dark in pagan lands long before we bring to them the light of Christ's teaching, why should this be in any way a scandal to some and not rather a source of immense consolation that the hand of the Lord is not shortened?

8

THE BASIC MORAL OPTION AND THE
AMBIENCE OF GRACE

The existence and nature of the basic moral option in man has already come to our notice in the discussion of radical openness as a condition for philosophizing thought, in the notion of a faith of pure intersubjectivity, and in the essay on "The Ways of Grace Outside the Church." The necessarily supernatural character of this option, even at the beginning of fully moral life, was seen in "The Faith of Pure Intersubjectivity." But it still remains for us to investigate more adequately the inner structure and dynamism of moral life as grounding, disposing for, and flowing from this basic option. Since charity and the supernatural life are indeed always at stake in this option, since therefore preparation for it, and its consequences as well, are relevant to the supernatural order of grace at every point, such an investigation of the option is at once also an inquiry into the ambience of grace in the moral life of every human being.

It was asserted earlier that such a basic moral option, the assumption of a freely chosen and fundamental attitude toward the ultimate good of human life, is demanded at the very outset of human moral life by the very metaphysics of finality. This was said notwithstanding the apparent absence of introspective psychological evidence of such an option in the child. In fact, the option was located at a level of human consciousness that in principle excluded adequate conceptual and propositional formulation, and did not require any explicit formulation at all, however inadequate this might be. It is good now to examine more carefully both the ground of necessity for this option and also the ground of its intrinsic obscurity in relation to formulating reason. The fuller understanding of these aspects of the option will in turn permit a better grasp of many of its supernatural aspects and implications.

How could a finite good terminate the infinite appetite of the human will for good? From the very outset, the activity of the will is directed toward the unrestricted good. If the first good-in-view is only the good of the agent himself, then it is this good that he desires in an unrestricted manner. And this desire is operative from the very beginning of human cognitive and appetitive life, however obscurely and non-reflectively. In man as he concretely exists this obscure desire is already such a disordered, self-centered love unless it be rectified by the grace of baptism or by some uncovenanted mercy of God. Were man in the state of original justice it would be otherwise, but what is done is done. Yet there is still a kind of quasi-innocence about such a disordered, self-centered childish desire, for the child "knows no better."

But it cannot remain so. Soon enough the child must become aware that completely unfettered self-will comes into conflict with another kind of good hitherto unseen – the moral good. At this point the moral good is still only one finite good among others, more or less attractive in view of many factors. The moral good itself, therefore, is seen as a good for the agent; the moral norm is only a relative norm in view of a certain good for the agent. At this point one can speak of knowing good from evil and of the use of moral reason, but this is so only in a qualified sense. The moral good is here only a certain relative "fittingness" with perhaps a certain relative sanction imposed by parental attitudes and physical means of punishment, and by the attitudes and means of others with whom the child must deal. But the crucial moment of the first moral choice in the full and proper sense, spoken of by St. Thomas in I–II, 89, 6, has not yet arrived.

This moment can only come when the moral good is seen as more than a relative and finite good of the agent. When its transcendent and absolute character as a good and as a norm come into view, however obscurely and on however minor an occasion, then one has reached the true use of moral reason, simply so called. At this moment, however small be the matter at stake at the level of formulated consciousness, a much larger, quasi-infinite issue is also at stake at a deeper level of unformulated consciousness. And the ground of possibility for the properly moral (in the full and adequate sense) resolution of the lesser issue is in some resolution, "final" at least for now, of the quasi-infinite question of that which one makes to be the freely chosen final goal of all his human choices.

There are then two first moments of moral choice and two uses of moral reason. But it is only the second that both permits and requires a basic option. This occurs when the person is, at least in his obscure depths, in possession of his total self and capable of disposing of himself in a free manner. Previous "moral" choices are only dispositions which can condition the exercise of the all-important option. More will be said of such conditioning for the basic option later on. And yet it must be emphasized that the basic option itself takes place at a level deeper than that of formulating consciousness and requires no explicit formulation at all, even as merely concomitant and dispositive. Indeed, one could even find explicit formulations of the issue of the basic option without a real option taking place at all at a deeper level of the person, as in some children who may be able to repeat the catechetical formulae, and perhaps even have a kind of purely cognitive grasp of them without yet seizing their valuative significance.

All this means that the actual moment of genuine moral option is necessarily very ambiguous, and may admit of wide variation in dependence on diverse factors such as personal, spontaneous growth, parental influence, formal education, etc. It could well be that one child might be able to take a moral stand at a very early age while another might perhaps await adolescense. There would, of course, be a certain appearance of morality and of moral choice before the basic option, an appearance which could well be misunderstood as meaning a moral life in the formal sense. But no true sin against a transcendent and absolute norm of morality is possible until the issue of transcendent morality is itself raised in at least an implicit and unformulated manner. Finite relative qualified claims of transcendence are not in themselves enough to specify simply moral reason and bring it into play, until they are set into the context and against the background of the infinite and absolute claim of the unqualified moral good transcending any other good of the particular agent. At this point, one could make a distinction between grave and slight sins; before this point, no such distinction could be made since the real notion of sin could not yet arise.

Thus "to know right from wrong" and "to have the use of moral reason" are not unequivocal in their meaning, and the date at which such expressions can be applied in their proper and full sense is ambiguous. Still, this date seems at all events to be early enough in the life of a normal human being, earlier in those educated in moral or religious matters from the earliest possible date, later in those who lack such education, but always allowing for wide diversity for exceptional cases. Clearly, the problem of early moral education is much more than one of imparting moral formulae and assuring their external observance. More than this is required to bring one to the most favorable conditions for the proper exercise of the basic moral option on which so much else depends.

Since the basic moral option is an act of the will, it is a conscious act itself and also presupposes some prior intellectual conscious act. But in order to discuss the modes of consciousness found here, it is first necessary to make a few remarks about some generic modes of knowing, about the distinction between preformulated and formulated intellectual knowledge. Logical analysis occupies itself with formulated intellectual knowledge: concepts, propositions, discursive structures. But prior to such formulations there is intuitive, preformulated intellection; and formulation could not take place except in dependence upon this prior mode of intellection. It is true that the finite intellect, by its intrinsic dynamism, moves toward formulation: finite intellectual knowing, as finite, achieves its own, relative, perfection in the clarity and distinctness of formulation. But at the level of preformulated intellection, there is already a distinction between an objectifying mode, which of itself and directly stimulates and leads to objective formulations in terms of conceptualization, and a non-objectifying mode, which leads to the partially non-objectifying formulation of judgment or to indirect, "constructual" formulations, which do not so much express the given contents of the preformulated non-objectifying intellection as merely designate, signify, point to it.

Primary moral knowing is a preformulated non-objectiying intellection arising in virtue of the inclinations and connaturalities, natural and acquired, of the existential subject. This is so in the knowledge of natural law, in more particular moral knowledge in which acquired tendencies of virtue or vice themselves guide the intellect and will toward the ultimate practical decision, and in the final, intuitive prudential perception of what is a fitting course of action in view of all the concrete circumstances. In all these domains, formulation is secondary; especially in the prudential domain it is inadequate, though this is also true in the other domains. The ultimate prudential judgment of what is finally to be done receives its adequate formulation only in the moral act itself, in a manner analogous to that in which the creative intuition of the artist receives its adequate formulation only in the work of art itself. Yet if explicit intervening formulations are unnecessary in the dynamism of the moral act, still they are possible and indeed are necessary for a reflective process of deliberation. Here the range of moral choices must receive formulation as a set of practical enuntiables, one of which is eventually to be selected. And yet the final decision depends upon the acceptance of a certain prudential way of viewing things as finally *the* way for this particular agent to view things

BASIC MORAL OPTION AND AMBIENCE OF GRACE 199

in this case, and this prudential intuition escapes adequate formulation. But if this prudential intuition itself escapes formulation, still it is possible to formulate the actual course of action to be followed, prior to the activity itself, and certainly in and after the activity. This final formulation is not so important, since it is the conscious performance of the act that matters; and yet it can bring a greater clarity, deliberateness, and consent to what one does. So too, at the more generic levels of moral knowing, the area of more or less general moral principles, formulation is most useful in order to bring greater clarity, deliberateness, and therefore a fuller degree of freedom, to the process of moral choice.

Analogous to primary moral knowing, the actual act of moral choice, an act of the will, is itself known in a preformulated, non-objectifying intellection arising in virtue of the spiritual reflexivity and auto-transparency, therefore consciousness, of the acts of the will. Again, actual formulation is secondary, although ordinarily possible.

When we return to the basic moral option, we can observe a certain difference between it and a moral choice subsidiary to it. While the fact of the basic option, as a moral act in the human will, is in principle formulable, its actual object, the good upon which one settles as *the* good for himself, eludes immediate formulation even in principle. For commitment in the basic option is a quasi-infinite commitment to a good regarded as infinite for oneself. Such a good, viewed in such a manner, necessarily eludes and transcends all finite formulations and therefore escapes our reflective view, even while it is consciously chosen in genuine freedom. It is true that one can come to a very solid conjecture, even a kind of "practical" certitude (which is not, however, true certitude) about the nature of one's option by examining closely the pattern of one's moral acts, which does truly depend upon the basic moral option. And yet there are many counterfeits of true morality which are difficult enough to distinguish from the genuine moral good in the supernatural order. It is also true that while commitment to the substantial moral good and to God is quasi-infinite in the manner described, it is not the same with commitment to some finite good which excludes God and the substantial moral good. Here at least one might think that the object of a basic option against God and for some creature would be accessible to formulating intellection and to our reflective view. But while this creature which is in fact the object of such a disordered basic option is in fact knowable as the object of moral commitment, and as the object of a moral commitment which seemingly excludes the possibility of a good basic option, still the quasi-infinite depth of the basic option itself remains obscure. If one does here often enough have the possibility of clear certitude about his state of alienation from God, this is not because he is immediately capable of formulating his basic option as such but rather because he knows "from outside" in his knowledge of choosing some finite good that is incompatible with a good moral option for God and the substantial totality of the moral order. And yet even here there is ample opportunity in many cases for deceptiveness, since there seem to be cases, perhaps quite frequent, in which a pseudo-God and a pseudo-morality are set aside in the interest of commitment to a true moral good and even to the substantial totality of the moral order, and therefore even to God Himself.

The above remarks about our knowledge of the basic moral option accord well enough with the lack of testimony about it from those reaching the use of moral reason, with the testimony of St. Paul that he did not know whether he was worthy of love or hatred, with the conclusions of theologians concerning our lack of full certitude regarding the possession of the state of sanctifying grace, with the growing view that the state of contrition, and therefore of justification and charity, is produced by the sacrament of penance in those who approach this sacrament with only attrition – even though there be no reflectively formulable psychological change observable. Such a notion of grace and of alienation from God in terms of the basic moral option, made with charity or in the rejection of this grace, enables us better to understand the distinction between "sin" as a general state of aversion from God and "sin" as a particular act contrary to the moral order, and how the former is itself already a principle of lawlessness productive of still further particular sins. For the option stabilizes one's whole mode of action in a pattern fundamentally centered on God and His moral order, or on the self and self-will which must come again and again in conflict with the divine order.

Such fundamental, radical sin is the primary analogate to which particular sin has a necessary reference, as either a disposition, cause, or consequence. One can hardly speak of this radical sin in the same terms as one does about particular sins. We speak of confessing sins according to species and number; we examine our conscience to note particular sins and habits of sin; we lament our "sins." But the basic option goes beyond such particularities: we do not confess the basic option; our conscience does not tell us directly of this option but only of acts and patterns of acts which lead us to a conviction of sin or, on the other hand, to a practical certitude or strong conjecture about the good or bad option we have made; we hope that despite our sins we are not now in the state of sin.

Every human moral act in the proper sense refers in some manner to one's freely adopted goal and basic option. Each such particular act either is in accord with, and in some manner strengthening, one's basic option, or not in accord with this option and preparing the way for a new basic option, or itself already necessarily requiring and manifesting such a change in the basic option. Since the issue of the basic option is always a supernatural one, the issue of openness to and acceptance of the gift of supernatural life, every particular moral choice in any domain whatsoever of human activity has some relation to the supernatural order. Either such a choice is in accordance with a good option and in some degree confirming this option, or it is not in accordance with one's good option and thus in some degree disposes one toward rejection of the supernatural, or it is in accordance with a bad option and confirms one in his rejection of the supernatural, or it is not in accordance with a bad option and disposes one toward an eventual acceptance of supernatural life. One might perhaps suggest that the entire possibility of a change from one bad option to another bad option had been overlooked. But in fact the bad option is fundamentally one in any case; it is fundamentally a choice that one's own self will should be the norm of what one wants. This bad option may of course have a vast range of modalities, in so far as diverse persons could center their affections upon diverse finite goods, and move about between them in the course of life; but fundamentally it is self and self-will that is the really ultimate good chosen in any case – one chooses to try to satisfy the quasi-infinite appetite of self-will in his own ways, as a law unto himself.

Every concrete moral choice of man thus moves him either toward or away from his supernatural end in some manner, at least in the line of disposition. At any moment when the basic option itself is in question, there is at least the offer of substantially supernatural grace; this same must be said for every subsequent moment of however particular moral choices by one who has made a good basic option under grace. In those who have not yet made a good option, or who have made a bad option, any positive disposition, whatever form it take, toward a good option is also substantially supernatural since it is a disposition for a supernatural option. Consequently, any opportunity for a moral choice which would constitute such a disposition must itself be called a supernatural grace in the line of supernatural finality and Providence.

But we must ask what such a disposition toward a good supernatural option might in fact be. There could of course be no merely natural moral choice which would constitute a positive disposition for the supernatural option in charity. Such an option is itself an escape from the entire domain of the merely natural in acceptance of radically supernatural life which transcends everything in the natural order. And yet, under the direction of supernatural Providence, one can be led to a series of moral choices which in fact removes various obstacles to a good option in the supernatural love of God. Such a process of negative disposition would consist in detachment, by whatever means, from some finite goods and some forms of self-will that would preclude even a merely natural opening to God, a recognition of a good and an authority greater than oneself, an acceptance of rather than a rebellion at the divine order of things here below. This kind of openness is not a positive but is a negative openness to the supernatural; it is already a gift of God leading one toward acceptance of His supernatural love. And if, even outside the limits of the visible Church and its sacramental system and profession of faith, one should finally come to embrace the moral good in a truly unqualified manner, however implicitly, he would in fact have already accepted also the divine offer of supernatural life as known in the faith of pure intersubjectivity. For such an embracing of the moral good is in fact acceptance of it as salvific and delivering us from the limitations of our condition, and such a salvific moral good is in reality the good of the supernatural order of grace and finally of the saving God. These last points of course refer us back to the earlier essay on the faith of pure intersubjectivity.

But the above remarks concerning moral acts which dispose one for a good supernatural option do not exhaust the possibilities in the line of disposition. In one who already has faith (and perhaps hope as well), but is without charity, something more than merely negative disposition is possible in the line of acts inspired by such faith and hope. Such acts would be only modally and not substantially supernatural themselves, but they can dispose one for justification in the manner indicated in Trent's decree on justification. And of course the very acts of such supernatural faith and hope themselves are more than just modally supernatural and exercise a very positive role in disposing one for the act of charity as a basic option. One could inquire further also into the more remote dispositions for charity in the first movements toward faith itself, but this has been treated in the long essay on the act of faith.

Such dispositive acts favorable to a good basic option of charity are important not only for those who must come to repentance for sin but also for those coming to the first use of moral reason in the proper sense, those who must either for the first time consciously ratify their previous reception of the gift of grace and charity in baptism and those who, not having been baptized, must now begin their fully human moral life by assuming some fundamental attitude, freely chosen, toward the transcendent and absolute moral good. The most crucial problem in the moral education of the very young is the problem of leading them to the most favorable state in which to exercise their basic option in the right manner. This means that moral discipline for them must be much more than the inculcation of submission to some exterior norm of action. Law and norm and command must be presented in a manner which is more likely to prompt genuine interior assent and consent rather than in a manner which might just as well provoke at least interior rebellion. Such considerations could never assure that the option be good, just as ignoring them could not assure that the basic option be bad; this option is after all radically free. But the question of dispositions and favorable conditions and of what is of primary importance is no matter of indifference; for we are our brothers' keepers, and especially of the very young. Thus arises the entire question of the moral dimension, the affective dimension of Christian catechetics – but this question would take us far beyond the scope of this essay. It is enough here merely to note the importance of a careful analysis of the negatively and positively disposing and preparatory factors for the basic option of charity, as applied even to the very young, in order to develop a catechetical pedagogy best suited to lead the very young not just to the beginnings of understanding of the faith but also to the solid beginning of living in supernatural love.

In view of the above considerations some general principles can be stated regarding the ambience of grace in the world, the extent of its presence in the life of every human being. Could we say that "all is grace," and mean by this supernatural grace leading men on to share in the divine life itself? Given our analysis of the basic moral option as necessarily supernatural and given the relation, dispositive or consequential, of every particular moral choice to this basic option, it can be said that every human moral act in the proper sense either takes place in virtue of some kind of grace or involves a proximate or remotely prior rejection of grace. A good, therefore grace-inspired basic option carries with it the assurance of at least the offer of elevating grace for subsequent particular acts, to say nothing of the helping graces of the supernatural providence with which God cares for His adopted children. A bad basic option, no doubt, forfeits in ordinary cases something of this helping grace and prevents the offer of elevating grace until the possibility of a new basic option is immediately present. And yet even for men who have made such a bad option God still has a supernatural providence which can lead them by helping graces, negatively or even positively dispositive, to a new opportunity for a good option through repentance. The very possibility and necessity of repeated moral choices in particular matters, the advent of reflective moments in which one realizes that all is not well with him or asks himself what it is he *really* wants, the changeability of the human state which enables a man to see in a different light as time goes on, all these are elements of the divine economy of mercy and of disposition for repentance. Even the merely negative disposition for new supernatural life, which comes from the attempt to respect natural moral values, is already a kind of openness to a God who is communicative and will communicate His supernatural life to those who will accept it. Whatever induces such a genuine moral attitude in man is already a modally supernatural grace in the present order of supernatural finality and providence in which man exists, a grace that at least negatively disposes the recipient for the option of supernatural charity. And of course the role of positive dispositions – faith, hope, acts inspired by faith and hope, etc. – in this economy of mercy and repentance is so much the greater by way of opening the sinner to the acceptance of divine life in a new basic option of charity. And yet it still remains possible that the result of such repeated offers and approaches by God will be repeated rejection by the sinner and a greater and greater hardening in sin. In any event, while our reflections prompt us to acknowledge a very wide ambience of grace in the world, both inside and outside the visible Church of Christ, they also warn us that to say "all is grace" is to say too much, or too little unless there be added some finely nuanced qualifications.

Two general problems remain to be considered in the light of this analysis of the basic moral option and of the consequent wide ambience of supernatural grace. The first concerns the relation of the basic option to particular moral acts. It is a commonplace of moral theology that the three determinants of the morality of a particular act are the immediate object, the end of the act, and its circumstances. But it would seem that a bad basic option must assure the immorality of any subsequent particular moral acts, by reason of the bad end, until the basic option itself is reversed. But this is to say that unbelievers and those in the state of sin are simply incapable of good moral acts at all and can only sin, that they cannot dispose themselves in any manner in their particular acts for an eventual change in the basic option itself, that as a consequence there is nothing for them but to sink ever more deeply into sin until God should in some manner lift them out without any cooperation on their part whatsoever. The whole notion of acts preparatory to justification, so insisted upon at Trent, would have to be abandoned, as would the condemnation of Baius.

It is necessary here to understand that the three determinants of the moral act are the determinants of its "substantial" and objective morality as evaluated in the light of directly or indirectly objectifying knowledge. The end in question is the end that is known to objectifying and formulating knowledge, not that end which is the concern of the intrinsically obscure basic option. Our particular moral acts, knowable at the objectifying and formulating level, are consequences of and dispositions for the basic option, carrying out, intensifying, weakening, changing our basic commitment; but their substantial and objective morality is independent of the option itself, since this substantial and objective morality of necessity must be determined and evaluated in the light of a knowledge that is at least in principle and indirectly formulable, while the end in question in the basic option itself necessarily eludes this kind of knowledge.

It is still possible to distinguish between the substantial, objective goodness of the moral act – which is independent of one's basic option – and the simple goodness of the moral act – which is dependent also upon the basic option itself. Simply good would be a substantially good moral act carried out under a good basic option. Simply bad would be a substantially bad moral act carried out under a bad moral option. Such a bad act could of course be either gravely or slightly so. But there would also be the possibility of acts that are (slightly) bad, but under a good basic option – neither simply good nor simply bad, and in fact venial sins. So also there could be substantially good acts performed under a bad basic option – neither simply good nor simply bad, but not sins at all in the sense in which the term "sin" is applied to particular moral acts. Both venial sins in the good man and such acts (good in themselves) in the bad man could be classified as deficient acts; or this latter term could be reserved for such substantially good acts under a bad option, while venial sins in the just man could be set into the category of bad acts, though not simply so. The precise terminology is not all-important; what is important is to see that something more than the simple categories of "morally good" and "morally bad" is necessary when moral acts are considered not only in relation to the ordinary three determinants of substantial morality but also in relation to the basic option.

The second problem is raised by our consideration of the ambience of grace in the light of our analysis of the basic moral option. We have found ample room for divine grace to work in the moral life of man, whether he be inside or outside the visible Church of Christ. The same question that occurred in the preceding essay arises once again – why should there have also been given a formulated revelation and a teaching Church at all? Grace could have worked in such secret ways through all the history of the world. Such an economy of salvation would have been possible, and perhaps might even exist on another world. But the fittingness and value of formulated revelation and the visible teaching Church have been pointed out in the preceding essay. Why then do we raise the problem again? In our human way of viewing things the Church appears as an interruption, a break, a radically new phase in the current of history. And so it is; for with it continues the eschatological time in which the grace of Christ works in a kind of light rather than in the darkness. This time began with Christ's own Passion, Death, Resurrection, and Ascension, and continues with the Church as with the visible prolongation of Christ's being in the world until the end of time. From this point of view, the Church is a kind of island of divine inbreaking in the world, to which all men must come unless they would be excluded from the economy of salvation. But there is another way of viewing the Church. She is, has been, and will be the center, source, and goal of all human entry into the divine ways on earth at all times and places. She is not an island in the midst of mankind but a continent in which all men of all times have met the grace of Christ. In coming to the Church, men do not come to a new economy of salvation but enter more fully into one which has always been with them, through which the grace of Christ has always been offered to all men. In this perspective the Church and the formulated divine revelation which it teaches do not appear as something foreign to the previous course of history but as the breaking out into the open of the force which has been all along secretly activating historical man and moving him toward his supra-historical fulfillment, the force which had already manifested itself in progressively clearer ways to men before Christ and which finally unveiled itself (to faith) in the coming of

Christ and of His Spirit. It is from this perspective that the Church can finally appear at home in the world and call for a welcome from the world as from her own, and that divine election can be seen not as a gathering that is just as much an exclusion but rather as a means to call all through a few in the course of salvation-history.

LITURGY AND THE SPIRIT OF MAN

The phenomena of liturgical and sacramental life can only puzzle the uninformed unbeliever. A series of sensible signs reminiscent of long-dead religions, men bent in adoration before what appears to be bread and wine, sprinklings of water, repetition of verbal formulae crystallized for centuries even if now at last translated into modern languages, solemn gestures and movements of various kinds, hymns and chants, incense, and all the other elements of liturgical worship seem curiously out of place in our everyday modern world. And indeed, they are out of place in a world which has lost the sense of the sacred and the holy at the heart of reality, which sees only a world of things to be used for the better well-being of an entirely autonomous man, which is no longer aware of the all-penetrating and all-powerful presence of God who sustains us and all that is in being at every moment.

Faith sees liturgical and sacramental life as an encounter with the mystery of God and of His grace, a mystery which utterly transcends the sensible signs and may therefore be said to be veiled by these signs, but at the same time a mystery which is manifested – but only to faith – through these same signs. God has freely chosen so to meet men, so to give His favor and His gifts, through an economy that is at once visible and invisible, evident and mysterious. And yet, though God could have arranged otherwise for His coming down to men and raising men up to Himself, we know that, since divine wisdom has so ordered things, this present economy is eminently wise and fitting.

It is the privilege of the theologian to contemplate this divine plan and to see something of its meaning and of its wisdom. The purpose of this essay is to consider some aspects of the harmony of liturgical life with the nature and existential reality of man, and some of the demands made upon us by this life.

Man rises above the other living creatures of the world above all in virtue of his openness to the spiritual world of the true, the good, and the beautiful, and to the presence of God. But although he is capable of sharing in the goods of the angels, he is still a little less than the angels. Openness to the spiritual in man means not clear vision but the ability to understand something of the existence and nature of invisible realities in virtue of the understanding of visible and sensible things. Even if there can be something of an experiential understanding of spiritual reality (and this is more than only possible), still this cannot be rightly appreciated for what it is without the use of ideas and judgments based ultimately on our sensible contact with the material world.

Indeed, we are not only dependent upon sense experience as the ultimate basis for all formulated understanding; we are also dependent upon the life of the senses and of the imagination in this very formulation. For we are not pure spirits but spirits incarnate in matter. Consequently, our thought itself must in some manner incarnate itself in matter – in material symbols, such as those of language or of the arts, and even in practical action in space and time. Every act of intellect and will, no matter how exalted its object or its mode, involves at least a stirring in the sense life of man and perhaps also a stirring in the exterior world. And this influence is reciprocal; if spiritual acts carry with them a stirring of the material world, it is also true that matter exercises an influence upon spirit, by providing an object of knowledge and love, but also by providing favorable or unfavorable conditions for the life of the spirit to flourish. To deny to someone all the opportunities for symbolic expression is also to assure an impoverished life of the spirit, while to expand these opportunities through education and favorable environment is at least to open the door for expansion of spiritual life.

So far we have been considering the natural being of man as a composite of matter and spirit. Existentially he is more than this, by the grace of God. A new object and a new mode of understanding and love enters his spiritual life as a gift from God. But here too, God respects the incarnate character of the human spirit and bestows His gifts in an appropriate manner. The life of faith employs, for its own higher ends, the sense-derived ideas and judgments of the human intellect, and strives to incarnate itself ever more fully in symbolic expressions of language and art and in practical action. Revelation itself makes use of the humble instruments of human language, human actions, and the material world, even to the point that God Himself becomes man in order to communicate the fullness of revelation to us. From this point of view, one may say that the life of faith has been grafted onto human nature in a manner connatural to that nature.

There are at once two connaturalities in the life of faith: a divine connaturality to divine things as regards the object of this life, and a human connaturality as regards the mode in which this life is to be lived by men. This latter has still other aspects.

If the fullness of revelation is given in the words and concepts of human language and human thought by a divine person become incarnate in human nature, this same Incarnate Word has instituted visible sacraments as efficacious signs of the giving of divine grace and a sacrifice mystically renewed under visible signs. Not only faith but also sanctifying grace and charity are communicated to us in ways to be manifested by visible signs. So also, Our Lord has also instituted visible government as a visible sign of His own authority and will.

A consideration of this very last point reveals still another mode in which the divine life is given to men in a manner connatural to human nature. Human nature makes each of us more than an individual; it includes within itself a demand for community, communication, and communion. No one of us can live alone or for himself alone; our lives and our destinies are mutually intertwined. So it is also in the life of grace. The most evident visible sign of our unity in the life of grace is the visible unity of the Church, in which the faith is visibly professed and grace infused through visible sacraments to the community of believers. And behind this visible unity is the vital, mystical unity of the Mystical Body of Christ.

But if we come to God in the Church not simply as individuals but as members of the Mystical Body, then it is for us under the guidance of the Church to manifest this communal aspect of our divine life in our worship of God, in our prayer of adoration, thanksgiving, petition, and satisfaction. This manifestation is above all to be found in the liturgy of the Church, the sign at once of our communal offering and of the descent of the Spirit and His gifts to those who are one in Christ, as well as of the coming of Christ to those who are gathered together in His name.

Through the liturgy we enter together into the mysterious presence of God, a presence simultaneously hidden under sensible phenomena and revealed through these phenomena to faith. Through the liturgy our hidden life of faith finds manifestation in public praise, public thanksgiving, public petition, and public satisfaction. Through the liturgy the invisible gifts of God are given to us hidden under sensible signs and yet revealed through these sensible signs to faith. Through the liturgy human language, human art, human action, all are used at once both to express and to foster the divine life in us.

But if the liturgy is so connatural to man that practically all cultures have evolved something similar to it, from primitive man down to modern man – whether its object be the worship of God or gods or science or the Leader – we could not of ourselves invoke, conjure up, magically produce, or enter into the supernatural presence of the gracious God. God Himself must mark out the way and reveal His dispensation, His economy of grace and salvation, whether He choose to do this as He did in the ages before the coming of Christ, or through the revelation of the Incarnate Word, or through the further action of the Church to which He has given the power to bind and to loose. The first suppositions of genuine liturgical life, then, are receptive faith and active obedience, faithful listening and faithful response to the voice and call of God.

But even after the reception of the pattern of liturgical life and the determination to follow it, there is still no question of an automatic or magical procedure. For the grace of the sacraments and of the liturgical sacrifice is a grace that comes only to faith, a faith which sees more than the sensible phenomena, a faith which perceives the sign-value of these phenomena in order to enter through them into the presence of the divine mystery itself. The mere letter of the liturgy of itself does nothing at all; that grace be given even *ex opere operato* demands more than mere incantation and blind ritual performance. (Even the baptism of an infant by a non-believer demands a minimum intention on the part of the non-believer, while the faith of the Church supplies for the inadequacy of the infant.) Another supposition of genuine liturgical life, then, is an interior spirit that gives meaning to the exterior letter. It is this spirit that alone can make the apparent opposition of liturgy (as active) and contemplation (as passive) disappear.

And this interior spirit giving meaning to the exterior letter enables us to pass through the liturgy into the presence of the grace-giving Lord and His Spirit who are greater than and in no way bound down to the forms of the liturgy. Our God has marked out these means of grace, but He has not limited Himself to them. Indeed, the same Lord Jesus who promises to come wherever two or three are gathered together in his name also urges prayer in secret, in the privacy of one's room. It would be most unfortunate for Christian life if the current appreciation of the liturgy were to lead, as it seems to have done in some cases, to a downgrading of meditation and other forms of private prayer. Despite out human tendency to set down limits as to where and how the Spirit of God can work, He breathes where He will, both inside and outside the visible communion of the faithful, both inside and outside the liturgical life of the Church. Here too, the divine life breaks in upon man in ways connatural to the human spirit. For man is not only a member of a community, but also an individual person with his own secret depths and with his own unique and personal life of love and of relation to God. And he must do more than use all the instruments of human language, thought, art, and action to bear witness to his secret life with God; he must also be silient before God, for it is only to the silent that God can give the fullest knowledge which transcends every human mode of understanding and the fullest charity which is at once the principle and the result of this knowledge. But at this point the life of grace has passed beyond a mode connatural to the human being who lives it and has now become divine not only in its object but also in its mode, under the regime of the gifts of the Holy Spirit. This mystical prayer is all God's work and as such is utterly beyond liturgy; liturgy and other active forms of prayer cannot produce it but can only make the soul open to the descent of the Spirit. And yet, even if such silent loving union is the greater gift, it too should lead back to a fuller sharing in the liturgical life. For one who has known the gift of God cannot keep still about it; all that is in him must bless the Lord, even in the human activity of the liturgical acts. And he longs to return again and again to the liturgical and sacramental encounters with Christ and with his Spirit.

SACRAMENTS AND ENCOUNTER

This essay proposes to consider the sacramental economy in the Church from a very limited point of view. Supposed is the common and well-known doctrine of the Church concerning the minister, recipient, rite, nature, etc. of the sacraments. Supposed therefore is the theological understanding that in the sacramental economy the Church is itself the primordial sacrament, the *Ur-Sakrament*, by which Christ comes to all men to offer them His Spirit and the grace of the Spirit, and this especially in the seven sacraments of the Church. These sacraments, by the institution of Christ, bring grace to the recipient in virtue of themselves; they are only special modes by which the grace-giving presence of Christ in the world, in the Church, encounters and is encountered by the Christian. But if grace is offered through the sacraments, it is still grace – for the sacraments are themselves free gifts of God rather than claims upon God for grace.

There are two possible perspectives on the Church and the sacramental system. The first, which is also inadequate, sees the Church and its sacraments as means by which, in which, we rise to God. They are efficacious signs, signs which produce grace in virtue of their finite and creaturely being as signs – although of course they had to be endowed with such a power by God Himself. From this viewpoint, one can see a certain "magical" quality in the sacrament, or at least what seems to be such. Because of the decree of God, a small and in itself insignificant material rite brings with it the greatest benefits in the spiritual order. If one inquires about the mode of sacramental causality from this perspective, he must explain either how a creature can as a creature be a true cause of grace or how mere occasionalism can still preserve some meaning for the causality of sacraments. There are difficulties enough in either of these two courses, since grace is always the grace of God, and since the sacrament is a cause of grace.

A more adequate perspective on the Church and its sacramental system sees these as signs of the descent of God to us. God descends to us in order to raise us up, to draw us more fully to Himself; He descends to us in Christ, in the grace-given encounter with the grace-giving Christ. Here the visible Church and its sacraments are seen as actually extensions, in the order of objective intentionality, of Christ's own incarnation. They are like the light from the distant stars, which in coming to us is an extension of the being of those stars in the order of objective intentionality, which makes those stars themselves present to us as sources (however feeble because of the tremendous distances) of light. Note that we are speaking of *objective* intentionality. Even though one might be oblivious to the presence of the light from the stars – or that of the visible extension of Christ's incarnation, the reference and the intentionality are still objectively there. But our comparison to light from the stars limps. For this light refers us back to, renders present, the star as it was when this light was emitted; we see the star as it was, however many light-years ago. But while the Church and the sacraments do really refer us back to, and render intentionally present, the historical Christ in the mysteries of His life, death, resurrection, and ascension, they are also and even more extensions, in the order of objective intentionality, of the incarnate but here and now resurrected and living Christ "yesterday, today, and the same forever." But from this aspect they do much more than render present Christ across the centuries, Christ present at a distance. They are means, instruments, by which Christ here and now is present in the world in the Mystical Body and in it in the sacramental encounter with each Christian. There is, however, no question of the finite and creaturely reality giving grace or some kind of claim to grace; rather, it is grace and the favor of the grace-giver that is absolutely prior, utilizing visible created signs as means of encounter in a manner analogous to that in which we use words to communicate to other men the truth that we possess. The visible created signs are necessary, not as some magical devices, but rather as instruments disposing for the encounter with the incarnate and risen Christ in a visible manner in accordance with the sacramental economy of the distribution of grace; the grace of Christ and of the Church has itself become incarnated in the spatio-temporal in accordance with the spatio-temporal reality of the incarnation of Christ and of Christian existence in the world. Yet this does not mean that we climb a spatio-temporal ladder to God, but rather that He (in Christ) descends to us in a spatio-temporal manner; the sacraments are not claims but means for the transcendent, loving God freely to bestow His own self and a share in His life as wholly unmerited gift – given in a manner connatural to spatio-temporally conditioned human existence.

In the light of this second, more adequate perspective on the Church and her sacraments, and especially with the help of a more refined understanding of the notion of encounter, we may hope to make a more fruitful consideration of sacramental causality, of the manner in which these sacraments are actually employed as instruments of the divine mercy. This consideration can be focused upon three problems.

(1) How can the sacramental sign be efficacious precisely as a sign?
(2) In what sense can the created reality of the sacrament actually be said to communicate grace? This question will also provide an opportunity to consider the meaning of sacramental causality as *ex opere operato*.
(3) What kind of effect is produced in the recipient of the sacrament immediately in virtue of the mere reception of the sacrament and independently of its ultimate fruitfulness?

Analysis of the Sacrament as Cause of Grace

The sacramental sign itself is already a visible, spatio-temporal conjunction between the recipient of the sacrament and Christ in the Church. As such, then, this sacramental sign is already a remote disposition for the reception of sacramental grace insofar as it is offered to one open to receive the sacrament by one intending to confer it. (It is not necessary here to enter into a discussion of the kind of openness required – the requirements for valid reception – or the kind of intention and other requirements in the minister of the sacrament.) But along with this visible conjuction in virtue of the sacramental sign (*sacramentum tantum*) there is a deeper, entirely spiritual conjunction, signified and effected by the sacramental sign, "visible" only through this sacramental sign, between the recipient and Christ in the Church. This interior conjunction, union with Christ the grace-giver, is itself a promise of further grace; for it is union with the source of grace at a privileged moment for the communication of grace in the economy established by the grace-giving God. This union is already a kind of grace, but it is the proximate disposition in the recipient for further graces – sanctifying grace and special graces proper to each sacrament. If the recipient is open to these further graces they begin to be given immediately. (This latter openness is described by the conditions for the *fruitful* reception of the sacrament.) If the recipient is not sufficiently open to these further graces, they can still be given later – if the interior conjunction remains – when the recipient removes the obstacle, with the help of grace. This interior conjunction, then, is the symbolic reality of the sacrament (*res et sacramentum*).

The interior conjunction is effected by Christ and His Spirit, coming to the recipient in and through the visible rite of the visible Church. This visible rite, the sacramental sign, is truly dispositive for the interior conjunction because of the ontologically intentional reference of this sign as sign to Christ in the Church. While a psychological perception of this intentional reference of the sign (a perception possible only for one who believes) is also in some manner required for adults to the extent that they are consciously capable of it, in accordance with the nature of each sacrament, it is the ontological intentionality of the sign that constitutes it as truly dispositive for the interior union with Christ, and not merely as some kind of juridical claim to this interior union. But the dispositive power of the sacramental sign only *opens* one who does not oppose it, who is already open at least to the reception of this sign, to the further symbolic reality and remotely to the subsequent grace which is the fructification of the symbolic reality. The sacramental sign does not of itself confer the symbolic reality, nor does the symbolic reality of itself confer subsequent graces. To think otherwise would be to slip into the first, inadequate, perspective on the sacraments, which sees them as means by which we rise to God rather than as means by which God descends to us to raise us to Himself. But we must always see the whole sacramental economy as a descent of God in Christ giving the Spirit, in which the dispositions produced by the sacraments are not means that are claims for us to grace but rather means that are instruments for God to employ in His giving of grace.

Insofar as the sacramental sign refers with objective intentionality back in history and also in the immediate present to the Sacrifice of Christ and to Christ present in the Church, this sign is itself already an "advance" of Christ toward man, an instrument of Christ disposing man for more (not in some merely juridical order but in the order of ontological state). The symbolic reality, the state of interior conjunction with the grace-giver, is from one point of view a further stage in the "advance" of Christ toward man, though in fact it comes concomitantly with the sacramental sign itself to any recipient who is sufficiently open (here again there is question of the requirements for valid reception of the sacrament). Still, an absolute priority must be accorded to the sacramental sign over the symbolic reality, since the recipient is in fact disposed to receive the symbolic reality through the sacramental sign.

The culmination of the advance of Christ toward man in the sacramental meeting comes when, to the man interiorly and ontologically conjoined with Christ in virtue of the symbolic reality, Christ and His Spirit communicate sanctifying grace and with it the divine indwelling, or better, the divine indwelling and sanctifying grace as its formal effect, or a fuller share in these, together with the special sacramental graces proper to each sacrament. This is the fruitive consummation and highest stage of the sacramental union. We shall return to consider it again only at the end of this essay.

It is apparent that the sacrament of the Eucharist calls for some special further remarks as regards the symbolic reality and its relation both to the sacramental sign and to the fruit of the sacrament. Only in the Eucharist is there a distinction between the moment of confection and the moment of reception – and to this distinction there corresponds a twofold symbolic reality, the reality of the real presence of Christ coming at the moment of confection and enduring so long as the sacramental sign endures, and the reality of the interior conjunction of the recipient with Christ coming at the moment of reception and enduring so long as the sacramental sign of *food* continues to endure. While it has been argued that this sign ceases to endure immediately upon physical eating, against the common view that it continues until the appearance of bread and wine is lost through the digestive process, it is unnecessary here to enter into this problem. Note that the interior conjunction with Christ in the reception of the Eucharist is more than the simple physical presence of the sacramental species to the recipient; how would such a merely physical conjunction in communion really be very different from that in a visit to the Blessed Sacrament? It is only a matter of a few feet! The interior conjunction in the reception of the Eucharist is comparable to that in the other sacraments, in that it is something real that is in and of the recipient as such. Here too, just as in the other sacraments, it is required as a disposition in the recipient, as a mode of union with the grace-giver, a union which is a necessary condition for the sacramental bestowal of grace by Christ and His Spirit. This interior conjunction in the reception of the Eucharist differs from that in the other sacraments in that its term is not just the grace-giving Christ and the Holy Spirit but Christ as bodily present. Accordingly no adequate description of the interior conjunction here can be given without reference to the real presence of Christ in the sacrament, unique to this sacrament. But it is still possible to focus attention upon this interior conjunction in a generic manner, in so far as it is found in all the sacraments, and only later to consider its diversity in the particular sacraments. This procedure will be followed in our treatment in greater detail below of the symbolic reality of the sacraments.

The foregoing analysis of the sacraments as causes of grace has already provided a general answer to the first two questions posed above, and indeed also to the third – but much more remains to be said about the latter below. In the light of what has been seen concerning the efficacy of sacraments a few remarks can be made the about the meaning of the formula that the sacraments produce grace *ex opere operato*. We shall not dwell upon the significance of this formula as regards the minister of the sacrament, in so far as it means that the sacraments produce their effects independently of the personal dispositions of the minister, so long as he has all the requisites for being a true minister of the sacrament. Rather, of special interest here is the significance of the formula as regards the respective roles of the recipient and the sacrament itself in the bestowal of grace by the grace-giving Son and Spirit. In ordinary prayer and good-works, the increase of grace is in some manner merited through the (grace-inspired) positive actions of the one who thus prays and acts. But sacramental grace as such is not thus merited by openness to reception of the sacrament and to the grace-giver who comes in the sacrament (however meritorious those acts of faith and charity, etc., which achieve or preserve such openness actually are). Rather, the properly sacramental grace is bestowed by the grace-giving Son and Spirit themselves in so far as their sacramental advance meets with openness in the recipient: first, openness to the interior conjunction which is signified by the sacramental sign and for which the sacramental sign is a dispositive cause; and second, openness to the bestowal of the further graces signified by the sacramental sign and (invisibly) the symbolic reality or interior conjunction, and dispositively caused (remotely) by this same sacramental sign and (proximately) by this same symbolic reality. Yet clearly, openness is a necessary condition; and where acts are necessary or desirable for such openness or for the increase of this openness, the *ex opere operato* manner in which the grace-giver bestows grace in the sacraments does not remove such necessity or desirability for these acts. The sacrament is not a mechanical device to increase grace but a visible union of persons in mutual openness, even though the openness of the finite person is itself already grace-inspired.

The immediate effect produced in the recipient of any sacrament in virtue of the mere reception (and not merely the appearance of reception) of the sacrament and independently of the ultimate fruitfulness of the sacrament is, as we have seen, that special grace of interior conjunction with Christ which has been called the symbolic reality of the sacrament. This interior conjunction with Christ is real, ontological, intentional, communicative, participative. Older Scholastics might have contented themselves with calling it a relation of union and fairly well have left it at that. But it is now possible to say much more about this relation of union in the light of some metaphysical reflections upon the modern notion of interpersonal encounter; indeed, this relation of union can be regarded as an ontological principle of interpersonal encounter with Christ in the Church. Such a relation, of course, is not just a pure relatiom devoid of all absolute reality whatever – there are no such pure relations in real existence. The ontological reality of this supernatural principle of union must be analogous to that of other modes of the finite (substantially) supernatural as they were described in an earlier essay. Futher reflections upon the ontological structure of this mode of created grace may better be deferred until after some rather detailed considerations of the nature of encounter, supernatural encounter with God, and sacramental encounter.

Encounter

The "grand tradition" of philosophical thought has always regarded philosophy as a study of all things according to their most general and ultimate causes as knowable to inquiring reason. But there is a domain of individual concreteness that seems to go beyond the scope of such universal knowledge. Still, every philosophical system of thought must take this very domain into account and integrate it into the system in some manner. The Hegelian attempt at the total absorption of everything into the self-generating system of pure thought was the occasion for Kierkegaard to rebel at such a design and to focus attention upon the individual "existential" predicament of man, not upon man as subject to universal law but upon man as standing personally on his own before God. Kierkegaard was surely not the first to direct attention to man as individual existential subject (one thinks immediately of Augustine and Pascal, but there are many others), but in fact Kierkegaard is looked upon as the forerunner of twentieth centuy Existentialism.

The protest of Kierkegaard against the excesses of the age of rationalism has struck many twentieth century men, with their experiences of chaos and disaster in two wars and the threat of still another, as much more than just a legitimate reaction against those who had gone too far. For many philosophers a whole new problematic has come to occupy the central place. The concern of the Existentialists is with the domain of the "tychic" (from the Greek "tychê"), those concrete events and happenings that "mean" a great deal to each individual and unique person: death, the call of grace, interpersonal meeting or encounter, communion. Such realities had been in large part overlooked or left only a minor place in rationalist philosophy, but for Existentialists they are the primary concern. Marcel is occupied with concrete moral life and with personal communion with man and God; Heidegger considers the *Angst* before finitude and the mystery of death; Sartre sees anxiety and nausea as fundamental life attitudes of man, who himself is a kind of sickness of being. Many Existentialists have thought it necessary to *replace* the grand tradition of philosophy with this kind of thought; but while Heidegger in fact is only trying to build a better base for metaphysics, both Marcel and Sartre have had second thoughts about their earlier rejection of the structures of philosophy in the traditional sense. Existentialism is wedded to phenomenology in Sartre and Heidegger, and even Marcel utilizes a phenomenology that seeks to uncover the fine detail and structure of the "tychic" facts.

It was inevitable that religious thought should meet and be greatly influenced by Existentialist thought. For religion too is much more concerned with the domain of the "tychic" than with that of universal structures and standards. Beyond all the fine formulations of dogmatic and moral theology is the need for each person on his own to meet God, to heed or to disregard the call of God at every moment, and above all at the moment of death. In fact, as was seen above, even from the start in the person of Kierkegaard, the Existentialists have been occupied with fundamentally religious problems. Could it, indeed, ever be otherwise in a world in which no death is merely natural death, no fundamental decision of merely natural significance, no encounter without some obscure relation to the encounter of man with God? The meeting of religious thought with Existentialism has, apart from the case of those religious thinkers who too hastily dismiss as emotionalism and illusion a mode of thought to which they are unaccustomed, resulted in three principal reactions.

Some have responded by calling for an abandonment of the grand tradition of philosophical thought, at least as regards its use in theological understanding. This "pendulum" response has perhaps been felt more forcefully among Protestant theologians than among Catholics. Certainly the stabilizing influence of the magisterium and of the weight of the intellectual tradition of the schools has contributed to diminish the likelihood of any large-scale move of this kind among Catholic theologians. But existential theology has not carried all before it among Protestants either, especially in America and in England.

Others have seen Existentialist thought as calling for the parallel development, alongside theological thought in the grand tradition, of an existential theology of divine-human encounter. Here would be a place for a "Biblical" theology of the historical encounter of men with the self-revealing God. (This is clearly a very special kind of Biblical theology – quite other than that positive historical study of the Bible simply to ascertain what it says and what it meant to the people of its times.) Existential Biblical theology would tend toward recreating a "Biblical aethos," as a context for our reading of the revealed word with a fuller appreciation of its total significance and affective overtones. Existential theology would of course be much more than Existential Biblical theology, since it would also consider the continuing encounter of man with God, especially in the privileged moments of divine inbreaking in salvation history after the time of Christ – as in the sacramental, mystical, and charismatic events in the life of the Church.

But one cannot consider the possibility of such an existential theology parallel to the structures of traditional theology without asking about the relation between these two modes of theological thought. It is not enough that they be simply parallel. Which one will exercise a control over the other? If the dogmatic formulae of the Councils and of the whole teaching authority of the Church must regulate those structures of traditional theology, they must also regulate the development of existential theology. And in fact a good deal of this regulation must be achieved precisely through the mediation of the traditional theological structures and formulations. All our understanding of the divine-human encounter is ultimately judged in the light of the dogmatic formulae and the formulated results of theological reflection. There can be no "free" existential theology emancipated from traditional modes of reflection upon dogmatic formulations.

Finally, many see an opportunity for the expansion of the body of traditional Christian theology in the consideration of the new problematic of the Existentialists. It is true that there is a kind of closed scholasticism that would seek to reduce whatever seems new to something that has been said long ago, but there is also the possibility that an open Thomism could really bring about organic growth of the grand edifice of Thomist theology in the light of new insight. And this is no mere possibility – as the names of Maritain and De Finance in philosophy, Rahner and Schillebeeckx in theology testify. Their reflection has contributed a great deal to the foundations of the phenomenological and metaphysical treatment of "encounter" which follows.

The fundamental point to grasp in the phenomenology of encounter and interpersonal communion is that besides universal, formulated intellectual knowledge, and besides sense knowledge, there is quite another way of meeting with persons, and even with things. Beyond sense experience and formulated conceptual, propositional, and discursive knowing there is given another generic mode of awareness and presence of reality to us – a non-objectifying awareness. There is, of course, a preformulated awareness in the act of intellectual insight that precedes conceptual, propositional, and discursive formulation; but it is not this kind of unformulated awareness that concerns us at present. Rather, we are speaking of a radically non-objectifying mode of awareness which is in principle not at all expressible (directly) in any neatly delimited formulation having such-and-such intelligible notes. Here there is an existential presence, an immediate union with concrete being, in an awareness that is obscure, easily disregarded, requiring a certain silence, openness, and listening.

In order to appreciate better the new element in such awareness and presence, beyond that objectifying knowledge with which we are more familiar, it is well to consider briefly an example of each, or rather instances in which one or the other is more predominant. It is better to choose cases that are rather far removed in order to see the contrast more easily and clearly. In fact there is an infinite spectrum of possibilities of more or less of one or the other; ordinarily one is never found without some at least of the other as well.

One might contrast the meeting with a bus driver who is a total stranger, with whom one must briefly deal in the course of a cross-town trip, and the meeting with a friend of many years which is the purpose of the trip. Unless we have an extraordinary degree of personal regard for others which dominates even our dealings on such occasions, the bus driver is for us present mainly in his *function* – a machine could conceivable replace him in the operations of collecting the fare, opening and closing the door, driving the bus, and indeed may eventually do so with the progress of automation. We do not ordinarily at such a moment see him as a personal value with all his personal relations to others such as his family and friends and with all his personal success, failure, and problems. This in certain respects is useful, since we deal more efficiently and quickly with objects than with persons. We should not want to see our bus driver distracted by warm, personal conversation with someone of his family or friends, for fear that his performance of his job might be less than adequate and even lead to an accident. Be this as it may, in fact the bus driver is as a bus driver primarily a function and not a person; and even our exchange of words is only a means to facilitate his function or perhaps a perfunctory and very subsidiary acknowledgement, kept in the background, that in fact this meeting *is* more than a mere dealing with a machine.

But it is not so at the end of the trip when we encounter our friend of many years. His presence is a much fuller presence to us, as is ours to him; here is mutual total presence in depth, in which heart can speak to heart, perhaps even without the necessity of words. This presence is, of course, not possible without the mediation of more or less objectifying knowledge in sense and intellect; but the presence of which we speak here is much more than the sum total of sensations, concepts, and propositions. This presence is surely linked with affective response; it is a kind of overtone of love. For this reason, some will insist that in fact it is nothing more than subjective emotion without ontological self-transcendence. But one must ask whether what is met with here is only a new modality of self or whether one does not also know the other in a new way. The former answer would seem to presuppose a prior determination and restriction of what one will accept as knowledge of the other, a limitation of knowledge to the domain of formulated knowing. The phenomenology of Buber, Marcel, and others carries us far beyond such a limitation. At this point we can recall our earlier treatment of knowledge through love in the essay on faith and intersubjectivity. The following discussion will recall some of its points and go on to some further developments in regard to the understanding of interpersonal encounter.

Marcel's phenomenology of participation and communion in interpersonal encounter, in which the frontiers between the self and other persons are broken down through a transcendence brought about through love, is greatly reinforced if we note that this special mode of non-objectifying awareness is not at all unique, is only a part of a rather wide domain of this kind of awareness. First of all, such awareness of another is also correlative with a similar awareness of oneself as a subject. Such self-awareness in fact has several levels and modes, into which it is not necessary to enter here; but these levels and modes all pertain to this domain of non-objectifying knowledge, and therefore offer a certain term of comparison for the appreciation of interpersonal encounter. Indeed, the simplest way to grasp the reality of interpersonal encounter in an analogical manner is to compare it with this self-awareness, by speaking of knowledge of the other as of another self. Closely related to such awareness of one's own subjectivity, indeed partially constitutive of such awareness, is awareness of one's inclinations; this awareness of inclination is the ground for formulated moral knowledge not only in the domain of the prudential judgment but also in the field of the virtues and in fact of even the most general formulation of natural law. The intuitive moral awareness of what "fits" one's being in the area of moral action is in the mode of non-objectifying knowledge. This is also true of the most formal and final element of aesthetic experience, of creative and receptive poetic intuition.

Also belonging to this domain of non-objectifying awareness is the obscure natural spontaneous awareness of the divine being, an awareness that Maritain finds in the Upanishads, that St. Thomas points our in *In Sent.* I, dist. 3, q. 4, a. 5, that Rahner, Schillebeeckx, Fuchs, and many others are noting in their contemporary writing. While the thinkers just mentioned, along with St. Bonaventure, find such an obscure awareness of God within the depths of self-awareness, the early Indian sages thought that such an encounter with the divine being could be had *everywhere*, in knowing the *Brahman* that pervades, and indeed is, all things – and which is finally identical even with the *Atman* that is the self and at once also the Infinite Self. This same pantheistic conception is found in Wordsworth's poetry, as in *Tintern Abbey*. But the list could be made much longer, if we were to speak of the Chinese concept of *Tao* or of many other Western pantheists. I have presented some account of such modes of awareness of the divine being in my *Inquiry Into Being* and in *The Christian Intellect and the Mystery of Being*, and we will not enter into them here. But it may be noted here that if such an encounter with God be given, on the plane of non-objectifying presence and awareness, then much pantheist thought can be conceived as an inadequate attempt to conceptualize such non-objectifying intuition in an indirect manner, and a ground can be given for an intuitive sacramentalism of natural being with respect to the divine being.

Still another manner of non-objectifying knowing is found in the presence of God in the Christian life of grace and prayer, and especially in that sense of presence of God that is the essence and central point of mystical experience. This latter will be considered in some detail in the essay on the ontological principles of mystical experience. At the very root of the Christian life of grace, the act and habit of faith, as has already been seen, are based primarily upon a supernatural interpersonal communion with the revealing God. Such a conception of the ground of supernatural faith has led us to see the possibility of a faith without explicit propositional formulation – the faith of pure intersubjectivity – in encounter with and acceptance of the self-revealing God.

It may be hoped that this brief survey of some other modes of non-objectifying knowing may serve to facilitate understanding of the phenomenological reality of interpersonal encounter between human beings. A few brief remarks about the metaphysical principles of such encounter and of non-objectifying knowing in general may also be helpful in order to confirm and to deepen this understanding – a fuller treatment of these metaphysical principles must be reserved for the essay on mystical experience. Some do not seek any understanding of such metaphysical principles; they are not a problem for anyone to whom existentialist phenomenology is the sum total of valid philosophizing and theologizing. But a Thomist metaphysician or a metaphysical theologian must raise the problem of the metaphysical basis for the reality of interpersonal encounter and of non-objectifying knowing in general.

Certainly something more than the traditional epistemology of sense knowledge and the triple intellectual knowledge of simple apprehension, judgment, and reasoning is necessary. It is necessary to pass beyond the level of formulated intellection to the analysis of the pre-conceptual, pre-propositional, and pre-discursive level of understanding, and even beyond the kind of pre-conceptual insight that could be directly formulated in a concept. In this "beyond" there is conscious union with and presence of, not the objective aspects of things, but the inner being, the subjectivity, the heart of things. (But note that this union presupposes, is controlled and directed by, the modes of objectifying union.) This subjectivity that is thus "known" may be the subjectivity either of persons or of things. Existentialists and phenomenologists generally use the term "subjectivity" only of persons; things are regarded as mere "objects," without any interiority of their own. But one can also speak of things in such a way; indeed, the Thomist notion of the "subject" lends itself to such a manner of speaking. Both things and persons have interiority in their unique affirmation of existence, and this affirmation is the very subjectivity of the person or thing. Such subjectivity is *conscious* in persons; it is the core-consciousness of dynamic self-presence at the heart (indeed, it is the heart) of the person. Subjectivity is further considered in a later essay. Interpersonal encounter is mutual presence not only in this or that objective or objectified manner but in subjectivity itself.

Diverse metaphysical explanations have been proposed for the modes of non-objectifying awareness, and of interpersonal encounter in particular. In general the explanations can be divided into those that find in some manner of intellectual intuition a sufficient reason and those that look beyond that to a knowledge in and through the medium of love as a necessary principle above and beyond purely intellectual intuition for at least some modes of such awareness. A mode of intellectual intuition is clearly present in the self-presence already mentioned (although it is grounded in an even deeper "substantial" self-presence). Some would consider such intellectual intuitive awareness of one's own subjectivity, whether only as acting or also as exercising existence itself, as the only mode of non-objectifying presence that is truly such, and would explain other apparent cases (even the mere pre-judgmental awareness of the actual existence of other things) as requiring some kind of projection of this one valid case – though perhaps a justified projection.

Others would recognize other valid cases of non-objectifying presence, of other persons (and things), and look to a further mode of intellectual intuition as an explanatory principle. Here one could point to the intentional existence that always goes with, and indeed constitutes, the intentional form by which the other is known as other. While the intentional form is the required principle for union of the knower with the objective aspects of the known, the intentional existence can refer the knower to other existential aspects which are not directly objectifiable – to the actual existence and activity and even subjectivity of the other.

It is not necessary to deny either of the above modes of explanation of certain modes of non-objectifying awareness, but they are not adequate to account for the full reality of human interpersonal encounter or of supernatural mystical experience or of poetic or moral knowing. These are more profound modes, in which more than intellect alone is required, in which love itself becomes a formal means by which the intellect knows – as was seen in the essay on faith and intersubjectivity. The affective "weight" in the will, which connaturalizes the will with the beloved, is a formal medium through which the intellect is led to the very heart of the beloved; in supernatural charity union with the beloved goes even beyond this, since charity is not only the principle of a mediated union but also the created term corresponding to a non-mediated union (in quasi-formal causality) of God and the finite will, as was seen in the essay on the finite modes of supernatural being.

The love that is a principle of interpersonal encounter is not necessarily a love of complete or very intense commitment to the other person. In fact, this love may be of a rather minimal kind, the kind that is only a spontaneous response to the natural goodness of any being that comes to be known as present. This is why some degree of non-objectifying awareness is always present along with objectifying knowledge. But this degree varies in proportion to the degree of interest and regard for the other. If the encounter is truly *inter*-personal then there must be some degree of mutuality in this interest and regard. If the spontaneous affective response and interpersonal encounter lead to a free and mutual commitment to some degree (which is already the seed of friendship), then mere encounter becomes interpersonal communion. But note that it is still love itself which formally sustains communion as well as encounter; these are not mere matters of intellectual knowledge alone. Communion is formally constituted by the free continuation and deepening of the affective response which gives rise to encounter.

Encounter, Communion, and Dialogue with God

Dialogue is communication of good in the order of knowledge and love, between persons. Presupposed for it is openness to the other as a center of value, whose good we ourselves would have and to whom we would communicate our own good. But here self and other must be present, not as two objects, self-enclosed and outside each other, but rather as in communion. Such affective communion between subjects has, of course, many degrees, ranging from the mere prolongation of initial encounter in mutual interest all the way to the heights of friendship. What is necessary here is only that minimal degree which prompts a willingness to listen and a desire to give something of one's own spiritual treasury of knowledge and love. These conditions are in fact verified in every human situation in which there is genuine communication, and it should be unnecessary to enter into detailed examples.

All our life is in fact opportunity for dialogue with God, for every human situation comes from the immediately present providential direction of God and calls for our response in a "yes" or a "no" to the divine call. For one who is open, by the grace of faith and charity, to hear this divine call, every moment is a moment of encounter with God calling, a moment of communion and of opportunity for still deeper communion in the dialogue of mutual exchange of goods – God's offering of Himself in and through the created goods of the situation and the created person's free acceptance of this offer which is at once also the gift of himself to God. In such a dialogue formal prayer tends to merge with a prayer of all times that finds God in all things. But of course for most men it is not a question of such a sustained intensity of affective communion and dialogue with God; rather, there are peaks and valleys in this life, perhaps even points where the communion and dialogue are broken off altogether through sin or renewed through repentance, and of course the moment of initiation of this dialogue with the beginning of truly moral life in the first moral act. The Christian baptized as an infant has, right from the moment of baptism, the germ of communion and dialogue, has in fact already given a radical *yes* to the first advances of God in the order of supernatural grace; but even this Christian must, at the beginning of real moral life, ratify this radical *yes* in a free basic moral option of supernatural charity or withdraw this radical *yes* by a free *no* to the solicitations of grace.

Sacramental Encounter

In the course, if not of the continuing dialogue, then at least of the continuing offer of dialogue, between man and God, there are privileged moments of encounter, special conditions, in which God intervenes and enters into our world and comes to us in ways that go far beyond those of ordinary life in the world. This was seen in the case of Adam, of

Abraham, of Moses and the Old Law, of Christ, and in the Church as an extention of Christ's being-in-the-world-with-us, especially in the Mass and in the sacraments. The sacraments are truly extensions of the incarnate being of Christ, by which he, from his own point of space and time, reaches out throughout space and time to approach us in a sensible manner, that is, in a manner connatural to and accomodated to our own spatio-temporal being. In the humble sensible reality of the sacramental signs it is the heart of God that reveals itself and speaks an offer to man, an offer that is at once also efficacious if only we are open to it. The Holy Trinity has revealed itself in Christ and communicates itself through Christ and His Spirit, but now through the medium of objective modes of sensible being that constitute the sacramental signs. Our encounter and communion with Christ and His Spirit through these signs goes far beyond the simple reality of the signs themselves to an interpersonal communion that is non-objectifying in its mode but nevertheless understood through the formulations of faith for what it is. Such encounter and communion is no warm sensible "glow," no "vision," but only a simple presence the understanding of which is formulated by faith alone.

But again let it be emphasized that the sacraments are not magical tools by which we may ascend to God or draw down in the manner of a conjuror Him to ourselves; rather, they are extensions of the incarnation of Christ and instruments employed by God in His descent to men with the offer of His love and the gifts that are the effect of that love. They are the signs of the immediate presence of the grace-giving Christ and His Spirit to whoever is open to Their advent, and the spatio-temporal presence of the signs to the recipient of the sacrament is the incarnate manifestation of the immediacy of Christ Himself. This incarnated, sacramental manifestation of this immediacy is at once the ultimate disposition for the interior conjunction of the recipient to Christ that is the *res et sacramentum* or symbolic reality, and the manifestation in a sensible manner of this conjunction itself.

Yet, as was pointed out earlier, it is not necessary that the incarnated, sacramental manifestation be apprehended as such by the recipient; it is enough that there be in the signs an objective intentional reference to the Church and to Christ, and in the recipient a genuine openness to the advent of Christ. This openness, however, must be a conscious openness when possible; for genuine interpersonal encounter is a reality of consciousness. It is true that in some cases (infants, the insane), Christ compensates for the deficiency of consciousness as regards some of the sacraments and achieves the work himself – yet even here there is openness, since freedom would be required in order to close oneself off by a bad moral option or by a refusal to accept an offered sacrament or at least by a failure to elicit the required intention, however implicit this might be. (Could not a good moral option of charity already be all the intention required in an adult for the valid reception – fruitful as well – of at least baptism?) But ordinarily, in those who are neither infants nor insane, there is required the openness to the sacrament that consists in faith (actual or habitual for baptism, habitual for the other sacraments, as a rule) and the required intention, as well as any other conditions of validity that may be required for particular sacraments. Faith itself could conceivably be absent in the valid reception of some sacraments, but ordinarily the requisite intention arises out of faith.

If the conditions are verified for such validity, then the sacramental encounter with Christ in virtue of the symbolic reality of the sacrament actually takes place. This symbolic reality is dispositively caused by the presence of the sacramental sign, as has already been pointed out; and this same symbolic reality is itself a disposition – proximate, if sufficient openness is present (conditions for fruitfulness), remote in the absence of sufficient openness in the line of faith and of affective attitude – for the further grace of the sacrament, that is, sanctifying grace and affective communion and the special graces proper to the particular sacraments in question.

The symbolic reality which mediates the sacramental encounter exists in the will. This must be said if the sacramental encounter with Christ is to be conceived by analogy with human interpersonal encounter, the immediate metaphysical and psychological principle of which is a connaturality in the will that has been induced by the *other*. Interpersonal encounter with the human Christ in his historical being would have taken place in this manner, and the sacramental encounter is with the same human Christ in the extension of his incarnate being. Moreover, since the symbolic reality is the proximate disposition in the open recipient for the infusion of sanctifying grace and for resultant affective communion, this disposition itself should be in the *will* of the recipient. Again, the very requirement of openness in the will in order that the symbolic reality itself be conferred in the sacramental rite indicates that it is in the will that this symbolic reality is received.

Since the symbolic reality is a true disposition, by way of positive conjunction to Christ, for the grace that is the fructification of the sacrament, this symbolic reality must be said itself to be a grace, a supernatural reality in the will of the recipient, a reality that is not yet charity and yet one that prepares the way for charity by unifying the openness of the recipient to the generosity of Christ and His Spirit. In its ontological reality it is a qualitative connaturalization of the will to Christ in his sacramentally incarnate presence, a grace-given connaturalization that could not be given without some minimal openness to the advent of Christ, be this only the openness of the infant who does not say no, or that of the adult who is only capable of valid reception without yet gaining the full supernatural fruits of this reception.

But this symbolic reality is not the same in each of the seven sacraments, and with its diversity there are diverse modes of personal encounter and relation to Christ. In the sacrament of Penance the symbolic reality is entirely transient in character, the principle of a privileged moment of encounter with Christ dispensing his forgiving grace. In Extreme Unction the symbolic reality is again transient, but not as transient as in Penance. A quasi-permanent personal relation to Christ is given that endures throughout the illness that called for the sacrament; this union with Christ disposes the recipient for a continuing stream of grace of help amd strength beyond whatever increase of sanctifying grace comes at the moment of fructification of the sacrament.

In the sacraments of Baptism, Confirmation, Holy Orders, and, so long as both partners live, in Matrimony, the symbolic reality is permanent. In the first three this permance is absolute and the symbolic reality is the indelible sacramental character. In all four the symbolic reality is the principle of permanent personal relation and continuing union in interpersonal encounter with Christ as the Head of the Mystical Body. In virtue of these relations and union with Christ in the Mystical Body, the baptized, confirmed, ordained, and married exercise determinate functions within the Mystical Body and are disposed for the infusion of sanctifying grace in the fructification of the sacrament and for all the graces necessary for them to carry out their functions in the Mystical Body and to grow in their Christian life in the exercise of these functions. Always of course the offer of such graces depends upon the degree of openness in the recipient; only one who is sufficiently open can be proximately disposed by the symbolic reality to receive the infusion of sanctifying grace, and only continuing openness and affirmative response can permit the maximum gift of the other sacramental graces consequent upon the reception of these enduring sacraments. It is possible to close oneself to these graces of the sacrament even while receiving the sacrament or after having received the sacrament, although one must expect that some healing graces at least will continue to be offered by Christ to those who still – despite their hardness – retain such an intimate personal relation to and conjunction with him.

The Holy Eucharist is an altogether special sacrament, in which we must distinguish a double symbolic reality. Since the Eucharist does not, like the other sacraments, come into being at the moment of reception, so that the symbolic reality would arise in the recipient at the moment of reception and only as something *of* the recipient, but rather is brought into existence at the moment of consecration – the moment of confection – a symbolic reality is found from this moment onward, a symbolic reality which is nothing other than the Real Presence of the Lord. This latter symbolic reality is not an encounter, not a conjunction of man to Christ, but the physical presence of the Person of Christ through his human nature under the appearances of bread and wine. At the moment of reception of the Eucharist, the second symbolic reality arises and is the conjunction of the recipient with the really and ontologically, though sacramentally, present Christ. While the former symbolic reality is relatively permanent, since the species of bread and wine could endure for a long time, the latter (subjective) symbolic reality is much more transient, arising only in the consumption of the species and enduring for only a short time. If the former symbolic reality is already objective Grace, the latter is the proximate disposition in the well-disposed recipient for the communication by Christ and His Spirit of subjective grace to the recipient. And of course this latter symbolic reality is similar to that in the other sacraments in so far as it *is* a principle of encounter, though not encounter with Christ through simple sacramental extensions of the incarnation but rather encounter with the very sacramental presence of the incarnate Christ himself. In the other sacraments Christ is spiritually present through the medium of the sacramental extensions of the incarnation; in this sacrament Christ is physically present in his incarnate being, though under signs that again are sacramental extensions of the historical incarnation. Accordingly, the Eucharist is that sacrament in which our sacramental mode of encounter with Christ reaches its greatest fullness; the other sacraments all look toward this fuller encounter with Christ, though it itself is a foretaste of the still fuller encounter in heaven.

But neither in the Eucharist nor in any of the other six sacraments is the mere encounter, through the symbolic reality, the term of the sacramental meeting of man with the grace-giving Christ and His Spirit. Encounter, even when it is more than transient – as in Baptism, Confirmation, Holy Orders, Matrimony, and to some degree Extreme Unction – is still only the beginning of interpersonal relation and tends toward fuller and fuller affective communion in those who do not turn away. Communion is mutual giving in mutual love and absorbing dialogue. The principle of communion between man and God is supernatural charity, the very gift which Christ first gives or increases in those who are open to the fructification of the sacramental encounter. And all the other modes of sacramental communion look toward Eucharistic Communion as toward the fullness of communion in the sacramental economy.

II

SOME ONTOLOGICAL PRINCIPLES OF MYSTICAL EXPERIENCE

This paper takes for granted the fact of "mystical" experience and seeks to reflect upon its nature. But there are difficulties at the very outset concerning the very evidence of the fact itself. For the purposes of scientific analysis of the nature of mystical experience, one cannot use purely private data gained from introspection, even if that should be possible. Rather, it is necessary to rely upon the testimony, chiefly written, that has been given to us by those who claim to have had such experience or whose words at least obliquely point to the fact of such experience.

But such testimony can be more or less clear, more or less accurate, even in some cases more or less honest. The gathering of valid testimony in this domain is in fact considerably more difficult than in the ordinary domain of history, which likewise must ultimately rest on human testimony. And even after the general validity of the testimony has been established, it is still necessary to make a judgment concerning the value of the experience to which it testifies.

In fact, a great deal of work has been done in collecting and arranging and classifying such testimony. Poulain's *Graces of Interior Prayer* remains a classic treatment, from the inductive point of view, of the various types of authentic Christian mystical experience. Marechal's *Studies in the Psychology of the Mystics* extends the inductive consideration to various kinds of "natural" mysticism and to pathological counterfeits of mystical experience. One can profit by reading Marechal's descriptions even if one does not necessarily agree with his psychological, philosophical, and theological interpretations in all their detail. I do consider his denial of positive and transcendent content to natural mysticism to be a mistake, as will be seen later.

The present essay seeks to point out ontological principles for the wide diversity of mystical knowledge attested to as a result of the studies of inductive and comparative mysticism. It therefore represents an effort in the same direction as that of Garrigou-Lagrange, in *Christian Contemplation and Perfection* as well as in later works, to explain more than to describe. But while Garrigou-Lagrange gives us in many ways a satisfying account of Christian mystical experience in the light of the Dominican Thomist tradition, his system now appears rather inadequate from three points of view. First, the entire treatment is restricted to mystical experience within the Church and makes no real attempt to account for such experience outside the visible Church or for natural mystical experience. Second, the approach of Garrigou-Lagrange depends far too heavily on the Thomist doctrine of the real distinction of the gifts of the Holy Spirit from the infused virtues, a distinction which can be called into question. One need not, as a Thomist, be committed a priori to every hypothesis put forth by St. Thomas. Third, Garrigou-Lagrange unfortunately wrote his treatises apart from the influence of modern Existentialism and before the advent of the Thomism of the existential subject of Maritain and De Finance; in the light of these recent advances we may hope to give a somewhat more adequate account of the principles of the diverse types of mystical experience. Yet these criticisms should not be permitted to obscure the fact that the work of Garrigou-Lagrange was itself a considerable step in the progressive understanding of Christian mysticism and of Christian spiritual life.

It is now necessary to delineate a little more sharply what we have so far been referring to vaguely as mystical experience. It would be easy enough to designate authentic Christian mystical experience as what we mean by the term "mystical experience" and in virtue of this limitation proceed to show that there is no other valid form of mystical experience. But this would perhaps mean an undue depreciation of certain forms of experience which seem to have more kinship with Christian mysticism than with the more ordinarilly discussed forms of knowledge; and it would certainly mean a disregard of contemporary usage, which applies the adjective "mystical" to forms of experience certainly distinct from that of Christian mysticism. While many Christian writers confine mystical experience to a certain privileged communion with God, and then discuss and ordinarily answer in the negative the question as to whether there is such a thing as natural mysticism, many modern philosophers speak of any experience of being which cannot be expressed conceptually as "mystical." My own reflections have led me to believe that such a usage is in fact fruitful, in the sense that it leads to the consideration of the kinship between a variety of types of experience and eventually to a coherent account of them which can be extended even to an understanding of the principles of grace-given mystical contemplation of God.

From this point of view, mystical experience is conscious communion with transphenomenal and transobjective being. Knowledge in the ordinary sense attains to being through its diverse objective aspects, its various faces, its exteriority. Even the affirmation of existence in judgment refers to the existence of the thing as "known from outside." Such knowledge of the real can be called union with the real but not communion. Knowledge of sensible phenomena and of intelligible essence, mathematical constructions, the mere affirmation of being as distinguished (can it ever be completely separated?) from consent to being, all these are modes of union with the object known. But beyond such partial union with being there is also entry into, conscious communion with, experience of, the plenitude of a being. Here one lives again, at least vicariously, the very exercise of being of the one which is known. In self-knowledge there is found the "warmth and intimacy of the contemplated me" of William James, in which one's subjectivity is, in the words of Maritain, "felt as a propitious and enveloping night." "Night," for the conceptually expressible insight into sensible phenomena, the constructs of the intellect, ordinary judgment in the field of conceptual knowledge—are all daylight knowledge as compared with this obscure sense of self-presence. It is the same in the intersubjective encounter with another person or even with non-personal beings, the "I-Thou" relation of Buber. The essentially fragmentary objectifying insight and conceptualization finds itself here complemented by a non-objectifying experience of plenitude of being, an at least vicarious attainment of the interiority and subjectivity of the other, in which the gulf that lies between self and other is actually transcended in communion. That such transcendence is in fact given is attested to in poetic intuition, in the phenomenology of interpersonal relations, in the testimony of "mystics" in the more restricted sense. The accounts given by psychologists of the sense of presence and of possible illusions in this regard touch only the material concomitants and not the spiritual reality of this transcendence. One must go not to the psychological analyses of Marechal but to the existential phenomenology of Marcel for a somewhat adequate understanding of this spiritual reality.

Such a broad use of the term "mystical experience" seems justified not only by actual usage among many philosophers but also by the nature of things. There is question here of knowledge in the dark rather that in the light, of entry into the domain of the transobjective and meta-problematic, the domain of the mystery rather than that of the problem, in the terminology of Marcel. Objective knowledge is experience of light, but transobjective communion is experience of mystery – or mystical experience.

While this usage cannot but seem at first to lead in the wrong direction for those who are primarily interested in the problem of mystical union with God, it enables us to focus attention upon a whole domain of "knowledge," of which mystical union with God is only one segment. This domain has been far too little analyzed by Scholastics, and as a result their attempts to understand its higher reaches of mystical communion with God have been somewhat crippled. But in focusing attention entirely upon conscious communion in the domain of transobjective mystery, upon the non-objectifying sense of presence rather than upon the objectifying understanding of phenomenal and transphenomenal objectivity, we are already at least in the general domain in which authentic Christian mystical experience is to be found. St. John of the Cross, Poulain, and Marechal, as well as other spiritual writers, are at one in asserting that essential mystical experience of God in the supernatural order is in the line of this sense of presence, and that the more objective types of knowing which are frequently found to be associated with this essential experience in the Christian mystics – such as visions, locutions, special revelations – are truly accidental to mysticism as such, which can exist without them altogether.

The remainder of this paper is devoted to a consideration of the ontological principles of mystical experience, in the sense we have given to this term. There is a mystical experience which is essentially contemplative and another which is essentially ordered immediately toward action. Here are treated the principles of mystical contemplation; only a few remarks will be made concerning the principles of mystical action. Phenomenology and the principles of natural mystical experience are treated first; in this light it is possible to approach the problems of supernatural mysticism with somewhat greater hope of an adequate treatment.

1. PHENOMENOLOGICAL INVENTORY: THE DIMENSIONS OF BEING

The domain of mystical experience has already been marked out in opposition to that of conceptual knowledge; but in order to understand it more clearly it is helpful to make a phenomenological inventory of the diverse dimensions of being as it presents itself to us, and in this light to mark out the area of mystical experience within the larger metaphysical context. I have already made such a phenomenological inventory in detail in chapter 1 of my *Inquiry Into Being*, and present here only a summary of it.

A dimension of being is a distinct aspect of being presented or presentable to the intellect in a distinctive manner. If there are several distinctive manners of presentation of being to the intellect, grounded in some diversity in being itself, then being has several dimensions. In fact, the being which stands before us and immediately reveals itself to us has at least seven such distinct dimensions. Not all of these dimensions are equally manifest to us, and a considerable degree of analytic reflection is necessary to disengage them all. Here we present simply the conclusions of such analytic reflection upon our total experience of the real.

Most evident to us are the sensible phenomena of things. While some philosophers have persuaded themselves that the phenomena are illusion as compared with some other world of true being, the being of phenomena of the material world strikes most men as the most evident of all. It is this phenomenal world that is the concern of the modern positive natural sciences. The very existence of such positive sciences proves that intellectual insight into sensible phenomena precisely as phenomena is in fact not only possible but given.

Quite another kind of insight and another mode of being are found when one turns inward from the phenomena dispersed in space and time to the phenomena of consciousness, to the conscious manifestation of consciousness as *my* consciousness. Such reflexivity is the distinguishing mark of consciousness in the full sense. All knowledge is knowledge of some thing, and this is also true of consciousness – consciousness is of its nature intentional; but at the same time consciousness is always reflexive. If sensible phenomenality is pure dispersion without intrinsic relatedness, psychic phenomenality is total reflexivity and essentially relative. One may also contrast the clarity

ONTOLOGICAL PRINCIPLES OF MYSTICAL EXPERIENCE 239

with which sensible phenomena are presented (so far as they are presented) to the obscurity with which psychic phenomena are given. This latter contrast is ultimately rooted in the fact that sensible phenomenality is the phenomenality of determinate sensible forms given as determinate forms (more or less confusedly relative to the actual detail independent of the knower, but clearly so far as they are actually given to the knower), while psychic phenomenality is not the phenomenality of forms but of a special mode of existence. It is true that this intentional existence is also the existence of a special type of determinate object, of objectivity which is essentially and totally relative or intentional in regard to the being which is the object of consciousness. Since such intentional objects, or intentional forms, are similar as regards their content to the being to which they refer, only the mode of existence being different, we have focused attention on intentional existence rather than intentional form in order to discern a distinct dimension of being.

But being has other dimensions than those of sensible and psychic phenomenality. For in both of these domains, besides the multiplicity and flux of phenomenality, there is also a certain clustering and permanence. This is especially evident in man, in whom one finds a certain interfusion of these quite disparate dimensions, an interfusion resulting not from these essentially disparate modes of being but rather from a third, deeper mode of transphenomenal being. Behind all the phenomenal manifestations of being there is the deeper, fuller, more real world of the being which manifests itself through phenomena. And this transphenomenal being does not present itself as one homogeneous mass, as Parmenides seemed to think, but rather as divided into the various nuclei of unity and stability which are the persons and things of the world. Nor are these various nuclei all simply "chips" from one block; besides diversity there is also difference in transphenomenal being. This is to say that through the phenomena we come to understand, by insight and conceptualization, that there are various essences or natures distinguished not only individually but also as to type in the world of transphenomenal being. Together, all these essences, natures, formal and material constituents of things, constitute the world of transphenomenal objectivity, a distinct dimension of being.

Note that transphenomenal objectivity has in common with sensible phenomenality that the contents of both domains are sufficiently discrete and determinate – both are domains of determinate form – that these contents are known through insight which can be expressed conceptually; this is to say that both are objectifiable domains of being. Together they comprise the world of objectivity. Since psychic phenomenality is a mode of existence rather than in the line of form, it does not belong to this world of the directly objectifiable.

But since the entire world of objectivity can be mirrored in knowledge by the forms of logical objectivity, intentional forms, actually existent objectivity must possess something else beyond objectivity. This new principle of being is transobjective existence, in fact a fourth dimension of being. This existence is what is affirmed in true judgment, but such affirmation presupposes some immediate grasp of existence pertaining to the order of intuitive understanding. Such intuitive understanding can be discerned most easily as regards the existence of the self; it is also given in regard to the existence of those things which act directly upon our senses (where the activity refers the knower back to its source in an existent reality); an indirect understanding of the existence of still other things is gained by reasoning back from the evidence of immediately given reality to the existence of other reality which is necessarily demanded by the immediately given.

A fifth dimension of being appears in activity, which is understood as a superexistence, an overflow or superabundance of existence, beyond the existence which gives reality to the primary objectivity of things, and giving being in some manner to further degrees of objectivity, the effects or products of the activity. Psychic phenomenality is, of course, a kind of activity and existence; but its distinct mode of manifestation is evidenced by the contrast that is noted between consciousness and "real" existence and activity.

If existence is a determination of objectivity, which gives being to objectivity and is at the same time possessed by objectivity, activity on the contrary is a determination of being in which the note of possession recedes into the background. While activity can still be said to be "possessed" by the agent, it is also exercised by, emanating from, the agent as a kind of thrust of new determinations into an already existent world; and it is this note of exercise, rather than that of possession, that characterizes activity as a determination of the agent. And yet this same note of exercise in addition to mere possession can be discovered in existence as well as in activity. Real things are not simply sets of objective notes held in being by the existence they happen to possess; rather, they assert themselves against nothingness and in the face of other being – they exert an existential pressure. This active thrust against nothingness and into being constitutes the objective existent as more than an objective existent, as an existent subject. Such actual exercise of existence makes existent objectivity the locus also of subjectivity, the sixth dimension of being. To subjectivity existence is no longer alien; indeed, existence as exercised may even be said to emanate from subjectivity (though only because it has first been possessed by objectivity), in a manner analogous to that in which activity emanates from the same subjectivity.

Since the here and now exercise of actual existence must be unique, the subject as such is unique – its subjectivity is as such incommunicable to any other being except God, who is the author even of subjectivity and who is closer to things than they are to themselves. On the other hand, objectivity is by its nature communicable; it is precisely what can be objectified in knowledge. Objectivity has a note of "exteriority"; it is a "face" of being, presented to or awaiting possible knowers. Subjectivity, on the other hand, is a kind of metaphysical interiority. In an intellectual subject, this interiority becomes conscious self-possession, which is the root of freedom. This attribute of self-possession characterizes all subjects, even those that are not really selves in the proper sense (only intellectual subjects are properly selves). Objectivity cannot be said to possess itself, since it is essentially communicable. But if objectivity does not possess itself, then it must be possessed by the subject, which, properly speaking, possesses all that the being is and exercises the dynamic determinations of existence and activity. Objectivity neither exists nor acts; the subject exists with a determinate degree of objectivity and acts in accordance with its degree of existence and objectivity.

Clearly, there are special problems concerning the manner in which we "know" the subjectivity of any being. Such knowledge of necessity lies outside the field of conceptual knowledge and of judgment within the field of conceptual knowledge. It goes beyond any intuitive understanding of the existence and activity of other things and even of one's own activity outside the field of intellectual consciousness in knowledge and love. If there is given any such understanding of subjectivity as such, it will fulfill the requirements for mystical knowledge as conscious communion with transphenomenal and transobjective being. To ask whether any immediate awareness of subjectivity as such is given is to raise the question of the existence of natural mystical experience.

There could be no question of such communion in regard to sensible phenomenality or transphenomenal objectivity, since both pertain to the sphere of the communicable exteriority of being. Psychic phenomenality, in the sense in which we have understood it, could not be the object (or rather the subject experienced) in such communion, since it is of the phenomenal rather than the transphenomenal order – but we must expect to find means to such communion, if it is given, in this order of psychic phenomenality. Neither existence nor activity as distinct dimensions of being are the term of mystical communion, since they are only known from "without" until one rises to the perspective of subjectivity.

Yet before embarking upon the formal discussion of natural mystical communion, it is good to complete the phenomenological inventory of the dimensions of being. The analysis of being has revealed a universe of discrete subjects, although the manner in which we can enter into communion with such subjects remains mysterious. But in fact something even greater than union among subjects seems to be given, a unity of all things, which transcends all differences and distinctions even of subjects themselves. Pantheism and monism have so stressed this unity as to destroy the true multiplicity already seen in the previous analysis. Especially in the *Upanishads* is found this absorption of multiplicity into deeper unity, with the confusion of the finite self and the Infinite Self. But granted that there is unity deeper than the diversity in things, this unity cannot exist on the same level as the diversity, so as to deny the diversity. The unity is really and not merely noetically prior to the diversity; it is found in the Infinite Being on which all other being depends for being. In this Infinite Being or Infinite Self is contained all the being of all other subjects in a higher way; but these other subjects in their subjectivity are still distinct from the Infinite Self. Such dependence in being must be called creation rather than monist or pantheist emanation; the obscure awareness of unity underlying all the multiplicity of things turns out to be an awareness of the createdness of things. This createdness is the seventh dimension of the being which stands before us.

But if this obscure awareness of unity is in fact an immediate awareness of the dependence of finite subjects on the Infinite Self, and of the supereminent presence of the being of finite subjects in the Infinite Self, then is there not required for such awareness of unity an immediate awareness of the Infinite Self? Such an immediate awareness of the Infinite Self must in fact be given — not a clear vision (which would be the beatific vision of the supernatural order), but an obscure felt presence. Here too there is perhaps question of a natural mystical experience, one which would exist at least in germ in every man, one which might by happy chance, ascetical effort, or the special gift of God come to the foreground of consciousness, at least for a time, in a poet, a philosopher, or a sage.

From the above phenomenological analysis, evidently subjectivity and createdness are the ontological arena of natural mystical experience, if it exists at all. Indeed, most properly it is subjectivity alone which is the term of such communion, since the intuition of createdness is between understanding of one's own subjectivity and an obscure presence, perhaps mystical, of the divine being, as a property of the former self-knowledge and a principle of the latter knowledge of God.

II. SELF-CONSCIOUSNESS

Doubtless there is a knowledge of subjects on a non-mystical plane; it may be said that all knowledge is ultimately of subjects. But neither objective insight nor objective conceptualization nor judgment of existence and activity refer to the subject as subject. Beyond all this, however, there is mystical communion – with the self, with other creatures, with God – conscious communion with transphenomenal and transobjective being, and this in the natural order without the necessity of grace. Let us consider each of these in turn.

We have first of all a very privileged intuitive understanding of self as self, in the transobjective depth of subjectivity. But even this understanding can be differentiated into several levels. First, since conscious activity is by its very nature reflexive, there is a knowledge of the subject as source of such conscious activity, a knowledge which arises in virtue of this reflexivity through which consciousness manifests itself to itself as exercised by a subject of consciousness. Closely akin to this knowledge is the conscious recognition of non-conscious acts as pertaining to the same conscious subject, as exercised by this subject though not precisely as conscious. Second, there is given an obscure consciousness of tendency and need in the conscious existential subject, a consciousness arising in virtue of lived tendency and lived exigency. Later, we shall note the important role of this kind of self-consciousness in ordinary moral life. But both of the modes of self-consciousness just described fall short of the deepest interiority of the existential subject. Prior to all exercise of activity and prior to the dynamic tendency toward activity is exercised substantial existence itself. Since the substantial existence of the human existence is a spiritual existence, being first of all the existence of the spiritual soul, it too must be exercised in a conscious manner in virtue of the reflexivity of spirit. Everything in spirit is consciousness and light, in virtue of this reflexivity, although in man this consciousness and light is at a minimum because his spiritual soul is also the form of prime matter. The intrinsic multiplicity of prime matter is a principle of non-reflexivity; for reflexivity is the total presence of a totality to itself and is therefore grounded in the complete unity of this totality. But the reflexivity of spirit could never be completely eliminated without the elimination of spirit itself, and therefore concomitant with all human activity at the very base of consciousness there is an obscure awareness of one's own existence as a substantial subject. And just as substantial existence grounds the ultimate unity of the existence me, so also this obscure awareness of the exercise of substantial existence grounds the ultimate unity of the conscious me. But this obscure awareness is ordinarily only in the background of consciousness, which is taken up with determinate activities, tendencies, and needs. Even the consciousness of tendency and need recedes toward the background as compared with the knowledge of the objective terms of such tendency and need. As a result, ordinary human self-consciousness appears principally in and through activity.

But in activity a fourth mode of understanding the self as self appears, when the self is seen as a center of value, an object of love, for the self. This mode of self-consciousness will be understood better later, when we have seen the principles of the consciousness of the subjectivity of the other.

While all these modes of self-consciousness can be regarded as forms of mystical experience, according to our usage of the term, it is especially the third that corresponds to some forms of natural mysticism. While this mode of self-consciousness ordinarily remains in the background of conscious life, it can be disengaged and brought to the foreground by an appropriate ascetical procedure, one which would eventually lead to withdrawal from particular activity of any kind and to the creation of a kind of void in conscious life. In this state of conscious unconsciousness one encounters the self. Some have regarded this as a kind of awakening to real being from the sleep into which the ordinary flow of phenomena and of other forms of knowledge has lulled us. For some such an experience has even been regarded as the height of human achievement, although apparently it can be induced by various drugs

ONTOLOGICAL PRINCIPLES OF MYSTICAL EXPERIENCE 245

and in any event requires no high spiritual culture or moral perfection. Evidently, ordinary sleep does not suffice for the required withdrawal from particular forms of activity; otherwise it would be sufficient to go to sleep to achieve this encounter with self. And yet perhaps it is achieved in a certain minimal way in sleep; some have thought that there is a deeper union with the ultimate reality of the self in the sleeping state than in the waking state. Some ascetical techniques of natural mystics, at any rate, do seem to lead to unconsciousness, whether this be the conscious unconsciousness mentioned above or some kind of unconscious unconsciousness like sleep.

III. UNION WITH THE FINITE OTHER

But while each of us has a privileged perspective from which to know his own subjectivity from within, the subjectivity of other persons and things in the world around us might seem at first to be completely inaccessible to us. It would seem that we can only know such beings from the outside, in their exteriority, and not at all in their incommunicable exercise of existence. Yet the situation is not altogether hopeless, for there does appear to be a new mode of awareness, of subjectivity, through the medium of love. Not that the will knows; rather, the intellect sees things in a new way in so far as they attract the will.

Poets and mystical writers have long testified to the power of love to lead us deeper into things than the unaided intellect can, and their testimony is confirmed by St. Augustine, St. Thomas Aquinas, John of St. Thomas, Jacques Maritain, Gabriel Marcel, Eric Fromm, Martin Buber, and many others. Love embraces its object in its uniqueness and incommunicability, in its transobjective depth in which is the source and spring of all its activity and existence, in its *heart*. Love, then, is a principle of intersubjectivity; and this intersubjectivity is not mere physical union but spiritual and conscious. This role of diverse forms of love can be seen not only in friendship but also in ordinary human interpersonal relations (which suppose a certain minimum of affective regard for one's fellow men), in poetic intuition (as has been described by Jacques Maritain, especially in *Creative Intuition in Art and Poetry*), and even in that minimum of open consent to being that the universe calls forth in us.

Since such spiritual and conscious intersubjectivity falls into the category of the mystical as we have described it, some reflection upon its nature, in at least a generic way, is called for. In fact, such reflection will provide valuable insights for an understanding of even higher forms of mysticism.

Such consciousness of intersubjectivity through love is not adequately explained by our general consciousness of the intentionality of the will in love. This intentionality of the will is directed toward the other, not in its objectivity but in its subjectivity, and therefore *presupposes* conscious intersubjective presence, since the will can only tend toward what is somehow known. And yet mere knowledge of the other cannot attain to the subjectivity of the other, which appears to present us with a dilemma.

At this point, the Thomist doctrine concerning "affective connaturality" offers a way out of the problem. Once any being is apprehended as a possible or actual good, the will is moved through this knowledge to the passion of complacent love. This passion in the will is an intentional form, like the object itself, since it has ultimately been produced by the object. In so far as it has this intentional form, the will is said to be connaturalized with the thing; this is affective connaturality. There is, of course, a still further degree of affective connaturality if the initial complacency is followed up by a free adherence to the good in question. But only the first complacency is considered in the following discussion, it being understood that the more intense degrees of intersubjectivity in fact require more than this initial complacency.

How is the will moved by knowledge? Cajetan holds for an efficient causality of the intellect on the will, while John of St. Thomas holds for a "metaphorical motion." The difficulties of Cajetan's position drive one to the alternative "metaphorical motion," which is the very motion of final causality itself. Even though this causality is more a causality by the known thing than by the knowledge of the thing, still this causality cannot exist apart from knowledge. And yet this causality is more than knowledge; this causality influences the will, not simply by producing a passion in the will, but in some manner by *being* this passion. This passion, as dependent ultimately upon the loved thing, is the final causality of the final cause; but this same passion, as flowing from the will itself as from an efficient cause, is also the effect of the final causality of the known thing. The passion of love is an induced activity in the will; but the influence which induces this activity, though dependent on something other than the will, is not distinct from the very activity itself.

This complex scheme might tempt one to place the causality of the final cause back in knowledge alone rather than in this induced passion. But if this were done, then everything would be desired precisely in so far as it were known. The final cause then must be a cause of desire not so much by producing desire as by being desired; this is why the motion of final causality is only a metaphorical motion.

But if this final causality is in the passion of the will, still it must somehow be exercised by the final cause itself – not in the physical being of the thing outside the knower but in the thing as representatively present in the intellect. This exercise of influence consists in the contact, not entitative or physical but merely representative, between the thing and the will, a contact arising in virtue of the spiritual compenetration of intellect and will.

The exercise of such contact, formally by the intentional representation of the thing and fundamentally therefore by the thing which is represented, is both the "attraction" (final causality) and the specification (formal) of the act of the will. The will itself acts as an efficient cause under such contact, in virtue of the natural dynamism of the will with respect to the good.

Through the intentionality of the induced passion of love, the will tends toward the real thing itself through the medium of its intentional representation in the intellect. But we have said that this tendency of the will is in fact a tendency toward the very subjectivity of things; this tendency therefore presupposes in some manner a cognitive attainment of the subjectivity of things. Again we must ask how this prior cognitive attainment is possible. But now, in the light of the foregoing remarks concerning the induced passion of love, some explanation can be given.

The affective connaturality of the will with the loved thing consists in the tendency of the will toward the loved thing. But presupposed to the connaturality itself is the connaturalization of the will by the "metaphorical motion." This metaphorical motion of final causality is fundamentally exercised by the thing itself in so far as the thing exercises its existence and activity; this constitutes the real attractiveness of the thing, for it is existential act to which all things tend. But the same metaphorical motion is exercised formally in the representative contact spoken of above, even though there is ultimate dependence upon the real thing itself. The thing as represented, therefore, is vicarious with reference to the real subjectivity of the thing, so far as the exercise of final causality is concerned. The subjectivity of the thing is now vicariously present in the intellect, as exercising final causality, but only in so far as the object in the intellect is actually connaturalizing the will by the metaphorical motion which induces the passion of love in the will. Thus the subjectivity of the other is known in the very moment of the affective connaturalization of the will, in a moment which endures so long as the other is being regarded with some degree of affectivity. As connaturalized, the will tends toward a subjectivity that is already revealed as subjectivity in the very connaturalization of the will.

This vicarious attainment of real subjectivity through affective connaturality is by no means as immediate as the privileged knowledge of self that was described earlier. And yet one must not underestimate its value. Because it lies at the heart of interpersonal encounter, of poetic intuition, and of the presence of being that flows from utter openness and consent to being, it can lead to a nature-mysticism (yet not the deepest type of nature-mysticism), that exclaims in its moments of highest exaltation, with Thales, "All things are full of gods!" Such a mysticism will emphasize the sacredness of nature, and perhaps especially of persons; but it falls far short of the flight of the alone to the Alone. While there is transcendence of the self, and encounter with a plenitude in the beings of the world, there is no transcendence of the finite itself. In a perverse case, there could even be a complete turning back on the self as the primary object of love, with withdrawal from the other, resulting in a special heightened form of self-consciousness above and beyond the three privileged forms treated earlier.

So such for the natural mystical knowledges of self and of other finite being. It is time now to consider the question of whether there is given in fact any kind of natural mystical experience of God Himself.

IV. NATURAL MYSTICAL EXPERIENCE OF GOD

If there is any natural mystical experience of the divine being, the most likely place to look for it is in the area of the awareness of createdness that was described earlier. This awareness is most obscure, most frequently lost sight of in the midst of all the stirrings of discursive reason and intellectual analysis. And yet there are many testimonials to the fact of such an immediate awareness, testimonials which themselves are frequently confused and distorted attempts to express what is radically unconceptualizable and ineffable.

Two distinct manners of approach to the "intuition of createdness" may be here pointed out. Below the superficial sameness and diversity of phenomena, below even the deeper sameness and diversity of essence, there is existence. Now although each thing seems to have its own existence, and even to exercise this existence as the existence of an independent subject, still even more deeply existence is *one*, one perfection. It is the diversity that is relatively superficial; at bottom there must be unity. There are many subjects, but there must also be one subject. There are finite selves, and there is the infinite self. One is sometimes able to see in the finite things before us that which transcends any one of them and is in all the others as much as it is in this one. From this viewpoint there is indeed a temptation to affirm the identity of all things in one being. Was this perhaps the intuition found in Wordsworth's "Tintern Abbey"?

A similar intuitive knowledge may be gained from reflection upon one's own subjectivity. Ordinarily, one is not thus preoccupied directly with the evidence of his subjectivity; but it is possible for him to withdraw from all the activity that distracts him from his selfhood and to focus upon this self, as we have already seen. But at the same moment as this withdrawal and concentration and recollection are achieved, there may appear not only the self but also that which is in all other things as well; and all of this is unified in one experience of self which is also experience of Self. Is this perhaps even a characteristic mode of contemplation among the Indian mystics?

And if one can retain this deep awareness of self and Self as he returns to the knowledge of other things, he discovers that the same Self is somehow revealed in the revelation of other things to him. If he did not understand this revelation before, it was because he was too taken up with the distinctions and diversities and uniquenesses of these things. But now he can see that, even while they are not the same, still the Same is found in all of them. This mode of contemplation may be found throughout the *Upanishads*.

Such an intuitive understanding of the self and God simultaneously was recognized by St. Thomas Aquinas in his commentary upon the *Sentences*, Bk. I, dist. III, q. 4, a. 5; and his failure to speak of such intuitive understanding in the *Summa Theologiae* can be explained as a change in perspective rather than as a change in doctrine. But whatever is to be said of the teaching of St. Thomas, the evidence calls for some metaphysical and psychological account.

One's own substantial existence, lived in the conscious reflexivity of spirit, is also intentional with respect to Existence itself, is a medium through which Infinite Existence itself can be understood in some manner. It is intentional because it exists in the spiritual soul of man and is at the same time in immediate dependence upon the pure existence. It is at the same time consciously (though obscurely) lived and exercised, and therefore a conscious (though obscure) union with pure existence. But this union is not an immediate vision of pure existence; pure existence is not seen in itself through the finite existence but rather is confronted (most inadequately) in another, namely in finite existence itself. In understanding my finite existence as dependent, I understand it as referring beyond itself to a pure existence of which I have some obscure apprehension in my apprehension of finite existence; but this is not at all to have a vision of pure existence in itself, for which no finite intentional medium could ever suffice. This paragraph will recall to the reader the similar analysis of Jacques Maritain in his *Ransoming the Time*.

But this pure existence is discovered not only in the lived intellection of substantial existence itself; it is also found in the existence of other things as intentionally lived in the intelligence of the knower. Here too is an existence in the spiritual soul of man and also immediately dependent, as is all existence, upon the pure existence; therefore this existence is intentional not only with respect to the known finite thing but also with respect to the pure existence itself. Again results a conscious union (though obscure) with pure existence, not seen in itself, but seen in this finite intentional existence.

Whether one looks into one's own subjectivity or into the being of other things precisely as known to him, he finds not only the finite existence but also in some manner the infinite existence. Everywhere, if one only learns to listen, there is immediate presence of pure existence in its activity of giving existence to things. Such conscious union with pure existence, however dark and inadequate it be, is nevertheless akin to sense experience, since it is a knowledge of this pure existence as acting here and now upon the knower in producing the influx of existence in the knower. It can therefore be called an *experience* of the pure existence or absolute being. Since this union with pure existence is in a way a supreme natural fulfillment of the tendency of the human spirit to ever greater degrees of intentional existence (whereby it acquires the being of all things and becomes all things), this union must be a cause of joy to the human spirit, a fruitive union. If this joy in absolute being is not found in most men, it is because they are so taken up with the many and the diverse in reality as to lose sight

ONTOLOGICAL PRINCIPLES OF MYSTICAL EXPERIENCE 251

of the all but sub-conscious experience of the One and the Same in all things. Nor is it easy for one to quiet all the faculties, the stirring of which is natural, in order to discover the Self through the self. But in fact, this discovery of the Self through the self is an all but necessary prerequisite for the discovery of the Self in the intentional living of the being of other things, unless one has already learned from elsewhere how to look beyond the things to that absolute being of which they are only the sacrament.

Is such a knowledge of the divine being as we have been describing mystical knowledge? There is here an obscure encounter with the divine existence, but it would seem to be encounter from "outside," an encounter with the exteriority of the divine existence, a union but not a communion. And yet although this conscious union with the divine being through the medium of created existence does not mean an immediate and proper attainment of the divine subjectivity in the human soul, yet it does mean a mediate and vicarious attainment of this divine subjectivity. Through the obscurely conscious living of one's own existence (or of the intentional existence of things) *as exercised*, one is referred to and enters into union with the divine existence as exercised. Here there is proper attainment of the exteriority of the divine existence (through the medium of consciously lived finite existence) and vicarious attainment of the interiority of the divine existence (in and through this same medium). This mode of communion with the divine being is in a way analogous to the mode of communion with others through affective connaturality that was described earlier, although this new mode of communion is entirely outside the order of affectivity in itself. Yet it is quite possible that this mode of communion be intermingled with other, more affective modes of communion with creatures and with God in the concrete order. Thus there can arise hybrid forms of natural mystical experience.

By now the reader may have become aware of a difficulty. Earlier, there was considered a form or forms of self-consciousness without any reference to communion with the divine being in the depth of such self-consciousness. Yet here one of the characteristic modes of coming to such mystical communion with the divine being is discovered in and through profound self-consciousness. Is it possible that this self-consciousness could in some cases lead one beyond itself to the divine being, while in other cases it would remain the ultimate term of experience?

In the light of all that has been said so far, this does seem to be the fact of the matter. It seems possible to account for this fact by introducing the concept of the focal point of consciousness. In our surface conscious life, the focal point of consciousness is in the object of consciousness – so much is this so that the reflexivity of consciousness hardly appears at all in young children, and even in some adults attention is for the most part directed to the object. And yet all the while the reflex awareness is there; it is simply left in the background. But interior souls, as they are called, begin to focus their attention upon this background; it is possible, as we have seen, even to bring it into the foreground of awareness by appropriate techniques of withdrawal and recollection. Here result the more profound modes of self-consciousness that we have seen.

Yet why should it be that in one case self-consciousness should be the ultimate term of the experience, while in other cases this self-consciousness should be the means to obscure communion with the Infinite Self? Again it seems to be a matter of the focal point of consciousness. What is given in the profound consciousness of the self is a certain global reality of the self with all its existential attitudes, whether natural or acquired, and of this self as dependent upon and essentially relative to the ground of its being in the divine being. Whether one rests in the finite pole of this global reality or through it rests in the infinite pole (and in either case it is a matter of groping in darkness and obscurity) depends on the sum total of existential attitudes of the finite subject. These attitudes serve to orientate, to focus, even his most profound consciousness, to open out his attentiveness and awareness even toward the Infinite Being or to close in this attentiveness and awareness on the finite self. Here, then, moral attitudes are of great importance. What degree of moral purity is actually required as a condition for such natural mystical communion with God? Is it possible that this degree will never be achieved without the workings, at least in secrecy, of supernatural charity? If this be so, then such a natural mysticism would not appear in the concrete order of things except as a result of a life directed toward a far more intimate communion with God. Still it would remain true that this mysticism is in itself an essentially natural mode of experience, attainable by efforts themselves entirely natural, at least substantially.

The danger in the practice of technique to lead to this mode of experience is evident enough. May one not easily mistake the term of this obscure experience, and take for communion with the divine being what is only a most profound experience of self? In each case there is an encounter with a certain plenitude of being, an encounter in darkness and obscurity. It seems that the encounter with the Infinite Self carries with it its own guarantee, but perhaps this guarantee will not be adequately understood without light from theological or at least philosophical reason. In any event, what of those who have not actually attained to this communion, who have no guarantee of anything, but who lead themselves to think that their encounter with self is an encounter with God? Perhaps the Quietist forms of contemplation, and other similar forms outside the Christian tradition, are for the most part victims of this deception. It may be that ordinarily the best course is not to seek for this kind of communion with God, but to accept it if it occurs as a kind of by-product of the life of grace and recognize it for what it is.

The general remarks that have been made concerning mystical communion with God through profound self-consciousness, to explain the role of diverse focal points of consciousness and to point out the danger involved in seeking this mode of communion, can also be applied to the approach to the same mystical communion with God through the consciousness of the existence of other things as intentionally lived in the intelligence of the knower. Here again, the encounter with God can be confounded with an encounter with some creature or creatures.

But, after all these cautions, it must still be admitted that even the encounter with the depths of the self and of other creatures is itself a very great good and can be referred to the contemplation of God, who is revealed in all His works. And if one should somehow mount through the darkness of self-consciousness and of the consciousness of the intentional existence of other things to a meeting in the dark with the Infinite Self, One and the Same at the heart of all things and of all experience, this too is a gift of God.

There yet remains another natural approach to mystical communion with God, that through the affective connaturality induced by a natural love of God. Such a connaturality is similar to that induced by love of creatures, but it also differs in accordance with the difference in the mode of knowledge of God and of creatures which is the principle of such connaturality. The natural mystical knowledge of God which has just been described can itself lead to a further, affective communion with God in so far as the plenitude of the Infinite Being, even attained in darkness, immediately and properly present in the soul in a conscious manner, connaturalizes the will to itself. Yet even here the divine subjectivity itself is attained only vicariously, since it is only vicariously that it connaturalizes the will. This affective connaturalization must needs be only vicarious, since the mystical communion which was its principle was only a vicarious attainment of the divine subjectivity, as was seen earlier.

The objective and discursive knowledge of God through a constructed idea of God and the demonstration of its foundation in reality lead to another kind of love of God, mediated through creatures and through such objective knowledge (or knowledge of objectivity). Since this love must have a non-immediate and unlimited term, affective connaturality here is a kind of project toward unlimited being, a tendency which cannot be terminated by any of the finite modes of being and which remains a kind of completely open grasping. Were it to fasten upon any of the special modes of being as a term, an ultimate term, this openness would disappear. But if the openness and projection are maintained, then there is an objectifying knowledge of God suffused with affective regard; and this affective regard is the principle of a *mediated*, vicarious presence of the divine subject. This is communion with the divine being, and yet it is *communion across a gulf* if we may so speak. Although it fulfills the requirement laid down at the beginning for mystical knowledge, it stretches the standard to the limit.

Is it possible that such an attainment of God through affective connaturality could be found even without any explicit objectifying knowledge of God as its principle? Jacques Maritain has pointed to the possibility of such a mode of attaining God in his essay on "The Immanent Dialectic of the First Act of Freedom" in *The Range of Reason*. But discussion of this mode of communion is better left to some remarks at the end on mystical experience in the life of action as opposed to that of contemplation; for it is in the dynamism of moral life that this mode or communion with God is to be discovered.

V. CONTEMPLATIVE SUPERNATURAL MYSTICAL EXPERIENCE

Since descriptions of the supernatural mystical states, to the extent that description is possible, abound, it is unnecessary here to repeat them even in summary form. The problem here is to offer some explanation for them in terms of principles drawn form philosophical psychology, metaphysics, and theology – even more specifically, in terms of the understanding of the supernatural life of faith and grace already presented in the preceding essays. But it is necessary to emphasize the hypothetical nature of the theory to be presented – at present it is a tentative account looking toward the possibility of modification and refinement in the face of ever more detailed examination of the mystical states. The most that can be said for the theory is that it is consistent with the philosophical principles of the earlier essays and that it does provide an account of such mystical states both as regards their continuity with common Christian life and as regards their unique newness in the life of the Christian. At the present moment it seems impossible to do much more than this in the face of the mysterious states of the mystics. Yet, if the aforementioned philosophical and theological principles be valid, the theory can claim a good deal of ground for itself and a fair degree of probability.

Be it noted once more that in speaking of the supernatural mystical states we focus attention precisely on non-objectifying modes of grace-inspired conscious communion with God and of self-consciousness and consciousness of other things in the light of such conscious communion with God. Such a grace-inspired, non-objectifying sense of presence of God is not simply continuous with that of ordinary Chrstian life; there is some continuity in the life of the Christian who is elevated to the mystical states, but there is also discontinuity and genuine newness. There may well be other elements of newness besides the new sense of presence, such as visions, locutions, etc.; but these accidental elements must here be set aside entirely in order to focus on the new mode of divine presence which specifies the mystical states.

In Scholastic accounts of the nature of such mystical experience, some authors have considered its formal principle to be in the intellect, while others have located this formal principle in the will, in a kind of loving taste. The object of such experience has been regarded by some as primarily God Himself in His uncreated being, known either mediately or immediately; others have considered the object of such experience to be primarily the created supernatural grace of God, which also refers beyond itself in some manner to God. Such general theoretical positions about mystical experience are determined in the light of general philosophical and theological contexts; and this must be so, since the problem of mystical experience for the philosopher and theologian is always one of explaining its nature in terms of what is already known from elsewhere about the psychological, metaphysical, and theological relations of man to God. The same method must be followed here, but we may hope to achieve a more adequate account with the help of the earlier analyses of various aspects of Christian life in faith and supernatural grace in general.

1. *Faith and Mysticism*

Since supernatural mysticism, from the very meaning of supernatural, is produced by principles that surpass the natural order, by grace, the only adequate perspective from which it can be considered is the Christian one. For all grace since the fall of man, and perhaps the grace of Adam as well, all grace up to the end of time throughout all human history, all this is the grace of Christ and can be known for what it is only through the teaching of Christ and his Church. Such grace could be found outside the limits of the visible Church even where the message of the Gospel has hardly been preached; but always it is from, of, and tending toward Christ and the Church. And the root and foundation of supernatural life, wherever it be found in the world, is always supernatural faith – be this faith found in a perhaps wholly inarticulate form in a good basic moral option made by one who has never heard the Gospel preached or to whom its mystery has never been opened, or be this faith found in the articulated profession of the Christian doctrine on the authority of the revealing God.

The nature of supernatural faith has already been considered in detail in the long essay on faith and intersubjectivity, but it is well to recall some points relevant to the present consideration of supernatural mystical experience. Faith was seen to consist in an intellectual assent presupposing an affective commitment to the revealer. Ordinarily, this faith is articulated in a set of formulated affirmations grounded on acceptance of the authority of the revealer. This acceptance of the authority of the revealer is first of all the just-mentioned affective commitment, even before it is expressed in a determinate affirmation. The manner in which the articulated assent can be actually grounded in an affective commitment through which the authority of the revealer calls for such an assent has been considered in the essay on faith and intersubjectivity. Through the very formulations of the faith in the preaching of the Church in the context of all the signs of credibility, a grace-inspired affection (*pius affectus credulitatis*) tends toward and also obscurely renders present the *locutio increata*, the revealing God as the primary and infallible motive for articulated commitment both to God Himself as the Supreme Truth and to the affirmations which express something of His revelation to men. In virtue of this grace-inspired connaturality and obscure knowledge through connaturality, one can both be aware that the assent of faith is in accordance with and called for by his now-elevated being and cling to the obscurely present *locutio increata* as the formal motive for the freely elicited articulated assent of faith. The free assent is grounded on the free commitment, which in the line of affection and connaturality goes far beyond the first grace-inspired affection already mentioned, deepening and stabilizing the union of the believer with the present *locutio increata*, perhaps even immediately disposing for the reception and possession of the infused virtue of faith. This infused virtue of faith renders the union of the believer with the present *locutio increata per se* permanent, so that he may easily elicit acts of faith at appropriate times and live his life in the context of faith. This description obviously has had in mind the adult who comes from non-belief to belief; baptism of course brings with it the habit of faith, both for the infant and for the adult, and necessitates a revised account – but enough has already been said to indicate in general the relation between articulated assent and affective commitment and the formal motive or ground of the assent of faith.

But we have also seen the possibility even of an inarticulate faith, one that is not formulated in revealed affirmations but rather is only an adherence, inspired by grace, to the being and goodness of God as the saving good, known obscurely through the grace-inspired affection for and connaturality with the unqualified and unlimited moral good. Such adherence, much deeper than and too obscure for expression in formulated affirmations, nevertheless is an obscurely conscious possession of the saving truth and must be included within the possibilities of an appropriately analogical notion of intellectual *assent*, such as is required for the reality of supernatural faith. If there be no articulation here, still there is genuine attainment of the very ground of articulation and formulation, not express faith but not merely the intention of faith – rather, a radical and inarticulate, but true faith.

And between the poles of adequately articulated faith within the visible Church, and wholly inarticulate faith such as has been described, there remains the possibility of inadequately articulated, but genuine faith – encounter, commitment and assent to at least some of the formulated affirmations of faith, such as the existence of a saving God under whatever name and however conceived, with whatever heretical or pagan additions as may be found in all the diverse religions of mankind. These additions need not mean the absence of faith and hope and charity, which focus not on such additions but on the kernels of divine truth which can shine forth in the midst of error and even sin – not only within the visible Church but everywhere in all the world.

The three possible states of the life of supernatural faith – inarticulate, inadequately articulated, and adequately articulated – point also to possible diverse states of mystical experience itself, and also to possible diversity in the natural accompaniments of such mystical experience in the line of images, concepts, physical effects, reflective interpretation. Yet such diversity does not mean inauthenticity in the profound life of grace and even of mystical states among separated Christians, Jews, Mohammedans, Hindus, Buddhists, or others. The same grace of Christ can call men through the *Koran* or the *Bhaghavad-Gita* or the *Analects* of Confucius, even though it is adequately revealed only through the Church and its Scripture. But here we focus attention only upon mystical experience in the Church, in which alone is found the adequate state for the flowering of mystical life and of supernatural life in general.

A precise conception of supernatural faith is most vital for the proper understanding of supernatural mystical experience. If supernatural mysticism is truly a part of supernatural life at least in some Christians, this must be because it is in some manner an extension of the life of supernatural faith. Fot the supernatural life of the wayfarer on earth is at every point a life of and through faith. If, in some rare instances, someone like St. Paul might be in a transient manner elevated beyond the state of the wayfarer even to the beatific vision itself, this still remains a rare exception to the ordinary rule even for mystical states – these too in their beginning, middle, and end are part of the life of faith.

In many theological circles, divine faith is regarded as a free but purely intellectual act. An act of the will is presupposed, but faith is formally constituted only by a set of intellectual affirmations. It is not necessary here to dwell upon the difficulties of such a purely intellectualist conception of divine faith; they have already been met in the extended treatment of faith and intersubjectivity. But it is useful to consider the problem posed by such a view of faith in the relation of supernatural mystical experience to divine faith. Whether the formal principle of mystical experience be placed in the intellect or in the will, it is difficult to sustain the continuity between mystical experience and the life of such an intellectualist faith.

If the formal principle of mystical experience is thought to be non-affective, rather more like an infused intelligible species, mystical experience lies outside the domain of faith to the extent that such an experience would be fundamentally non-free as to its mode – contrary to the radical freedom of the act of faith. This difficulty indeed holds against any purely intellectualist view of mystical experience, no matter what idea of divine faith is accepted. Supernatural mystical experience is always conditioned by this freedom of faith, and indeed also by the freedom of charity. Even the intellectualist theory of divine faith must recognize the freedom of faith and so cannot accept a purely intellectualist theory of mystical experience.

If the formal principle of mystical experience is thought to be affective – in the line of charity – so that mystical experience is a knowledge through a supernatural affective connaturality, then the object of mystical experience is simply outside the object of the divine faith of the intellectualist theory of faith. A new knowledge appears here, mediately dependent, it is true, through charity upon faith, but still a really new knowledge beyond the object of faith. Such a knowledge might well be "interpreted" in the light of faith; but it is not continuous with faith, not really a growth of the life of faith. Here would appear to be a rather fundamental break between the ordinary Christian life and the mystical state, a break which is finally unacceptable – the mystic too is through and through a man of faith and not a gnostic.

But if the intellectualist theory of faith is set aside in favor of the view that Christian faith even while being intellectually articulated yet rests upon an affective relation that is already the principle of a knowledge through affective connaturality, in which the very formal motive of faith itself is attained in a non-objectifying intersubjective communion, mystical experience can be understood as a kind of extension within the life of supernatural faith. Here such experience is in no need of an extrinsic "interpretation" in the light of faith, for it is never separated from this faith and from its articulations, never outside the object of faith, and indeed itself articulated in terms of faith itself – so that the very mystical experience itself can be in some manner expressed in terms of the dogmatic formulae and the formulae of theological reflection. The formulae of faith in such a view are not at any point to be regarded as pure intellectual affirmations without any element of intersubjective encounter with the revealing God, and therefore are able to aid even in the expression of the content of mystical experience. Faith attains to the divine plenitude beyond the propositional formulations, and mystical experience only reaches further in the same line, and across the same formulae.

The latter view of faith is of course the view that was presented in the essay on faith and intersubjectivity and therefore rests on a much broader base than its ability to provide a more satisfactory relation of mystical experience to faith. But if mystical experience can be well integrated with this kind of faith, provided that this mystical experience itself be conceived as not purely intellectual but radically affective in nature, it still remains necessary to explain in detail the ontological structure of such mystical experience.

2. *Charity and Mysticism*

Supernatural mystical experience presupposes not only faith and hope but also charity. It might be possible to discuss at length the possibility of exceptions to this law, but it is at least the ordinary law. Moreover, analytic reflection in the light of the earlier essay on the finite modes of the supernatural will tend to confirm this ordinary law. The presence of God in the mystical states is not just His ordinary presence by causality (whether natural of supernatural), nor just a vicarious presence such as is found in ordinary love, in which the beloved is said to be in the lover by affective connaturality. Rather, mystical union presupposes divine indwelling and quasi-formal union of God to the soul – with charity as the primary formal effect of this union and also the ultimate material disposition for it. The affective element in faith – affection for God as the Supreme Truth revealing Himself – is not a sufficient disposition for the indwelling and is only a remote preparation for it; though God becomes present to the believer in virtue of faith, as the *locutio increata*, this presence is still the presence of a completely *other*, mediated through a vicarious presence in virtue of a created act or habit. Similar comments must be made in regard to the affection of supernatural hope for God as good for us and willing to give Himself to us. But it is quite otherwise with charity. Charity too does give the presence of God as an *other*, mediated through a vicarious presence in virtue of affective connaturality; but it is also, as has been said, the ultimate disposition for the indwelling and quasi-formal union, and consequently for a non-mediated presence (to the will – not to the intellect, for this would be the beatific vision).

This non-mediated presence cannot be simply unconscious, for it is immediate presence of the supremely intelligible being in finite spirit. It is true that this presence is non-mediated only in relation to the will; but the will is in the intellect, and the reflexivity and auto-presence of spirit render at least obscurely conscious whatever is thus present. But such consciousness and presence of God must remain in the background and only on the horizon, in a manner analogous to that in which substantial self-presence and presence of God through such substantial self-presence must remain in the background in ordinary human consciousness. Indeed, the inaccessibility, the impossibility of bringing such consciousness and presence into direct focus is even greater in this case of the indwelling. The problem is analogous to that of the beatific vision; how can there be non-mediated presence of God at the focal point of consciousness when the very nature of created knowledge seems to require that it be mediated?

3. *The Mystical Light*

But if the focal point of consciousness can be supernaturally moved by the light of glory outside the created order, then perhaps something analogous is possible in the domain of mystical experience, through some kind of "mystical light." If such a mystical light in the intellect were to open a man to the non-mediated presence of God indwelling in quasi-formal union with the will, then he might well speak in the language of the mystics of immediate "felt" (rather than seen) presence, even of "fusion" with God, of man "becoming God," of the processions of the Trinity taking place in the soul, of abysses of inexhaustible goodness, of an ocean in which one loses himself, and on and on without end. Note that such a mystical light would have for its formal object (on the side of the thing itself) the same aspect as does ordinary supernatural knowledge of God through affective connaturality in charity, namely, God as felt and tasted in love – and in this respect a continuity would be preserved between the mystical light, charity, hope, and even the affective encounter at the basis of faith. But the mystical light would be a genuinely new formal light (on the side of the knowing subject) on that formal object – in this respect the real newness of the mystical states in relation to ordinary Christian life is safeguarded. The difference in formal light here is precisely the difference between a mediated, vicarious attainment of God as felt and tasted in love (therefore of God Himself as thus lovable, touchable, tasteable) and an attainment of His non-mediated presence under the mystical light. This difference is analogous to that between the formal light of divine faith and the formal light of the beatific vision (the light of glory).

The nature of the mystical light will occupy us further on, but it is first useful and profitable to consider briefly some aspects of ordinary supernatural knowledge through the affective connaturality of charity. If the mystical light focuses attention precisely on God as present in the will, as lovable and tasteable by the will, then mystical experience can be viewed in a way as a prolongation and deepening of that ordinary knowledge – though of course the *mode* is now quite extraordinary.

4. *Ordinary Charity and the Presence of God*

In ordinary charity there does arise a presence, vicarious and oblique, of God through affective connaturality, a presence mediated by charity itself. The non-mediated presence already spoken of remains very much in the most obscure background of consciousness, as has already been pointed out. The mediated presence itself remains far in the background when there is question only of habitual charity; but in actual charity the mediated presence comes toward the foreground of consciousness (although it still remains a presence mediated through love, conscious through the consciousness of love, felt and tasted only vicariously in love, known through love as through a *medium in quo* and therefore always known obliquely rather than directly). This mediated presence of God may or may not be more or less attended to, depending on differences in one's state of activity or formal prayer and on differences of psychological temperament, circumstances, etc. It is possible that such a mediated presence can remain very much in the foreground of consciousness even when charity is operative in the direction of external activity – this is an ordinary (non-mystical, in the strict sense) state of contemplation in action. Clearly the mediated presence of God through supernatural charity will intensify with the intensive growth of charity itself, even to the point at which an affective prayer of simple regard could become the most attractive and dominant occupation of a soul.

It is perhaps unnecessary to point out again that the Christian attains this mediated presence across the formulae of faith and understands it in the light of these formulae and those of reflective theological penetration of these formulae. But this is in no way arbitrary, since charity as the principle of mediation is itself rooted in this same faith and could not exist without it. The reality that charity attains is the same reality that has revealed itself to faith.

The inclination of charity has two aspects; the objective aspect, or term which the inclination has, and the subjective aspect, the ontological and psychological reality which *is* this tendency in the one who has it. The first aspect of charity was the concern of the preceding paragraph and must of course be of primary interest in the study of the mediated and non-mediated presence of God through charity. But the second deserves a few words here also; the consideration of this aspect of ordinary supernatural charity, apart from the mystical light, in fact provides some ground for understanding, not the mystical union in itself, but the mystical states in the subject of such union.

Subjectively considered, the inclination of charity is the most important and dominating factor in the moral decisions of one who has charity, since these decisions are to a great extent grounded on the affective connaturality of the moral agent. This aspect of the subjective inclination of charity does not concern us here; it will be recalled in the brief discussion later of mystical experience in moral action. Here we are concerned with contemplative mysticism.

Rather, here we focus upon the subjective inclination of charity insofar as it grounds a certain overall awareness of oneself, an attitude toward one's state of being. Obscure awareness of this fundamental inclination, simultaneous with awareness of defects, but also of subsidiary good inclinations, gives a certain tonality to one's self-awareness, one which varies somewhat depending on which aspects of this sum-total of affective attitudes are more central in one's self-knowledge at a given moment or a given period. Of course, this tonality and its variation would be present even without charity; in such a case the ground of overall awareness would necessarily be some other fundamental inclination, ultimately egocentric in nature.

It is possible for a man to immerse himself to such an extent in external concerns as to be hardly aware for long periods of this complex affective tonality in his self-consciousness, but it is always there. The reflective Christian cannot help but face this complex affective reality of the self before God, the discordance as well as the concordance between so many inclinations and what he thinks and hopes to be the fundamental inclination of charity. This is why ordinary Christian self-knowledge cannot be the occasion either for unmixed joy or for unmixed sorrow, but must rather be a reason for both at once.

If the mystical light opens the mystic to the unmediated presence of God as loved and thereby tasted, it must also result in a great intensification in the awareness of one's concordance, but even more of one's discordance with the demands of the love and the lovableness of God, and of the disparity between any creature, created light, or created consolation, and the infinity of God. It is along these lines that the explanation of some extraordinary subjective states and dark nights of the mystics must be sought.

Apart from any question of the mystical light and of the mystical states, the affective tonality of self-consciousness and its dependence upon one's fundamental inclination also afford a ground for understanding the psychological rules for the discernment of spirits, judging inclinations that may arise, according to the agreeability or dissonance ("ease" or "violence" of entry) of such inclinations with the fundamental affective tonality of self-consciousness. But a detailed discussion of this point would take us far away from the central question of the nature of the mystical light itself.

5. *The Nature of the Mystical Light*

It is time now to attack that question and to say what can be said, at least by way of hypothesis, concerning the nature of this mystical light. One may begin by considering the ontological and psychological situation in the soul advanced in Christian life and living with intense charity. The non-mediated presence of the indwelling Trinity in the will by quasi-formal union is far in the psychological background, although no real presence of spirit in spirit can fail to be at least obscurely a conscious presence. This obscure non-mediated presence to the will and in the will is mediated to the intellect by the will itself, in the consciousness which the intellect has of the will and whatever is in the will. But to know the indwelling Trinity in this manner, with no medium save the will itself, is hardly to know it at all – the being of the will is a most disproportionate medium and the presence of God here is indistinguishable from the other elements of one's ground-consciousness. The mediated presence of God through habitual charity also lies in the remote psychological background, in the most obscure consciousness of such a *habitus*, connaturality, and the "object" of this connaturality. But the mediated presence of God through actual charity is more toward the foreground of consciousness, although even here the presence is necessarily oblique (since the knowledge of God here is entirely in function of the reflexive knowledge of love and connaturality as subjective states of the lover – this reflexive awareness is a *medium in quo* in relation to God as lovable) and vicarious, rather than direct and proper. Knowledge through affective connaturality is necessarily thus limited, by its very nature as being through *con*naturality.

All the same, God is present in one who has charity; and the intellect of such a one seeks to know more of God, being led by His love. And yet the radical impossibility remains, the radical impossibility of focusing directly upon the thus present God so as to let Him occupy the foreground and focal point of intellectual consciousness without the mediation of any creature. Only the light of glory enables a creature to transcend this impossibility in the beatific vision. But still short of such a vision, the mystics testify that a much fuller cognitive union with God is possible to one who is led by love and given the further gift of the mystical light of infused contemplation. And if God is indeed already present in one who has charity, in the manners described, then it is unnecessary for the mystical light to do anything but to illuminate in some manner this divine presence, to open the intellect to a much fuller, though still not face-to-face, awareness of the indwelling Trinity.

If we consider supernatural mystical experience as a further self-communication of God to men, then it can be set into the context of His other self-communications – not as a manner in which man rises to God but rather as another manner in which God descends to man. His self-communication in faith and hope, and then in the quasi-formal union which has charity as its primary formal effect, as preparation for the ultimate communion of the beatific vision, has been considered in detail in preceding essays. There is a great gulf between the obscurity of the presence of God in His quasi-formal union with the will and through charity as the primary formal effect of this union, and the clarity of God's presence in the beatific vision. Mystical experience and the mystical light stand between these two as a testimony to and promise of the full vision, not only for the mystic himself but often enough even for other men.

The function of the mystical light is to elevate and open the intellect to God's presence in the will. This light then is not a *medium quo* or *medium in quo* but rather a *lumen sub quo*, analogous to the light of glory in the beatific vision. But unlike the light of glory, this mystical light only opens the intellect to the presence of God as mediated, and therefore also veiled, by the will; the will itself here remains a *medium in quo*, so that what the mystical light unveils is the will precisely as conjoined to God in quasi-formal union and through charity.

These are in fact two distinct modes of presence of the same reality of God, two "levels" of this presence; and the non-mediated quasi-formal union still remains, even under the mystical light, in principle more obscure than the mediated union through the affective connaturality of charity. Even without the mystical light this latter is more toward the foreground of consciousness, although not yet directly at the focal point of consciousness. Consequently, with the progressive increase in intensity of the mystical light, the mediated union through affective connaturality comes toward the center of psychological consciousness more rapidly than does the non-mediated union. The more direct awareness of the Trinity indwelling in the will in quasi-formal union will come only with greater intensity of the mystical light.

In the lower degrees of intensity of mystical light, when love begins to pass over into the condition of object and actually does so – but with the presence of the indwelling Trinity itself still in the obscure background of consciousness – the presence of God through love grows in consciousness; but paradoxically this is a presence in the dark, so far as the lower levels of human understanding are concerned. No natural understanding, no formulations of understanding, can directly grasp what is not so much seen as felt in the darkness of love. In this great darkness of a presence that seems more like absence, so far as the psychological order is concerned, the soul learns in a passive manner, and perhaps with intense suffering, the tremendous gulf between God and every creature.

In this dark night of passive purification, detachment from creatures can be perfected and love for God grow to new intensity, thus disposing the soul for the higher degrees of the mystical light which can illuminate (by opening the intellect more fully to what is already present in the will) the consciousness of the divine indwelling itself in the non-mediated quasi-formal union with the will. Although this illuminated consciousness transcends even more completely all the activity of our lower understanding, still this presence of indwelling is not a presence in the darkness any more but a presence in mysterious light – which the metaphors of the mystics strain to describe and cannot help but fall short of. All along it was this presence toward which the mystical light was tending, as its proper formal object; but the lower degrees of mystical light could not bring it into direct focus yet, but rather first focused attention on the formal effects of this indwelling – charity, acts of charity, and the mediated presence of God through affective connaturality. To the extent that the indwelling presence enters the focal point of consciousness under the mystical light, to that extent presence in the darkness (mediated by love) becomes presence in the light (of the "substantial touch" of God in quasi-formal non-mediated union with the will).

Would it be strange if such an awakening from darkness to light should hold one fast, in total absorption of ecstasy and suspension of faculties – at least until the psyche should adjust itself to such brilliant illumination? Until that adjustment such illumination could only be transitory. But the day might come when the lower operations of intellect and will would be integrated under such a mystical perception, still growing in intensity along with growth in intensity of love, so that the permanent state of mystical union in spiritual marriage could come into being.

Such is the hypothesis I offer to understand the essence of contemplative supernatural mystical experience. But it is perhaps unnecessary to point out how generic the hypothesis is. The question of the actual succession of stages in the mystical life has only been most lightly touched upon, and with it the whole question of the fluctuations, gradual or sudden, and even possible withdrawal, temporary or permanent, of the mystical light. Here I would repeat the cautions of Truhlar and De Guibert against too great an emphasis upon the classification of stages – these classification differ from one descriptive analysis to another, although there is no denying some kind of very generic similarity. Further questions are endless. What of the life of the imagination and of formulating reason, and even of lower intuitive reason, in the course of the increase of mystical light? Mystical writings themselves testify to many aspects of these matters; but it is impossible to enter upon any detailed study here, and I feel no security yet with any generalization that might be made. But I have restricted myself to a very limited task, to construct a reasonable hypothesis to account for the general fact of mystical experience of God in the supernatural order. The further, more detailed development of the hypothesis must wait for another time.

But one question does require special attention here, that of the role of the gifts of the Holy Spirit in the mystical contemplation we have been describing. These gifts have been favored by many as the media of mystical contemplation, and of mystically inspired action as well. It is necessary to make some remarks concerning the reality of the gifts and their position in relation to mystical experience.

6. The Gifts of the Holy Spirit and Mystical Experience

The gifts of the Holy Spirit are here understood in the manner in which John of St. Thomas understood them in his writings on them; this idea of the gifts has in fact been dominant in the Thomist attempt to make them the principles of mystical experience. The enumeration of Isaias 11 is taken to present seven really distinct, both among themselves and also from natural and infused virtues, modes of supernatural being – seven *habitus* which render their possessor docile to the inspirations of the Holy Spirit. The infused virtues are thought to give man a capacity for supernatural action, but an action that still must be performed in an all too human way; it would be necessary to think about action in the light of supernatural principles, to reason it out, and then finally to act in the light of the conclusions. But such a mode of action is in fact inadequate; it is more like limping along. We are actually much better equipped to act in the natural sphere, according to rapidly formed prudential judgments made according to the basic moral inclinations of the agent. The gifts of the Holy Spirit are thought to supply the supernatural counterpart of such basic moral inclinations – they are a set of supernatural instincts, modes of openness to the illuminations and inspirations of the Holy Spirit that are essential for all supernatural action.

Without inquiring at all into the question of the actual enumeration of the gifts and whether there are not six or ten or some other number, it is important to ask whether the reality of the gifts must be that of really distinct *habitus* or whether thay can be really identified with the organism of the infused theological virtues of faith, hope, and charity. It seems that two suppositions would have to be verified in order to necessitate a real distinction from the theological virtues. First, man would have to be seen as living a still completely autonomous life with grace simply being an internal elevating principle that is more the property of man than the property of God. Such a man would in his autonomy feel the necessity of passing a rational human judgment in a simply human way on every illumination and inspiration of grace that is offered to him, and consequently would need added supernatural instincts in order to be easily and readily moved by such actual graces. Second, a very narrow conception of *habitus* would be necessary, so that the theological virtues of faith, hope, and charity would be narrowly regarded only in terms of their formal objects and not in terms of their adequate object and the state which they induce in the one who has them. It would be as though the inclination of charity to love God in Himself above all things had absolutely no effect on the whole dynamism of every aspect of moral life apart from the introduction of further *habitus*. This is to be so preoccupied with the formal nature as to forget that the whole state of the faculty is modified by the infusion of this *habitus*. Such a narrow conception of *habitus* is in fact evidenced by John of St. Thomas

But against the first supposition, man does not autonomously possess the theological virtues as his own property; this was seen in the earlier treatment of the finite modes of supernatural being, which remain more of God than of man even as they are given to man. Man by grace lives God's own life in himself, and from another point of view God by this grace lives His own life in man – with man's consent. But such a man does not stand off in autonomy to pass judgment on the illuminations and inspirations of grace that are offered. These actual illuminations and inspirations are only fructifications of the life that has already taken hold of this man (with his consent); this man has already committed himself into the hands of the Spirit in accepting the gift of divine life, and is already in readiness for the impulses of the Spirit – though he remains free to reject them.

Against the second supposition it must be emphasized that faith, hope, and charity, in themselves already connaturalities to God and God's action, also connaturalize the *faculties* to God and His supernatural action. The entire dynamism of the faculties is modified by the primacy of faith in the intellectual order and of charity in the moral order, so that these faculties are rendered docile to the divine movement in every respect. (Yet this does not preclude the possibility of free rejection.)

This means that the addition of really distinct gifts as supernatural instincts is quite unnecessary. The gifts are only aspects, logically distinct (with a distinction that is grounded in the superabundant richness of the theological virtues and the inadequacies of human conceptualization), of the life of faith, hope, and charity. Similar remarks could be made about the infused moral virtues spoken of by Thomists and others. Why should their reality be anything other than the entirely new state and dynamism of the entire moral life in a will that is fundamentally oriented by supernatural charity?

What the doctrine of the gifts points to is a certain readiness in intellect and will, a readiness that comes only with the love of charity, although it also presupposes faith and hope. There is an attentiveness in the intellect to what charity tastes (and this is the scope of the gifts of understanding, wisdom, science, and counsel), and a readiness in the will for what charity demands (and here is the scope of the gifts of fortitude, piety, and fear of the Lord). The doctrine of John of St. Thomas on the gifts points up his tendency to ontologize some logical entities, to transform logical into real distinctions – a tendency which is very marked in his metaphysical analysis in the *Ars Logica* and in the *Philosophia Naturalis*. But if this too hasty and uncritical ontologization must be noted, the excellent phenomenology on which it is based must also be noted. To criticize the real distinction of the gifts in the doctrine of John of St. Thomas is not at all to minimize the value of the phenomenology of the spiritual life that he presents in the light of this sevenfold division – a division that is surely grounded not only in Isaias 11 but also in centuries of Christian tradition and spiritual experience.

The gifts can also be regarded as aspects of the "galvanizing" effect of charity on the entire life of the "new man." If the affection at the base of faith is finally for the good of the intellect (and therefore leading to a notional assent to the truths of faith), the affection of charity is for the good of the total man (and means a real assent, the meaning of which is partially understood in each of the gifts, a readiness for ever greater fullness of divine life and for the movement of the Spirit).

If some have used the names of the gifts, and especially those of understanding, wisdom, and science, to designate various aspects of the mystical light, this is not surprising. Since these three gifts are supposed to refer to various modes of attentiveness to what charity tastes, and since the mystical light is a special means of such attentiveness – although in fact the mystical light goes even farther than this to the non-mediated quasi-formal presence of God in the will – it is not difficult to use the doctrine of the gifts to account for at least the lower levels of mystical experience. The same is true as regards the other four of the seven gifts, although their role concerns not so much contemplative mystical experience as the mystical experience in active life that will be briefly considered below. But even apart from the seeming inability of the doctrine of the gifts to provide an account of the higher levels of mystical experience, experience of the non-mediated indwelling, we have already seen that there is not sufficient basis for even considering the gifts as distinct real principles in themselves. Accordingly the doctrine of the gifts does not seem to be a sufficiently fruitful conception to merit further consideration in this treatment of the principles of mystical experience.

VI. SOME REMARKS ABOUT MYSTICAL EXPERIENCE IN ACTIVE LIFE

Apart from any consideration of the supernatural life, two modes of moral knowing should be distinguished: the objectifying knowledge of moral principles through formulated concepts and propositions, and the primary moral knowing through the consciousness of affective inclinations and of the fittingness or non-fittingness of certain objects or courses of action with rightly ordered inclination. This primary moral knowing can itself be the ground for moral knowledge in the objectifying mode by judgment through affective connaturality. Indeed, all genuine moral knowing in the objectifying mode must ultimately correspond to primary moral knowing in the non-objectifying mode, although one can come to such formulated moral propositions in another way by a kind of deduction from metaphysical and other speculatively philosophical knowledge, or from divine revelation.

But in fact non-objectifying moral knowing through affective connaturality plays a part in every concrete human act, at least at the level of the prudential judgment regarding the individual case as such. The standards – including objective norms at least implicitly – are part of the global situation which must be considered before any moral act; refusal to consider moral standards is itself already a bad moral act, if such consideration is seen to be called for here and now. But one fundamental standard is the very being of the moral agent as such, as endowed here and now with a whole set of concrete inclinations that have been accepted as his own or against which he is striving (and therefore inclined) to set up a contrary inclination. It is possible for the moral agent to engage in deliberate rational reflection before the moral act, and this is necessary at times for a particular case or with a view to avoiding acting according to an acquired inclination that is no longer accepted as desirable, or in order to evaluate inclinations that one finds in oneself. But frequently enough in daily decisions the concrete being of the moral agent with his various inclinations is the principal standard for moral decision, with none but an implicit reference to objectively formulated principles. But even when such principles are explicitly brought to bear on the question of moral choice, the ultimate prudential decision remains unmade until the existential inclinations here and now of the moral agent are consulted in the face of the possibilities here and now; the prudential judgment concerns what here and now, in view of the possibilities, the standards, the total situation, befits the moral subject who must act.

Most important of all is the primary moral inclination of the agent, the basic moral option of the end, which dominates the entire affective tonality of self-consciousness. In the concrete there is always question of the option in supernatural charity or some finally egocentric inclination. Secondary inclinations, conflicting or harmonious with the basic inclination, also modify the affective tonality of consciousness – so as to make it easier or more difficult to choose in accordance with the fundamental inclination, perhaps even disposing one for the act by which he changes his fundamental option. And we cannot overlook the transient inclinations that spontaneously arise in the moral agent precisely in virtue of his consideration of the diverse possibilities for action and pursuit of value at the present moment. All these inclinations can be consulted at the moment of prudential moral decision; but the moral agent himself decides in freedom which inclinations and which fittingness shall prevail in the concrete action, perhaps even to the point of forsaking one basic option for another in the process. But ordinarily one would expect that the already made basic moral option would exercise a dominant role as inclination and connaturality in the prudential decision as to what is most fitting for the moral agent at this moment.

All that has been said concerns ordinary moral knowing in men who are either with or without ordinary supernatural charity. Interesting though it would be to follow up these observations with a more detailed analysis, especially of the dynamics of conversion to supernatural life in charity, we shall not do so but will rather move immediately to some remarks about the effect of the supernatural mystical light, spoken of in the preceding sections, on primary moral awareness. In fact new aspects of mystical experience do appear in the moral activity of one who has the gift of mystical light.

In so far as charity itself becomes illuminated by the mystical light, in the "dark illumination" of the lower degrees of this light, there arises a new mode of primary moral awareness through this now more conscious basic inclination of charity. The theology of the gifts of the Holy Spirit would consider this new mode of moral awareness as due to counsel, fortitude, piety, and fear of the Lord. In such a circumstance a fuller integration is possible of all aspects of moral life under this charity that is now much more consciously at the center. This integration will be even more stabilized and complete if the higher degrees of mystical light eventually lead to a state of permanent centrally conscious union with the indwelling Trinity. For here charity becomes focused on the illuminated presence of God, and charity itself is felt still more consciously as flowing from and tending toward God above all, through all, and in all. The entire moral life is now lived according to the dynamism of illuminated charity focused above all on the indwelling and grace-giving Trinity. Immediate serious sin becomes a practical impossibility, although a fall little by little through gradual disintegration is still possible in a moral being so complex and mutable as is man. But for one who has been raised by God to such an intensity of charity in such illumination this possibility remains most unlikely

Finally, in these brief remarks upon mystical experience in the active life a few words should be said about the case in which God is known only in the dynamism of moral life. This is the case of the wholly inarticulate faith of pure intersubjectivity that has been considered in earlier essays. Even here it is not impossible that the dynamism of moral life in charity in a truly generous soul may be so illuminated by the gift of mystical light as to give the profound experiential awareness of love in the manner of an "object." And with the growth in intensity of the mystical light there might even come to pass the experiential awareness of the indwelling Beloved, in a manner that is inexpressible because even the formulae of faith that might begin to speak of it are lacking. I speak here only of possibilities and not of concrete cases, but it is well to consider the possibilities before attempting to understand all the concrete cases. In this manner it may be possible to approach more sympathetically the modes of both ordinary and extraordinary religious experience not only within the Church but outside it even to the farthest reaches of mankind.

NAME INDEX

Adam, Karl, 49
Alfaro, 36
Aristotle, 117, 177, 190
Aubert, Roger, 28, 35–37, 39–42, 47
Augustinus, Saint, 20, 220, 245

Baius, 205
Bautain, 35
Beraza, B., 79
Billot, Cardinal, 37, 40–43, 45, 47, 102, 104, 140f.
Blondel, Maurice, 47f.
Bonaventurus, Saint, 224
Bonnetty, 35
Buber, Martin, 54, 223, 236, 245

Cajetan, Cardinal, 55, 79f., 99, 101f., 104, 139, 141, 246
Capreolus, 99, 102, 104, 139, 140f.
Clement of Alexandria, 185
Confucius, 190, 258
Congar, Yves, 83

De Broglie, 36
De Finance, 222, 235
De Guibert, 267
De la Taille, 36, 103f., 139–141, 143f., 156, 158, 181

Eminyan, M., 89

Fromm, Erich, 53f., 245
Fuchs, 224

Gardeil, P. Ambrose, 48f., 82
Garrigou-Lagrange, 235
Gilson, Etienne, 9f.
Guardini, Romano, 68

Harent, S., 36f., 79
Hegel, G. W. F., 219
Heidegger, M., 220
Hermes, 35

James, William, 236
John of St. Thomas, 55f., 117, 135, 245f., 270
John of the Cross, Saint, 55, 237
Journet, C., 83
Justin, Saint, 89

Kant, Immanuel, 22
Kierkegaard, 219 f.,
Klubertanz, George, 117
Krempel, A., 111, 117

Lao Tze, 190
Labourdette, M. M., 82
Lercher, Ludovicus, 37
Liege, P. A., 83
Lombardi, R., 79
Lonergan, Bernard, 104, 117, 136, 139–141, 156
Lossky, Vladimir, 110

Malavez, 36
Marcel, Gabriel, 53, 220, 223f., 263f., 245
Marechal, 234, 236f.
Maritain, Jacques, vi, 10, 52f., 55, 78, 82–85, 99, 101, 104–106, 138, 141, 181, 192, 222, 224, 235f., 245, 250, 254
Mohammed, 190, 258
Molina, L., 37
Mouroux, Jean, 50
Murphy, John L., 36 f.

Newman, John Henry Cardinal, 47
Nicholas, M. J., 82

Parmenides, 239
Pascal, 220
Plato, 117, 190
Plotinus, 126, 190
Poulain, 234, 237

Rahner, Karl, 143, 156, 181, 222, 224
Rousselot, Pierrre, 49, 71

NAME INDEX

Sartre, 220
Scheeben, 183
Scheler, Max, 49
Schiffini, 79, 80, 87
Schillebeeckx, 222, 224
Schlagenhaufen, F., 37
Scotus, Duns, 99f., 139
Sikora, Joseph, vi, 1, 3, 6, 51, 55, 58, 106, 117f., 174, 224, 238
Stentrup, F., 37
Straub, 37
Suarez, 79, 99–101, 139

Tertullian, 96
Thales, 248
Thomas Aquinas, Saint, 29, 32, 41, 77–79, 87, 89, 91, 96, 98, 110–112, 116, 141, 159, 177, 196, 224f., 249
Tiphanus, 99f., 139
Truhlar, 267

Vignon, 36

Whitehead, Alfred North, 107, 117
William of Champeaux, 117
Wordsworth, William, 224, 249

SUBJECT INDEX

Absolute, the 119f., 114–16, 118f.
Absolute and relative, 109
Activity, 57, 64, 81f., 240, 242
Affective connaturality, vii, 50f., 55, 58f., 62, 66, 73, 75, 91, 246–48, 251–54, 256, 260, 262, 265, 271
Analects, the, 258
Analogy, 120
Atman, 224
Autonomy, 60
Awareness, 51, 53, 222, 227

Basic option (cf. also First act of freedom), 88, 195, 197–206, 272.
Beatific vision, 137, 150–57, 168–175, 178f., 242, 260, 261, 265
Belief, 58–60, 62, 74
Bhaghavad-gita, the, 258
Bonum honestum, 65, 83–88
Bonum salutare, 85, 88f.
Brahma, 65
Brahman, 65, 224
Buddhism, 258

Causality, efficient, 55–7, 65
– emanative, 142
– final, 55–57, 65f., 247
– quasi-efficient, 142
– quasi-emanative, 142–45, 161, 168, 170, 172, 176f., 181
– quasi-formal, 143f., 168, 170, 173, 181, 182
Certitude, metaphysical, 62, 76
– moral, 61, 76
– relative, 38, 44
Character, sacramental, 231
Charity, 152, 176, 178, 260, 262–64
Church, 184, 186–190, 193, 202, 204, 206, 213f.
Circumincession, 133, 164
Cognitio matutina, 154
Cognitio vespertina, 154
Commitment, personal, 31, 45, 60, 62, 70

Communion, interpersonal, 43, 50, 55, 65, 66, 68, 70–73, 82, 91f., 152, 224, 227–29, 233, 237, 241–43, 253, 259
Community, 210
Connaturality (cf. Affective connaturality), 28, 57f., 67, 70–72, 87, 257
Consciousness, 51, 120f., 124, 126–129, 134, 224
– absolute and relative, 123, 127f., 132f.
– being-, 122, 124f., 135, 147f., 154
– of Christ, 136–155
– focal point of, 252
– reflexive (act & being), 147, 243, 251–53
– supernatural, 73
Contemplation, 211f., 228, 262
Council, Eleventh, of Toledo, 113
– First Vatican, 23, 29–33, 41f., 46, 76, 90f.
– Second Vatican, 31
– of Florence, 113f., 119, 123
– Fourth Lateran, 97
– of Nicea, 97
– of Trent, 29, 202, 205
Councils, ecumenical, 18, 221
Created actuation by Uncreated Act, 103f., 144, 158, 161f., 164
Createdness, 242f., 248
Creation, 130
Credibility, 61
Culture, 190–192
– non-Christian, 185, 191, 193
Cultural adaptation, 18, 192

Death, 220
Dialogue, 59, 62, 82, 227f.
Dimensions of being, transobjective, vii, 238, 240–42

Encounter, 213, 215–17, 219–21, 224, 226–30, 232f., 248, 257
Esse a se, 114
– *assumptum*, 158, 161–63, 181

SUBJECT INDEX

Essence and existence, distinction, 81, 100f., 105, 107, 139
Eucharist, 217f., 232f.
Ex opere operato, 211, 215, 218
Existence, 54, 64, 82, 104, 162, 241f., 249, 250
– act of, vi, 57, 97, 105–107, 164
– exercise of, vi, 57, 81, 105–107, 122, 160–162, 174, 181
– of God, 23, 43f., 53, 119, 122
– possession of, vi, 161f., 181
– reception of, 106, 145f.
– transobjective, 240f., 243
Existential choice, 1f.
Existentialism, 29f., 43, 50, 81, 219–221, 226, 235
– Thomist, 81f.
Existential state, 107

Faith (cf. also Belief), 24, 27, 29–31, 41, 67, 73f., 257, 259
– authoritative and scientific, 41f., 45, 47, 61, 63
– Christian, 15
– confidence, 32
– formal object of, 40, 45–47
– intellectual assent, 29, 32, 40, 74, 90–92
– interpersonal, 31, 46, 90–93
– intuitive, 47
– motive of, 38f., 42, 47
– natural, 37, 39, 69
– as personal committment, 31, 45, 74
– of pure intersubjectivity, 70, 76f., 89f., 92, 94, 186, 202, 225, 273
– scriptural, 28, 32, 51
– supernatural, 37, 39, 45f., 258
– trial of, 44
– of Vatican I, 30f., 33, 41f.
Fallacy of misplaced concreteness, 107, 117
Fideism, 35
Fides fiducialis, 27
– *ut assensus*, 27
Finite supernatural, 156–183
First act of freedom, 83, 87, 89, 196
First moral choice (see First act of freedom)
Freedom (cf. also First act of Freedom), 39, 41f., 168, 259
– of choice, 167f.

Generation, 131
Gifts of the Holy Spirit, 267–70, 272
God, duality in, 126–28
– relative and absolute being of, 112
Grace, 71, 88f., 137, 157, 159, 162–67, 175–77, 179, 184, 187–189, 206, 232
– entitative, 159, 162–68, 176f., 179

Hinduism, 191, 258

History, 188f., 206, 230
Hope, 176
Humanism, christian, 5
Hypostatic union, 103f., 108, 136–58, 168f., 175, 178

Infant and age of reason, 86
– unbaptized, 77f.
Infidelity, 71, 74
Inspiration, 14, 17
Intentio fidei, 82f.
Intentionality, 57, 65, 214, 216, 246f.
Interpersonal relation, 59, 233, 248
Intersubjectivity, 27, 51, 53, 58, 63–66, 68, 70–73, 83, 91, 227, 245, 259
Intuition, moral, 82, 87, 198f., 271f.
– poetic, 82, 245, 248
"I-Thou", 31, 50f., 54, 58, 62f., 82, 236

Jews, 258

Knowledge, pre-conceptual, 30, 85, 198, 225
– pre-propositional, 30, 225
– through living, 52f.
Koran, the, 258

Light of Glory, 151, 169f., 172, 175, 261, 265
Liturgy, 208, 210–12
Locutio increata, 51, 63, 66, 70f., 178, 256f., 260
– *testificans*, 72–77, 178
Love, 54–58, 59, 62, 87, 91, 124–26, 134f., 187, 223f., 227, 245–48, 261

Magisterium, 19
Materialism, 22
Metaphorical motion, 55–57, 246–48
Metaphysics, 20, 22, 25
– of existential subject, 83
– of finality, 87
– objectivist, vii
– of person, 103
– theological, 8f., 23
Missions of the Trinity, 157f., 163
Mortal sin, 87–89
Mystery, 54, 237
Mystical body of Christ, 210
Mystical light, 261–66, 270, 272f.
Mysticism, 55, 82, 227, 234–38, 241f., 244, 246, 251, 253f., 258f., 260, 262, 265, 267, 270–73
– natural, 66, 243–45, 248, 251f.
– supernatural, 254–56, 258f., 272, 267

Nature, 98f., 102f., 105–107, 110, 113, 115f., 119–123, 138
Nihilation, 167

SUBJECT INDEX

Objectivity, 54, 239–241
Openness, 2f.

Pantheism, 22
Passive testimony of God, 38f.
Perichoresis, 133f.
Person (see also "supposit"), 59f., 60, 62, 72, 96–99, 101–108, 110–117, 119f., 122f., 127, 138–40
Personality, 97, 139
Phenomenality, psychic, 238–40, 242
– sensible, 238–41
Phenomenology, 220, 223f., 226
Philosophy, 9, 21f.
– Christian, 9, 11, 22
– perennial, 19, 22, 192
– of science, 24
Pius affectus ad credulitatem, 85, 256
Practical judgment, 39f., 68, 71f.
Presence, 51, 65, 83, 262
– non-objective, 52, 86, 225f.
– objective, 52, 86
Problem, 54, 237
Propositional knowledge, 43

Quietism, 253

Rationalism, 35, 47, 220, 259
Relation, accidental, 117f.
– of opposition, 109, 112–15, 122f., 125–130, 135
– predicamental, 111–113, 116–118
– subsistent, 110, 112
– transcendental, 111
Relative, the, 109f., 114–116, 118f.
Reformation, 36
Revelation (see also Scripture), v, vi, 4f., 13f., 18–24, 30, 38f., 41f., 50, 63, 69, 206

Sacrament, 208–210, 213–219, 228f., 230–33
Sacramentality of creatures, 4, 225
Salvation, 184, 186, 189, 193, 200, 202, 205
Sapiential function of Theology, 23–26

Scripture, 14–20, 41, 46, 91, 95, 110, 137
Separated Christians, 190f., 258
Species, impressed & expressed, 171–174
Spiration, 132f.
Spirituality, 64, 122, 209, 244
State, the, 24
Subjectivity, vi, 52f., 55, 57f., 65, 82, 105f., 122, 160f., 168, 226, 241–251
Subsidiarity, principle of, 24
Subsistence, 99f., 102–106, 112
Supposit, 96, 98f., 101, 104–107

Tao, 224
Theology, 5, 7–9, 13, 16, 18f., 21, 23–25
– Christian (see also Wisdom, and Christian Philosophy), 10, 11
– existential, 221f.
– metaphysical, v, 20–22, 25, 47
– and philosophy, 1, 8, 21
– positive, 11, 13f.
– reflections, v-vii, 1
– system of, vii
Thomism (see also Thomas Aquinas), vif., 19, 22, 34, 36, 40, 45f., 48f., 55, 65, 80–82, 101f., 106, 117, 140, 176, 192, 222, 225f., 246
Transobjective reality, 82, 236
Trinity, 95–139, 141, 155, 157, 164f., 168, 170, 177, 261, 264, 266, 273
– processions of, 109, 114, 123, 127–131, 133, 157f., 261
Trustworthiness, 61f.
Tychic, 220

Upanishads, 66, 224, 242, 249
Ur-Sakrament, 213

Western expansionism, 192
Will, the, 56–58, 67, 246–248
– divine salvivic, 86, 185
Wisdom, 1
– of the flesh, 3
– Christian, 4–6, 8–12